*The Creed
in
Christian Teaching*

BOOKS BY JAMES D. SMART
Published by The Westminster Press

The Creed in Christian Teaching

The Interpretation of Scripture

Servants of the Word: *The Prophets of Israel*
(*Westminster Guides to the Bible*)

The Rebirth of Ministry

The Teaching Ministry of the Church

The Recovery of Humanity

What a Man Can Believe

A Promise to Keep

Jesus, Stories for Children

In Collaboration with David Noel Freedman
God Has Spoken

The Creed

in

Christian Teaching

by

JAMES D. SMART

THE WESTMINSTER PRESS

Philadelphia

Contents

Foreword

This book represents the convergence of two interests that have been in dialogue with one another in my mind for many years, the doctrinal and the educational. The former came to expression fairly early in my ministry in a book for laymen entitled *What a Man Can Believe,* written in 1939 in an attempt to bring order out of the confusion of my own beliefs, but not published until 1943. The latter, while present early, was not deepened and organized until I was conscripted as an editor of curriculum materials for the Presbyterian Church in the U.S.A. in 1944. Returning in 1950 to the pastorate where I could work at close quarters on the educational problems of which I had become more acutely aware as an editor, I ventured in 1954 to publish a book, *The Teaching Ministry of the Church,* in which I attempted a theological critique of the existing order in Protestant education and a sketch of what education would be like in the church if it were to take seriously the implications of its central doctrines. While it has been gratifying that the second book has been so widely used, it has been disappointing that it has not provoked more discussion of basic issues among educators.

The present book brings these two interests together in a new way and is really a continuation of the discussion begun in each of them. On the one hand, there was the desire, after twenty-two years, to spell out again in detail the meaning of the faith to which we are committed, this time dealing not with a selection of beliefs but with all the elements in the Apostles' Creed. On the other

7

hand, it seemed possible that to go through the Creed drawing attention to its implications for the educational task might do more than anything else to sharpen the theological issues in education and to counteract the sterility that seems to afflict the so-called " new theological era in religious education."

I have to thank Prof. Robert Lynn, of Union Theological Seminary, New York, for his kindness in reading the manuscript and making a number of valuable criticisms.

JAMES D. SMART

Union Theological Seminary
New York, New York

1.

Theology
and
Christian Education

Theology is inescapable in the educational enterprise. It can be ignored, with confusion as the inevitable consequence, but it cannot be eliminated as a factor in any educational situation. Someone may be inclined to interrupt at this point and say, " Of course, you mean, in any educational situation in the church," as though it were only in religious education that theology is a factor. But this is a false approach. It seeks to confine theology — and God — within the domain of religion. Theology is concerned, however, with the relations between God and man, and the corresponding relations between man and man, that form the substructure of existence in every realm of life. A man's theology is the ultimately determining force in how he deals with other men in society, for it brings to expression not only his conception of what it means to be a human being but also some conviction concerning the purpose of life in this world. The educator is particularly concerned with ultimate questions because the character of his work depends upon the answers that he gives to them. He is dealing with human beings in the period of their lives when they are most readily shaped in one direction or another, and he would be irresponsible if he were unconcerned about the direction in which education is sending both them and the society of which they are a part. But the question of direction is the question of the goal of human life, and this is one of the primary concerns of theology. The fact that we speak of " secular " education conceals from us the true state of affairs — that all education, whether it is called religious or sec-

ular, proceeds on the basis of convictions concerning man's true
nature and destiny that are basically theological.

The secular educator, then, though he may validly disclaim any
responsibility for religious teaching, cannot escape responsibility
for the character of the basic convictions that he consciously or
unconsciously communicates to his students in his contacts with
them. He needs to know in what total theological or philosophical
context these convictions belong and what their implications are
for the future of human society. In other words, he needs to know
in what direction his influence is taking his students. Let him
set this down on paper in an orderly fashion, and what he will
have will be his creed. But if the question of his creed is important
and decisive for the secular educator, it is much more important
and decisive for the religious educator.

Education in the church is from beginning to end education
in the Christian faith. Theology is no longer merely hidden in the
assumptions on which the education is based, but forms the very
content of the teaching. Religious education is " the church teaching," just as the ministry discharged in the pulpit is " the church
preaching," and consultations with individuals in the pastor's
study or in their homes is " the church exercising pastoral care."
Theology may be defined as " the church taking thought whether
or not it is true to its own nature and calling in its teaching,
preaching, and pastoral care." The preacher, when he comes down
from the pulpit, frequently is distressed by the consciousness that
what he has spoken has not been an adequate proclamation of
the church's gospel; therefore, the focus of theology for him is
upon the problem how he may more adequately grasp and be
grasped by the gospel that sounds forth from the Scriptures and
how he may escape from the misconstructions and inadequate
forms of expression that conceal the gospel in his preaching. So
also the teacher, whether professional or volunteer, must take
thought concerning what has been taught and how it has been
taught. Has the content of the teaching been distinctively Christian? Have the problems that are involved in it been faced honestly? Has the class session been in any real sense a fellowship in

the knowledge of the truth? Has it been such that not only the members of the class but also the teacher has been confronted with a word from God that calls for a decision of some nature? The teacher who asks such questions, discusses them with others, and searches in the existing literature for help in the answering of them is engaged in theological activity.

It is necessary to emphasize this point, because teachers, and even professional religious educators, have at times in the past been inclined to think of theology as an area that lies beyond them. In that area all manner of profound and erudite questions are discussed that have little bearing upon the problems faced week by week in a church school. "On the children's level we have nothing to do with theology," said an editor of children's curriculum materials some years ago. "We deal only with truth." But it is the question of truth with which theology is concerned. It is folly to conceal from any teacher the dimensions of the task on which he is embarked. Perhaps he becomes involved in teaching under the impression that there is no more to it than the preparation of a weekly lesson (for which ample materials are supplied) and the teaching of that lesson during an hour on Sunday. But the sensitive teacher is quickly made aware that the most careful study of a lesson is wasted unless there is an equally careful study of those who are to be taught. Each pupil then becomes a subject for investigation, and behind each pupil there emerge the various contexts in which he has his life — home, school, companions, and the community as a whole. The problem of the pupil is the problem of man in society and in the perplexing world of our day. Then the dimensions of the teaching office itself begin to appear. The church school teacher is not just an individual expressing opinions on various subjects, but to the group of pupils he represents the church of Jesus Christ and speaks for the church to them. There may be some members of the group for whom he is the only point of contact with the church, and the only person who speaks to them about the Christian faith. If he is to be a responsible spokesman, he cannot merely relay to the group statements that he takes ready-made from the curriculum literature.

What he teaches must be *true for him* if it is to have any vitality or authority for them. How could he ask his students to risk basing their lives upon something that he himself has not investigated sufficiently to be ready to commit himself personally concerning its truth? Therefore, once he has acknowledged this responsibility, there is no drawing back. He has to wrestle, no matter what it costs him in time and effort, with all the questions that his own mind and his students' minds are asking concerning the Christian faith. He has to know the truth of it that he may be of help to them in knowing the truth of it. In short, he is launched upon his own personal investigation of the limitless reaches of theology. Instead of standing before a neat little task of preparing and delivering a lesson, he stands between immensities — the infinite possibilities for good and for evil in the future that reside in the members of the class and in all the lives that are yet to be touched by theirs, and the infinite riches of God's grace and truth that reside in the gospel.

THE RUPTURE OF THE RELATION

This intimate involvement of education with theology has not always been recognized as it is today. In fact, twenty years ago the words " theology " and " education " were thought by many to denote two completely separate and widely different entities in the life of the church. Education was regarded as a science or enterprise having to do with human growth in which those who participated embarked on a journey into a vastly enriched future. Answers to life's questions would be found in the course of the journey, but the important thing was not so much the correctness of the answers as the experience of the venturer in the search for them. Education, so conceived, had in it an unusual excitement and fascination. Even a class of small children was conceived as a band of adventurers boldly interrogating the universe, under the guidance of a teacher, to be sure, but a teacher who would be ready to explore regions strange to him if the way should open up before the eager probings of his charges. The spirit and outlook of the theologian seemed then to be alien to this enterprise. His business was to provide ready-made answers, the correct Christian answers to life's questions. Moreover, some theologians were insistent that the educators' exciting search was a wild-goose chase that would lead nowhere. Anyone who was really in earnest about knowing the answers had best stop searching and begin listening. Why need there be any search if the church in its doctrines already possesses the truth? Was not the task of education to teach this truth to young and old alike and not to send them after a will-o'-the-wisp of truth that would ever elude them and might lead them into dangerous error?

Theology, in so far as it presented this rather somber and complacent visage, was an unwelcome intruder into the realm of education. Its unpopularity requires no explanation, for with one stroke it dissolved the excitement of the educational enterprise. Who will embark on a search for truth that may be strenuous and costly if he need only sit quietly for a few hours and have it presented to him in a few neat sentences? It is not surprising that educators should have been hostile to theology, seeing in it a deadly force that would transform education from a fascinating adventure into a dull and passive transference of theological propositions from one mind to another. But neither is it surprising that theologians should have looked upon the educators with distrust and dismay, especially when the latter expressed the confidence that in their search for truth and meaning they were already finding answers more adequate for life in the modern world than any the church had inherited from the past.

The pathos of this encounter between theology and education is that each participant was reacting against something in the other that was actually a falsification of its nature and function, and that each was defending as peculiarly its own something that was essential to the other. Educators were reacting against a theology that gave the impression that it was the custodian of a Christian truth that needed only to be imparted and that demanded an attitude of passive submission toward itself. But such pretentions are contrary to the very nature of theology. Simple-

minded people may think that the sum of all truth was entrusted
to the church in its beginnings in the form of doctrinal propositions and that the task of theologians through the ages has been
simply to repeat and explain these propositions in each new age.
But no one who reads the New Testament thoughtfully can fall
into any such error. The truth with which the Christian gospel is
concerned is strangely different from what we call "truths." Before all else it is a person, Jesus Christ. He is the truth, not just in
the words he speaks but also in his actions and in the things he
suffered, not just in his relations with other people but also in
his death and resurrection. Touch him at any point and you
touch truth, a truth that is alive like an electric current in a wire.
And as truth passes from him to other persons, it is not only his
truth but also his life that they receive. The same is true of the
Old Testament. The heart of the Old Testament is the covenant
between God and Israel, a personal relation between God and his
people that compassed the whole of Israel's life. It is both truth
and life. To know God is not just to know certain truths about
God, but to stand in a relation of openness and trust toward him
so that the light of God's presence illumines all the dark places
of life. This is the unique knowledge of the truth with which
Christian theology is concerned. Never can it claim to possess
the whole truth of God in its propositions without forgetting
what stands before all else: that Christian truth is a reality only
in a personal relation between God and man, and that to know
the truth is to know God. But this is a truth, then, that not even
the ablest theologian has at his disposal. It can be given only as
God gives himself to be the life and light of men. It cannot be
taken over ready-made from a past age. Those who have gone
before us can only point the way for us as faithful witnesses to
what they have known. We have to find our own way, painfully
or joyfully, step by step; we have to see for ourselves and believe
with our own hearts or we know nothing of the truth. It is
wrong, then, to think that theology lays a plaster of ready-made
answers over the eager questions of the young and old and robs
them of the excitement of going in quest of answers that will be

their very own. Theology has its own vital existence in each new age only as the questions are asked boldly and stubbornly in the form that belongs to that particular age and to no other, and only as the truth that is incarnate in Jesus Christ becomes the source of answers by which men find themselves alive in God. Far from having any quarrel with the educator's inquiring spirit, theology, rightly understood, merely widens and deepens the range of the quest and reminds the inquirers that they may waste their energies if they disregard the markers set up by past generations.

The protest of theologians against the trend of developments in religious education was valid only in so far as educators were untrue to their own principles, in their enthusiasm for the genuine revolution in educational method that they had effected imagining that they had also inaugurated a new era in the understanding and practice of religion. Modern religious education came into being as a multiple revolt against a form of education in the church that was almost entirely transmissive, against an approach to the Bible that was unhistorical and literalistic, and against forms of orthodoxy mingled with revivalism that identified religion with an experience of conversion followed by the acceptance of a specific code of doctrines and practices. The mood was one of liberation, and since religious education was now attempting to be scientific and up to date both in its methodology and in its use of Scripture, a scientific approach was also made to the defining of religion, the confidence being that the way was now opening for a wholly new understanding of man's religious life. In some quarters there was a naïve attitude toward scientific inquiry, as though science in the modern world had found a key that needed only to be used diligently to unlock all the secrets of the universe (including the secrets of God and man), all that men knew in the prescientific eras being deprecated as mere guesses at truth. But what actually happened was that the educational movement drew its concept of religion rather uncritically from what seemed to be the most progressive and scientific thought of the day. At this point it left itself most open to criticism. It failed to give to the investigation of the theological questions raised by its revolt against contemporary definitions of religion the care and attention that it gave to the educational questions, and yet it was as emphatic in its redefinition of religion as it was in its redefinition of education. Undoubtedly it was influenced by the unbridled optimism that was widely current early in this century concerning the prospect that education would transform humanity and open a new day in world affairs. The advance of the century has brought a sobering realization of the limitations upon what education can accomplish. It is the essential instrument whereby the knowledge and skills and insights gained by the human race in the past may be not only preserved but also enriched and augmented by each new generation. Through education the memory of humanity as the storehouse of all its treasures of experience becomes the memory of the child who was born only yesterday. Defective education means the impoverishment of life and the loss of large segments of our heritage. But let education break over these boundaries and claim that its task is to shape human character and to mold society, and the theologian must at once begin to ask from what source the educator draws his criterion of what man and society should be.

Education within the church is the essential instrument whereby we enter into the heritage of knowledge, faith, and action that belongs peculiarly to the church. We cannot possess any of it until we have made it our own, and in making it our own we have to venture out into the unknown, like Abraham. Our Christian education can be described as an expansion of our existence back through the ages and out across the world today as the life of God's people in all time becomes our life. Thus, when at last we find ourselves standing on the boundary beyond which lies the unknown future, the memory of God's dealings with his people throughout the past lights the way into the future. Christian education of itself does not make any man a Christian or give him a Christian character. " Faith cometh by hearing, and hearing by the word of God." It may be in an educational situation that a person first hears the gospel and responds to it, but in that moment teaching has become preaching. The word has been spoken in which God comes to us himself in Jesus Christ to bridge the gulf by which we have separated ourselves from him and to restore us to ourselves and to our rightful place in his world by reconciling us to himself. Reconciliation with God is frequently described in the New Testament as a new birth in which men are born of the Spirit and made new creatures, so that they enter a new world under God's immediate sovereignty. Christian education is the guidance the church provides that birth may be followed by growth, that Christians may not forever remain babes devoid of memory, knowledge, or capacity for action, but may grow up into their true stature as disciples of Jesus Christ, citizens of his Kingdom, servants of God. Education so defined is an indispensable function of the church and, far from having any quarrel with theology, lives from the same sources as theology itself. In fact, the church school in the local church occupies the place in the life of the Christian congregation that the theological seminary has in the church as a whole. Each on its own level is the training school for Christians that they may so enter into their Christian heritage that they may be equipped to share in some way in the ministry of Jesus Christ.

THE PERIL OF SUPERFICIAL THEOLOGIZING

To some readers this discussion of the relation between theology and education may seem superfluous. Have we not long since passed into a new era in Christian education in which no one disputes the importance of theology for the Christian teacher? Why thresh old straw? But the way in which theology is being related to religious education in some of the recent literature gives good reason for dismay. Only too often one has the impression that theology is being injected into education as a foreign substance, or appended to it as a kind of necessary decoration, rather than being discovered as the underlying reality in every aspect of education. A prominent educator reports that his students frequently introduce some theological paragraphs into their essays, not always too relevantly, as though the essay required a theologi-

cal trimming in order to be presentable. But they are perhaps
only following the example of more eminent practitioners who
assure them that, in a theological age such as the present, religious
education must provide itself with a good theology, and who
seem to think that this aspect of the task is not too difficult to
accomplish. A good orthodox theology is safest, at least in some
quarters — but there are other good theologies available if one
lacks a taste for orthodoxy! Not thus does vital and relevant theological thinking come to birth.

The transition from an antitheological age to a theological age
in religious education has been too painless. Before 1940 it was
typical for the religious educator to disclaim theological responsibility. In the early 1940's, theological issues had thrust themselves
so forcefully upon the minds of thinking men that they could no
longer be suppressed in any area of the church's life. Nevertheless, they were regarded as intruders from an alien realm by many
religious educators who saw the ruin of the structure they had
built, the sacrifice of its scientific character, from its invasion by
theology. The battle was sharp but brief. By the mid-forties the
opposition had already been broken and had faded into insignifi-
cance. There was no sustained discussion of the principles that
were at stake. The tide of theological interest swept all before it,
and soon it was being taken for granted that the religious educator must establish a relation between his educational and his
theological principles. " Theology is the order of the day; therefore we must be theological." Theology had become the new and
accepted style in religious education. Fortunately there are men at
work in this area who are unhappy with this situation and in rebellion against it. But they have the task of breaking through the
superficial and deceptive mask of premature solutions that conceal the desperately earnest and fascinatingly interesting problems that await investigation.

It may be of interest to compare the parallel developments in
religious education and in Biblical studies. Earlier in this century,
the Biblical scholar, like the religious educator, thought of himself as a scientist who by an empirical approach to the data of his

subject would be able to reach completely objective conclusions. He had to protect himself against theological influences that would interfere with the objectivity of his thinking. He was a scientific historian just as the religious educator was a scientific pedagogue. Since 1920, however, the viewpoint has made progress that the Biblical scholar must be both a historian and a theologian if he is to do justice to records of events in which not only men but also God is involved as an active participant. But there has been no quick or easy triumph of the theological concern. It has had to fight its way step by step. Old positions are not surrendered lightly lest valuable insights be lost, and new positions are more firmly grounded because of the many years of intense debate that has preceded their establishment. Religious education has known no such prolonged and thorough discussion. A new theological approach has been adopted rather than established. Therefore, the theological element has something of the aspect of a removable appendage. It sounds too much like what one thinks one ought to say rather than what has to be said under the compulsion of a truth that is so integral to one's thought and life that its abandonment would be the abandonment of life itself.

It has to be recognized in fairness to the "religious education school" of an earlier day, against which we are now so radically in reaction, that their writings had more vitality in them than the literature of Christian education today. Then, religious education was an exciting and passionate adventure; now, it seems gray and dull and cold. The earlier writers may have gone sailing off theologically into ultraliberal regions where belief in a personal god seemed an antiquated superstition, but what they believed they believed passionately and it was integral to the entire structure of their educational thought. There was no taking of anything for granted. They had had to fight for their principles in the beginning, and they would not abandon them without a struggle.

The theological interest and concern in religious education is endangered by the facility and superficiality with which it has thus far come to expression. There is likely to be a reaction against it when the awareness grows that in many quarters it has had a deadening rather than an enlivening effect. The laying open of theological issues in education should be the unlocking of new depths of interest and meaning and should bring to education a new vitality. Thus far this has been true in much too small a measure. We need to retrace our steps, to move back from premature solutions and let the problems open up to us in their full dimensions.

THE QUESTION OF TRUTH

We have already defined theology as the means whereby we take thought concerning the truth and validity of our teaching. We cannot take over truth ready-made even from the Bible itself. Truth in the Bible is concealed, so that we cannot grasp it until we are willing to be grasped and ruled by it. Until it is truth *for us*, it is not truth at all. We open our New Testaments and read the passage in which Simon Peter confesses that Jesus is the Christ, the Son of the living God. We seize upon this as a truth because it is in the Bible, or because Jesus plainly accepted it as a true confession, or because the church through the ages has constantly proclaimed it as a central truth of the gospel. But if we study the passage more carefully and learn what is said here and elsewhere in the New Testament about confessing Jesus as the Christ, we shall recognize that we and our pupils are in the same situation as was Simon Peter, that we cannot know Jesus as the Christ until the Father in heaven reveals it to us in our hearts and lives. Therefore, if we are to make known to others that Jesus is the Christ, something much more must be done than merely speak the words. Our very familiarity with the name " Christ " for Jesus may be an obstacle to knowing him in a living way as the Christ of God.

Perhaps we are satisfied with the truth of any statement concerning which we ourselves feel a strong conviction. It stirs us deeply. We would be ready to fight for it. But do we not know other people with strong convictions, which we recognize to be only deeply rooted prejudices? Not only truth but also attractive falsehoods have a way of stirring people deeply. We have only to think of the power that nationalistic propaganda, strongly interlaced with lies, has exerted in recent years in many countries. We are much more ready to accept as true a statement that flatters our ego and fits neatly with our existing point of view than one that disturbs us and forces us to reconsider our attitudes. Self-interest exerts a constant pressure upon our thinking even where religious convictions are concerned. Also, there is the unconscious influence of what the society in which we live takes for granted. Untruth that is so well established that it passes unquestioned as truth is still untruth and ruinous in its consequences. Add to all of this the fact that each of us is a blind and sinful mortal in spite of all that we have known of cleansing and enlightenment through Jesus Christ, that our light is broken light and our understanding a broken understanding. How, then, can we teach with confidence unless at every step we let the question, Is it true? come out into the open to shake us loose from all superficial religious speech and all cheap secondhand religious knowledge?

We need also to take account of the fact that the religious atmosphere of our time in America is genially uncritical, and unfriendly to the making of sharp theological distinctions. Religion is popular, but there is an unwillingness to define with any exactness what is meant by religion. There is a widespread impression that religion is good in any form and irreligion bad. Above all things, religion of some kind is essential to the national well-being and security. Good church people are rarely forced to give an account of their faith by confrontation with agnostics or atheists. In fact, so vague are the supposedly Christian definitions of religion in some quarters that even the agnostic and atheist can give assent to them. Tolerance seems to many to demand the viewpoint that all religions are merely diverse expressions of the one religion to which we all hold. In this atmosphere any religious viewpoint that is set forth with clarity and passion and with appropriate illustrations is likely to win a following. It is looked upon as narrow and ungenerous to ask, " Is it true? "

Yet this is what we must ask with thoroughness and stubborn

pertinacity if we are to be responsible Christian teachers, contrib-
uting to the clarification and deepening of the Christian faith in
our time and not to the increase of its confusion. And we begin
our inquiry not by asking what is true in general or by questioning the truth of what those around us are saying and doing, but
by interrogating ourselves, examining our own statements and
actions, which we have assumed to be Christian, that we may
discover wherein they are something less than or even contrary to
the truth as it is revealed in Jesus Christ. An irresponsible teacher
is one who never submits himself and his teaching to this self-
examination, and an irresponsible church school is one in which
the staff never takes time to perform this essential task together.
How can there be any fruitfulness in the life and work of a
church school in which there is carelessness at the very point on
which everything depends — that it should be actually the gospel
of Jesus Christ to which witness is borne in all that is said and
done? But irresponsibility concerning the truth of the gospel is
also an irresponsibility toward those who are taught. They live,
and for years to come they are to live, not by bread alone, but by
every word that proceeds out of the mouth of God. They live by
truth, the truth of God, which opens to them the possibility of
having the life in fellowship with God for which they were created. But if teachers, who are to these persons the spokesmen of
the church of Jesus Christ, bring to them not the truth of God
but religious half-truths or falsehoods that they have carelessly
absorbed from the life of their time, they become obstacles in
God's way, more by far than if they did not undertake to teach
at all, and, if truth is life, they become purveyors of death among
those whom they teach.

Too often we are unwilling to follow out the logic of the
Christian teacher's responsibility lest we discourage some timid
souls from teaching. But is this fair to the teacher, not to be told
that Christian teaching is a perilous occupation in which one can
by carelessness bring damnation upon one's own soul? And, moreover, does the dangerousness really discourage anyone who should
be encouraged to teach? Does it not, rather, for the first time

make Christian teaching exciting? It is a dull occupation as long as the question of truth remains unraised and undiscussed. But once it comes alive, Christian teaching becomes an unending and often breath-taking adventure out of darkness into light, out of falsehood into truth, out of isolation into fellowship, because at root it becomes our journey out of the godlessness and self-imprisonment that is the basic problem of our being into that life in reconciliation with God through Jesus Christ which is perfect freedom.

Only a false and unchristian conception of truth can lead anyone to say, " Then until I am in complete and perfect possession of Christian truth I cannot responsibly teach," or " Since there will ever be sin and misunderstanding and unbelief in me and in all I say or do, I shall never be in a position to teach." It is true that to our dying day there will continue to be darkness and unbelief in us, but if we are not careless about that darkness and unbelief, if we repent not only of past sins and falsehoods that have come into the open but also of present sins and falsehoods that are as yet concealed from us, God is gracious to forgive us our sins and to use us and our stumbling imperfect words to achieve his purpose. It is only a carelessness about the truth on our part that convicts us of irresponsibility.

The Criterion of Truth

We ask, then, " Is it true? "; but by what criterion do we recognize the difference between truth and falsehood? Again we have to be reminded that Christian truth is not primarily a set of true propositions or statements that we have merely to accept but rather a reality of life in God that confronts us in Jesus Christ. To be in the truth or to have the truth dwelling in us is to be united by faith with Jesus Christ in a relationship in which he is Lord and we, acknowledging ourselves subjects, are accepted as friends with whom he shares the fullness of his life. We can know the truth only in so far as we know him and have our life from him. In Jesus Christ alone is truth, and apart from him there is only untruth, darkness, and death.

Two consequences follow from this definition of the criterion of truth. First, if we are to take the question of truth seriously, we shall be forced to become students of Scripture, since only through the Scriptures do we have the possibility of knowing Jesus Christ. The function of the Scriptures in the church is not primarily to provide literature for devotional reading, as one might think from the customary use of them, but to bear witness to the truth and life that are manifest in Jesus Christ. The whole Bible is witness to him. The Gospels portray his birth, ministry, death, and resurrection, but the remainder of the New Testament is equally important for our knowledge of him. And, since the word of God incarnate in him is the same Word that lodged in the heart of Israel marking out the way of life and giving promise of that which was yet to come, we never rightly know him except in the context of Israel and the Old Testament. To know truth in Biblical terms is to know and love and serve the true God and in his service to be true men and truly his witnessing people in the midst of the world. In that knowledge we are given eyes to see the line that runs through the whole of life but, before all else, through our own lives, between truth and falsehood.

Secondly, if we are in earnest about the question of truth, we shall be anxious to hear what the church of Jesus Christ has had to say about it in the most solemn and decisive moments of the past when it has had to take its life in its hands and confess before the world the faith by which it lives and for which, if need be, it will die. In a very real sense the New Testament is the original apostolic confession of faith, the witness of the church to him in whom it had its origin. But in the dilemmas of its life the church found it necessary and useful more than once to state in briefer form the essence of its faith. The earliest of these confessions seems to have been simply " Jesus Christ is Lord," although there are in the New Testament a number of simple formulas that may have served as confessions. But as the church met challenges from various quarters, it had to say what it believed in a form that would guard against misunderstanding. Thus, in the second century the nucleus of what is called the Apostles' Creed came into being, although it was not to reach the fuller form in which we now have it until the seventh or eighth century. It has a right to the name " Apostles' " not because it was written or used, so far as we know, by any of the apostles but because it distills into a brief compass the faith that, according to the New Testament, was believed by the apostles. Later creeds and confessions are important to us also, since in them we hear the church speaking with deliberation in the face of serious threats to its life and standing guard over the truth of the gospel. But creeds and confessions do not settle the question of truth for us once and for all. They have always to be heard and examined in the light of the primary witness to the truth in Scripture, therefore critically as well as reverently, and with the consciousness that, however much the church of the past may help us and point the way for us, it has to be *our own* confession of faith that comes to utterance in our teaching, our own but within the great fellowship of prophets, apostles, and all who through the ages have been called to the task of teaching the Christian faith.

2.

I Believe

THE FREEDOM OF BELIEVING

We must at the very outset reckon with a basic repugnance that many people feel upon hearing the word "creed." It suggests to them something narrow and confining, a dull formula inherited from an ancient world. Religion itself is a spiritual reality as broad and deep as life itself, so beautiful, so vast, so majestic, so constantly growing in its meaning, that reducing it to the statements of a creed seems to be like trying to capture the beauty of the sunset in a bottle. Let every man have his own understanding and enjoyment of religion, they say. Do not chain him to a creed. "Not creeds but deeds" is the motto of some who make a false distinction between faith and action. Man must be free to find the truth wherever it shows itself in the life of humanity; he must not be constantly impeded by a dead hand out of the past. But this point of view has in it a subtle dishonesty. It is itself *a creed,* a statement of belief, a distinctive approach to life!

A large, Midwestern church places in its pews a card for visitors on which it states, "This church is not bound by any creed but requires of its members only loyalty to the truth." Beneath this heading is a list of "truths" such as the divinity of the human spirit, the perfectibility of character, and the certainty of man's progress in history. Jesus appears in the list as man's greatest teacher and example. This is a creed, one that stands in contradiction not only to Scripture but also to all the historic creeds and confessions of the church. To attempt to pass itself off as

26

something else reveals an unwillingness to stand the test whether or not its content is Christian truth.

In recent years the most persistent critics of the development of theological concern in religious education have been several Unitarian educators who repeatedly insist that a doctrinal concern entails a narrowness in which one is no longer unconditionally open to the truth. But surely, without being rude, one may ask whether they themselves have ever shown an openness to truth that would set their Unitarianism in question. Are they as open-minded as they profess to be, or are they, like all of us, bound by convictions, that is, by a creed, that they cannot surrender without becoming other than what they are? For Christians, to be open to the truth is to be open to Jesus Christ, which means nothing less than to be willing to have their convictions, their thoughts, their conduct, and their very existence, set in question by him. Whether one is Unitarian or Presbyterian or Lutheran, to ask the theological question in earnest is to have one's present position set in jeopardy.

Far from being an instrument for the enslavement and the bludgeoning into submission of the human mind and spirit, a truly Christian creed is a banner of liberty, a bulwark of the freedom of the Christian man. The New Testament has much to say concerning freedom. Jesus' mission is to set the captives at liberty. His promise to his disciples is that his truth will make them free. To Paul, the life of faith is life in the freedom of the sons of God. It is the unbeliever who is the prisoner, bound by the chains of his sin and ignorance and unable to take one step in freedom. Christian salvation is liberation. This is no empty rhetoric but penetrates to the heart of the human problem. Man's destiny is freedom, not freedom *from* God and *from* his fellow man to be and to think and to act in isolation, but freedom *for* God and *for* his fellow man, that in fellowship with both he may have his life. The drive to self-assertion and self-sufficiency which is so often mistaken for the way to freedom leads rather to a rupture or entanglement of his relations with both his God and his fellow men in which he realizes not his true humanity but an inhumanity that is an ugly caricature of a man. The man who isolates himself imprisons himself in death.

Life from its earliest moment is life-in-relation. That we ever exist purely as individuals is an illusion. It has been proved that a baby, sealed off from human relations, does not thrive. So, also, adults of mature development, when placed in complete isolation, experience an emptying out of the content of life and a severe disturbance even of their conscious identity with themselves (as experiments have proved). We are what we are because of what has come to us from others and remains with us only when our relation with them is unbroken. But preceding our relation with persons about us and closely interwoven with it is our relation with God. The witness of the Scriptures is that man is a creature made for fellowship with God. This is not a relation into which he may one day enter through a religious experience; it is a relation that exists before he is born and in which he has his life. He is what he was made to be only in this relation. He does not choose to have a Heavenly Father any more than he chooses to have an earthly father. His life, therefore, is a life in relation with God, and the character of his life is determined by the character of that relation. An assertion of freedom, therefore, that ruptures or entangles the relations on which his life depends is a form of self-enslavement and self-destruction.

The creed, then, is a bold assertion of man's freedom for God and for his fellow man. It is the man who believes and confesses his faith before men who has freedom to live. This was vividly true in Israel. Israel's covenant relation with God bound the Israelites to him so that they had no freedom to serve other gods; nor had they freedom to choose whatever way of life might please them, for their way was marked out for them by the implications of their relation with God. They were bound as no other ancient nation was bound. Yet they were free as no other ancient people was free. It was the bond between God and all Israel that gave the Israelite citizen courage to defend his right even against the king and made him the enemy of political tyranny. His point of security in God gave him strength to be free. So also in the early church the remarkable freedom of the Christian man to think and act in wholly new ways was the fruit of the inner binding of his whole being to God through Christ. Because he was the slave of God he was enslaved no longer to persons or powers in the seen or unseen, and he was unwilling that anyone should be enslaved to him. And more recently we have had it demonstrated to us in our modern world, where totalitarianism in various forms, some more easily recognizable than others, overshadows the life of man, that the man who has a creed in which he has committed himself unconditionally to his God proves ultimately to be the indestructible defender of human freedom. He is not free to be other than free. He has a freedom in God to do justly, to love mercy, and to speak the truth, which he cannot surrender without surrendering life itself. His life in God is beyond the reach of any human authority. Thus, ultimately, the defense of all our human freedoms depends upon the existence of men who think and act in freedom not because someone or some government permits them to be free but because their life in relation with God is of a nature that compels them to be free.

A teacher need have no fear, then, that in introducing the creed to his pupils, he is guilty of an act of spiritual coercion or is perverting education into indoctrination. Rather, to leave them ignorant of the creed, that is, ignorant of what it means to say Yes to the Christian faith and therefore No to all the other faiths that clamor for their allegiance, is to leave them defenseless in the confusion of creeds that characterizes our modern world and helpless before all the forces in their world and in themselves that conspire to enslave them. The creed must be so interpreted to them that when they repeat it in worship they will know who it is to whom they are committing themselves and what follows from that commitment, so that it will be an act of faith and decision and not an empty form. The better they understand what they are saying, the clearer it will be to them that it is a courageous act that may be very costly to them, that it is a corporate act that binds them into one with Christians through all the ages and across all the world, but above all that it is a liberating act in which they claim their rightful place in the world in relation to God and to their fellow men. It is only when the creed is misunderstood and misused that it becomes an instrument of spiritual and intellectual tyranny. But in the past, so often has it been presented as a code of beliefs which one must accept unquestioningly or risk eternal damnation that for many people this is the impression that conditions their responses. We need, therefore, to give some attention to possible misunderstandings of the creed.

WHAT WE OUGHT TO BELIEVE?

Few teachers are likely to be troubled by the fear of being damned eternally for disbelieving any article of the creed. But there is among Christians in general, and among teachers in particular, the idea that the creed tells us what we *ought* to believe as Christians. If we believed everything in the creed, we would be completely Christian believers. But if there are some elements in the creed that we do not as yet believe, we are not yet really Christians. The repetition of the creed in worship usually leaves some members of the congregation with a guilty feeling that they do not believe all that they ought to. Teachers who have not considered sufficiently what believing really means are likely to take for granted that what is in the creed is what their pupils ought to believe, and by this attitude they communicate to them the impression that believing is one among many duties of a Christian, with the implication that it is something they can do if they will.

This attitude contains within it a denial of the very nature of Christian faith. There is no " ought " in believing, as though believing were something a person could do at will, and only refrained from doing in carelessness or stubborn willfulness. A man cannot by an act of will believe in God or in Jesus Christ or in the church. He may for certain reasons, such as fear of the consequences of unbelief, or the desire to please someone dear to him, or the necessity to escape his own inner uncertainties, compel his mind's submission to certain articles of faith, and he may even secure a measure of spiritual relief and satisfaction thereby, but this is not what the New Testament knows as faith. There, faith is possible only as man's response to God's grace and mercy and truth. The initiative is God's, not man's. The disciples become men of faith only because in Jesus' words and person the Kingdom of God has come nigh to them. They do not choose him, but rather he chooses them. The seed of the Word has to be planted in men's lives before faith can grow. God speaks; man hears and responds with his whole being. This is the order in which faith stands. Therefore, to give anyone the impression that he ought to believe is to mislead him. It is better by far to tell him that of himself he cannot believe, that believing is a work of God in the human soul, God's greatest work. All that we can do is to be open and receptive soil for the seed of the Word, to acknowledge the hunger and thirst that we cannot satisfy, the emptiness that we cannot fill.

If there is an " ought " in this matter, it belongs with the teacher and not with the pupil. Believing is a response to the truth that meets us in the gospel, the truth that is nothing other than God himself in his truth and love coming to us to take away our darkness, to fill our emptiness with his own presence, and so to awaken us from death into life. But this gospel has to be *heard* if there is to be faith, and it cannot be heard unless there is faithful witness to it. But words are not of themselves sufficient witness. It is never rightly heard unless the witness to it is in both word and life. How can the pupil believe in the love of God if something other than love meets him in his relation to the one who speaks to him of God's love? How can he believe in the truth of God unless the mind and heart of his teacher are so possessed by that truth that the integrity and aliveness that belong to it belong also to him? The responsibility of the teacher is to let the gospel be heard. But here also there must be a warning that the teacher has no power to invoke faith in the pupil. The outcome is not in his hands, and if he becomes impatient for results and uses devices of his own to get the response he desires, he may sacrifice the deeper and more lasting response for a shallower one. Teaching, like preaching, has to be done with an eye only to the integrity of the word spoken. Is it the word of God, the word that God has given us here and now specifically for these pupils? Have we spoken it faithfully, putting ourselves in the situation of those to whom we speak so that we hear it with them and let it master us, that through us it may master them? Are we willing to remain servants of this word in relation to these pupils, watching for its fruits in their lives, which is another way of praying for the coming of the Kingdom? If this is what it means for us to teach, then we shall be free of all impatience concerning the response of our pupils; we shall be content to sow our seed and leave the mysterious growth of the seed to God, rejoicing at each sign of growth and not obstructing it by expecting to find the full corn in the ear before the plant is half grown.

Another frequent error is to judge the completeness of one's faith by the extent of one's acceptance of the articles of the creed. It is not unusual to come upon people outside the church who have the idea that they cannot honestly acknowledge themselves Christians because there are some parts of the creed that they cannot accept, perhaps the virgin birth or the resurrection of the body. To them it must be said that were they to accept all the articles in the creed without question, it would not make them Christians. Faith is not an intellectual agreement, or even intellectual plus emotional assent, to the articles of the creed. Faith is an unconditional openness to the living God to whom the creed bears witness. We do not believe certain things *about* God; we believe *in* God. To believe is to be so mastered, redeemed, and possessed by God that we no longer have any life of our own apart from him. Unbelief is the resistance of our life to God, our unwillingness to have all our life from him as our Creator, our self-sufficiency in which we act as though we had no need of a Redeemer, our determined self-centeredness in which we refuse to give up the place of rule within us to his Spirit. Therefore, just as assent to the articles of the creed is not faith, neither is the questioning of some of the articles necessarily unbelief. It may be a sign merely that a person has ceased to take the Christian faith for granted and has begun to think about it for himself. Or it may be a consequence of misunderstanding what the creed really intends to say.

THE RIGHT TO DOUBT

It is shocking how rarely churches and church schools are recognized as places where people can frankly and freely bring into the open their questions and doubts concerning all that has to do with the Christian faith. Sound educational psychology teaches that people learn most quickly and vitally at those points where questions have been rising spontaneously for them, not trifling, superficial questions, but deep, distressing ones. But it is notorious that in our churches these are the questions that people are most reluctant to ask. There is frequently an atmosphere that discourages and inhibits them.

Two stories will show how this atmosphere is created. A junior high class was studying the story of Jesus' rejection in the synagogue in Nazareth. One boy, who had the impression that Jesus had asked to be recognized as Messiah in his home town, expressed the judgment that if Jesus came to our town today claiming to be the Messiah, we would think him crazy. The teacher's reaction in horror at what he had said may well have played a large part in keeping that boy outside the church for twenty years. It was an honest question that should have shown the teacher a probing mind and should have led to a discussion of what it is that makes it so difficult for us to know who Jesus really is. But all the boy learned was that church was not the place to ask such questions. The second story is that of a college student who took a course in philosophy in her last year and had almost everything set in question that from her childhood she had assumed to be the truths of the Christian faith. In her distress she went to a minister who, after listening to her narrative, informed her that she was an atheist and had better get down on her knees and ask God to forgive her. She too carried away the impression that the church is not the place to let really serious doubts and questions out into the open. These are extreme instances. But a teacher has only to show the slightest sign of shock or disapproval when a pupil blurts out some emphatic expression of disbelief to send all the honest doubts of all the pupils scurrying like frightened mice into the dark back rooms of their minds, perhaps to hide there for years. How frequently this happens is evident from the number of Christians for whom it is the most unusual liberation to find themselves in a fellowship where *any* question may be asked and *any* doubt expressed without fear.

A church that is faithful to Jesus Christ should be the place before all others where every false pretense of faith or virtue is cast aside, where no one pretends to believe what he does not or to be what he is not. Jesus was himself the friend of publicans and sinners because they were, with him, simply what they were, sick men in need of healing, sinners in need of cleansing and forgiveness, blind in need of sight, unbelievers hungry for the truth. They had no pretentions to keep him from getting directly at their point of need. Why do we not understand that it is only in so far as we are sinners and unbelievers that Jesus Christ has anything to offer to us in his church? He is uninterested in the correctness of our beliefs or the virtue of our conduct, because he knows that for all of us, Christians and pagans alike, the sickness of our existence is that we do not believe in God in such a way as to have our life made whole in fellowship with him and that even our religion and virtue can be part of our defense against God's claim that we should belong wholly to him.

Perhaps the difficulty lies in an oversimplification of the problem of belief and unbelief, as though it should be possible to draw a line between the two, as though all persons should be classified as either believers or unbelievers. The leaders in a youth conference several years ago found themselves in an impasse on policy. Some wanted a program that would assume that all the young people were Christians who needed only some further training. Others wanted a program that would assume that many of the young people were not yet Christians and therefore needed conversion. Both needed to be reminded of the confession of faith offered by one man in the New Testament and recognized by Jesus as a genuine and honest confession: "Lord, I believe; help thou mine unbelief." One program is sufficient for Christians and non-Christians, because all of us, no matter how far we have gone in the Christian faith, have to confess the presence in us of both sin and unbelief. The continuing problem of sin is recognized by the prayer of confession in Christian worship, but the continuing problem of unbelief is often unacknowledged. And yet it is the unbelief of Christians, unbelief not merely as an inability to accept certain doctrines but as failure to respond to some of the truth and reality of God, that lies at the root of all the weaknesses and failures of the church. We cannot get at the crucial points of need in the life of the church until our unbelief is brought out into the open and conquered.

These distinctions are important because children at an early age begin to have false conceptions thrust upon them. They need to know their right to ask honest questions. As they grow, acquaintance with Jeremiah and Job will be an encouragement to them, letting them see that a real faith has courage to question God boldly concerning his dealings with us. And they need also to know that the sin and unbelief that they find in themselves as soon as they become conscious of their own existence is not evidence of some unusual corruption in them but is the sickness of all humanity and the basis of their claim upon the compassion and care of Jesus Christ.

The Unity of the Creed

Another frequent misunderstanding is that which takes the creed to be a list of separate items of belief, each of which stands by itself. Thus, to believe "in God the Father Almighty" is one thing; to believe "in Jesus Christ his only Son our Lord," another; and to believe "in the holy catholic church," quite another. It is true that each article, and often each word, adds something essential to the creed, but all are parts of one single act of believing and have their meaning from one center. It can be said that the Apostles' Creed simply draws out the implications of the original Christian confession, " Jesus Christ is Lord." We believe in God the Father Almighty, not apart from Jesus Christ as though we had some understanding of God's existence and Fatherhood and power in independence of him, but rather because of Jesus Christ. We go quite astray in thinking of God's almighty power when we think of it as some other power than was present in the weakness of Jesus upon the cross. As Christians we have no sure knowledge of God except as it is revealed to us in Jesus. So also the Holy Spirit is the life-giving Spirit, whose nature and works are known to us in Jesus' earthly life and in his resurrection from the dead, and not some vague divine entity of which we have dim glimmerings in our more uplifted moments. For belief in the church to be no more than a declaration of loyalty to the existing church would anchor us in its perversions as firmly as in its excellences. But when it becomes a concrete expression of our belief in Jesus Christ and of our openness to the Spirit that dwelt in him, it makes us members of his body through which he continues his ministry in the midst of the world. Belief in the forgiveness of sins, separated from faith in Jesus Christ, becomes an easygoing confidence that no matter what we do, God will forgive, in short, an incitement to sin. Only when we know the costliness of sin to him, and that in sin we are his enemies who crucify him, are we ready to hear the word of forgiveness that actually reconciles us with God. But perhaps at no point do we so pervert the Christian faith as when we separate belief in the life everlasting from belief in Jesus Christ. Thereby we give ourselves the hope of a blessed future in all eternity quite apart from any decision of faith that he requires of us. We assume our immortality and thereby build for ourselves an impregnable bastion behind which to hide from God. And yet in hiding we rob ourselves of the only security worth having, our share in the triumph over death that is reality in Jesus Christ.

The doctrine of the Trinity would be less a source of bewilderment to Christians if they knew to take as their starting point the church's faith in Jesus Christ. They try to understand it as a conundrum in theological arithmetic, three yet only one, one God yet three names for him, three persons in the Godhead. But what they should ask is why the early church came eventually to state its faith in God in such a seemingly illogical fashion. It is true, as one hears so often repeated, that the doctrine of the Trinity is never specifically enunciated as a doctrine in the New Testament, but that dare not conceal the fact that the way in which Christians confess their faith in God in the New Testament writings makes the doctrine of the Trinity inevitable. The early church was intensely conscious of knowing God and being possessed by God in a wholly new way through what had happened in Jesus Christ and what was being wrought in them through his continuing presence and power. The God whom they knew in him was the Creator God of Israel, the Lord of history, who was bringing to fulfillment in Jesus Christ the purpose for man that had been his from the beginning. So one was he with Jesus, yet in personal relation as a Father with his own Son, that they could not say who Jesus was without identifying him with the Father while still distinguishing him from him. And when they confessed the truth concerning the Spirit of God who now possessed and ruled them and was the source of their new life, they had to say that he was none other than the Spirit of the Father and the Spirit of their Lord, Jesus Christ.

Becauses the creed has its center in Jesus Christ, so that it is with him that we begin our understanding of it and not with God the Father, and in him that it finds its only right conclusion, we need to be reminded of the insufficiency of all human words to speak of Jesus Christ. No words even of a solemn creed can adequately grasp and comprehend the reality of what God has done and does for us and for all mankind in him. For this reason we have the sacraments in the church: Baptism, in which we are ever reminded that we have no share in him and no knowledge of him unless we die with him in his death and are raised into newness of life with him in his resurrection; and the Lord's Supper, in which Jesus offers himself to us in the bread and the wine and it is driven home upon us that there is no other Christian life than his life in us, the life for which he sets us free when he comes to abide not just with us but in us.

3.

. . . *In God*

On Taking God for Granted

The assumption of most teachers as they approach their classes is likely to be that all these well-dressed, well-washed, well-fed boys and girls at least believe in God. It would be discourteous to suggest anything else. Do not most of them come from the homes of church members? And the others would not be there if there were any hostility to religious belief in their home environment. Atheists are not accustomed to permit their children to attend church school, though it may happen. Moreover, for many teachers it would be a frightening prospect to anticipate the presence among their pupils of some who honestly and frankly confessed their disbelief in God. This would be a situation with which they would not feel competent to cope. It is a great comfort to them that, so far as they and their pupils are concerned, they can take belief in God for granted and start their teaching beyond that point.

There could be no greater mistake. That which dooms Christian preaching and teaching to the dullness of irrelevance is that anything should be taken for granted concerning the relation between God and man. A preacher who prepares his sermon and preaches it on the assumption that all his hearers will at least believe in God, so that he can start beyond that point, no longer speaks to the real distress of even his most Christian hearers. If he could look behind the polite façade that they maintain before the world (or if he would even look behind his own polite

39

façade), he would find that at the root of the weaknesses, conflicts, anxieties, and fears that afflict human life is a deep uncertainty, confusion, and darkness in man's relation with God. So, also, with children, God is the great question mark of their existence. They may answer readily when asked and say that they believe in God, but within themselves they are torn between different answers if they are conscious of the shifting phases of their own minds. There are moments when they are gripped by the fear that there is no God, nothing beyond themselves, although they would not dare to say it. At other times they tremble before a strange mysterious presence or are caught up into an ecstasy that seems to lift them above the world and themselves. How can they be sure? It troubles them that they should be so uncertain when all about them people seem to be so sure. The teacher must know that he speaks to persons whose whole existence is shaken and set in question by the word "God."

An opinion poll several years ago revealed the surprising fact that ninety-three per cent of the population were prepared to mark themselves down as believing in God. Far from rejoicing at this as a sign of what a God-fearing nation we are, in comparison with some others we could name, we should recognize in it one of the chief obstacles in the way of a genuine Christian faith. "Of course I believe in God," says the man whose every action and thought is a repudiation of God, and thereby he feels that he has warded off any further claim that God might make upon him. What more does God ask than that one should say Yes to his existence? This cheap admission of God's existence can be a kind of inoculation against a more virulent and costly kind of faith. For us as Christians there is only one true belief in God. It is not a belief that any human being can conjure up out of his own experiences of life or arrive at by a process of reasoning. It is no mere intellectual or emotional positing of a supreme being behind the phenomena of life. It is the faith that possesses the whole being of a man when God the Father comes to him through Jesus Christ and makes him his child, in his Spirit laying hold upon the inmost center of his being and giving him the promise of a new life in Christ. There is no Christian belief in God except as Father, Son, and Holy Spirit. And this is a belief that no preacher or teacher is ever likely to take for granted as already existing in his hearers. What, then, we must ask, is this belief in God which they are so inclined to take for granted? Surely, since it is not Christian faith in God, it stands revealed as some kind of false substitute for faith that men, even Christian men, take to themselves in order to conceal from themselves the emptiness that only the one true God can fill.

The Gods That Pass as Christian

The problem that confronts us here will appear more clearly if we consider what a series of men really mean when they say that they believe in God. First is the man who means that he believes in God's existence and considers this to be sufficient to remove him from the category of atheist, regardless of the character of his life. But the Scriptures of both Testaments are remarkably uninterested in the question of God's existence. The enemies of God, and even the devil himself, grants God's existence. The men who sent Jesus to his cross were all believers in God and did what they did because Jesus seemed to them to speak against their God. Some of the greatest crimes in history have been committed by men in loyalty to their religious faith. The Scriptures show us all manner of faith in God that stands in direct antithesis to a true faith in God. Sometimes today it is a sentimental mooning about "the man upstairs." Sometimes it is a product of meditation upon the necessity of a first cause as the origin of all things. All these flimsy substitutes for faith are left behind when the Christian confesses "I believe in God. . . ."

A second widespread meaning of the words is an assertion of the divine in man. As science has taken over the universe and seemingly emptied its infinite spaces of God, man is driven more and more to seek the divine in the recesses of his own spirit. Nineteenth-century religious thought was saturated with immanentalism. It had many popular forms. Christian Science and other more recent religious groups have built their teachings around the central affirmation of the divinity of man in himself. Aldous Huxley and other popular writers have set it forth as the basis of the one universal religion that is possible for modern man, the core of true religion within all of man's religions. It has always been, and still is, sweet to human ears to hear that we need look nowhere else for God than deep within ourselves. This faith insinuates itself into the minds of young and old through countless channels and may well be what a pupil means when he says that he believes in God. And yet this stands at the opposite pole from Christian faith. The Christian knows that all his life, its heights as well as its depths, must be redeemed. His confession of sin is confession that he is without God, cut off from God, lost in his godlessness except God have mercy and restore him to his fellowship. What need has a man of Jesus Christ if he already has God in the depths of his being?

A third form of popular faith identifies God with the interests and values of our civilization or of our nation. The adherents of this faith are usually quite sure that it is the Christian God in whom they believe. Are we not the chief representatives of the Christian heritage in the world today? Do we not stand for Christian freedom against totalitarian tyrannies and for Christian brotherliness among nations that, like beasts of the jungle, seem intent only on swallowing each other up? Where are men free to speak the truth as they are among us? What nation is so quick to play the Good Samaritan after a war and to bind up the wounds of its former enemies as we? Some would go a step farther and ask: " What nation has God ever blessed so bountifully or prospered so mightily as he has us? Or in what land are there so many churches and church members to sing the praises of God? " Surely we are his people and he is our God. We place his name upon our coins, that all the world may know wherein we place our trust. But when this faith is confessed it is never quite clear whether it is really God in whom we trust or just the order of life that we have made peculiarly our own and hope to see extended across the world in time to come. God seems to have become confused in our minds with the ethos of our society, so that it is doubtful to us whether any nation can worship our God without having an order of society like ours. Again we recognize here the face of a deity who is distinctly not the God and Father of Jesus Christ but much more like the god of the ancient Roman Empire, who was the very image of that society's hopes and longings, fears and prejudices, and could be incarnated in the emperor. Jesus Christ, who was crucified because he cut so sharply across the passionate interests of the nationalism of his place and time, can never be fitted comfortably into a cultural or nationalistic faith of this kind.

These three examples of what may be meant when faith in God is confessed are sufficient to show the acuteness of the problem that confronts the teacher. He has to ask what the nature is of the faiths that already clutter up the ground where he would sow the seeds of Christian faith. Allegiances have already been established; gods are already being worshiped; so, to say Yes to God in Christ will require the breaking of an existing loyalty and the surrender of another god. When Jesus Christ comes upon the scene, all the images, even the most beloved, that man has made for himself must go. The command still holds, " Thou shalt have no other gods before me." The inclination even of the child is, like that of the Hindu, to add Jesus Christ to the number of his gods. We are all of us at heart polytheists who want to worship at all the altars, that we may have the benefits of all. We do not like to be brought into the narrow pass where we have to worship one God alone. Yet it is only in this narrow pass that we learn the joy and strength and freedom of having our life unified and fulfilled in the worship of the one true God.

No God Except in Christ

Most of the difficulties that arise in the understanding of the Christian faith have their origin in ideas of God that we draw from some other source than the revelation of God in Jesus Christ. We are reluctant to concede that we know *nothing* of God except through Jesus Christ. Has not God implanted in us a knowledge of right and wrong, which is in essence a knowledge of his will and so of him? Has not God set in the hearts of all men a longing for himself, which accounts for the diverse forms of worship in the religions of the human race, and is there not in this longing itself an elementary knowledge of him? All we can answer is that in the conscience of humanity and in the religions of the world it is a wavering and uncertain light of knowledge that appears, flickering and pointing in contradictory directions, a dim candle when once the sun of truth and righteousness has shone in Jesus Christ. Yet Christians persist in the conviction that they have some knowledge of God from within themselves that they bring to the Christian faith.

Two places where this causes them great difficulty are the doctrine of the Trinity and the doctrine of the divine yet human nature of Jesus Christ. They approach the doctrine of the Trinity with the assumption that they know what the word "God" means. God is a spirit, unseen, infinite, eternal, omnipotent, omniscient. Their minds are already out somewhere in space attempting to grasp the reality of this unseen being when they are told that he has a threefold nature: Father, Son, and Holy Spirit. They try then to formulate some plan whereby their infinite, eternal, omniscient, omnipotent, unseen being can be present on earth in the man Jesus and can be known in the church as the Holy Spirit. They become hopelessly entangled, because they assume that they know the nature of God apart from Jesus Christ.

The first Christians were men who might have claimed for themselves a knowledge of God that was only enlarged and deepened by their experience of Jesus Christ. They were Jews, in whose midst God was known and worshiped as in no other nation. Yet all that they knew of God and man was set in question by what met them, confounded them, and transformed them in Jesus Christ. It was as though they had known nothing before and now had to be led by the hand as children to learn who God was and who they themselves were. Who would have dreamed that God would come among men in human flesh, would take man's sins and sorrows upon his own heart, and, dying at the hands of sinful men, would conquer the powers of evil and death? All their thinking about God had to start from this center, the reality of a new life and a new world that God had brought into being in the life and death and resurrection of Jesus Christ. In this wholly new situation, how could they speak the name of God without speaking of the Father of their Lord, and of their Lord, through whom alone they knew the Father and knew themselves to be his sons, but also of the Spirit of the Father and of their Lord, who had been sent into their hearts to quicken his life in them? So also today our starting point to understand the Trinity must not be any abstract conception of God, but must be a retracing of the steps of the first Christians as we spell out the name of the God who meets us and redeems us in Jesus Christ.

A similar difficulty arises in a similar way in regard to the divinity and humanity of Jesus Christ. How can he be fully human if he is divine, or how can he be fully divine if he is really human? This conundrum has plagued the church for centuries and plagues Christians still today. It begins early in a child's life. At first he is likely to think of Jesus as a divine being, not really of this earth, and then, when he discovers how human Jesus was, this seems to throw his earlier ideas of Jesus' divinity into the discard. The adult attempts a compromise. He thinks of Jesus as omniscient and omnipotent but of course not omnipresent, or he divests him of all these attributes of divinity and retains for him only the perfectness of his love and truth and holiness. But the source of our difficulty is that we assume we already know the nature of God on the one hand and the nature of man on the other. We try, then, to fit the two together in order to arrive at the nature of Jesus Christ as both God and man. But Jesus Christ is the point in the life of the world where all men have to come to know what these two words mean: " God " and " man." In him, God is truly God and man is truly man, not in separation but in union. This is what never entered into any mind before and what no man can ever know until he learns it here — that there is no other God than the God who lives for us, speaks to us, bears our sins, and triumphs over darkness and death in our flesh in Jesus Christ, and that only here, where our humanity is possessed wholly by God, is man truly man. We only confuse ourselves and darken the light of revelation when we approach this place of its revealing assuming that we know anything rightly either of God or of ourselves. Again and again a teacher will find that the difficulties of his pupils arise from this source, that they approach the Christian gospel with conceptions that entangle them in contradictions and that they have to learn to make Jesus Christ the starting point in all their thinking.

THE CHANGED SITUATION IN THE MODERN WORLD

A realistic assessment of the situation our pupils will face as they move out into the world must take account of the fact that in wide areas of modern culture it seems as though God had vanished. It is not that anyone takes the trouble to deny his existence; it is just that they proceed to think and speak and act as though there were no such reality to be reckoned with. And what makes it all the more perplexing is that people who would, if questioned, assert that they believe in God, and who may even be regular worshipers in church, may in their everyday existence think and speak and act as though there were no God except in the so-called spiritual realm, by which they mean within the confines of the church and in the inner life of the soul. They live between two worlds, one in which God is present and one from which he is absent. It is this which makes it so difficult to speak of God outside the specifically designated religious areas of life. It also creates an intolerable inner tension as men attempt to live in two contradictory worlds at once.

We can perhaps get at this problem best by noticing the contrast between the ancient world and ours. What we call the ancient world still exists in some regions of our world that have been untouched by modern culture. The ancient world was full of gods. All men were acutely conscious of the existence of two realms, the seen and the unseen, and the source of events and happenings in the visible, tangible world was constantly traced to the agency of unseen powers: gods, demons, angels, impersonal forces, fate, fortune. When Paul spoke to the cultured Athenians on the Areopagus, his problem was not to persuade skeptics to believe in God, but rather, among men who were hospitable toward all gods, to secure a hearing for his claim that in Jesus Christ alone could God be truly known. The antipathy to the Jews in many regions was resentment at their narrowness in refusing to worship any god except Yahweh, thereby setting in question, if not denying, the existence of the other gods. The Christians were attacked as atheists in the Roman Empire because of their denial of reality to the gods whom most men worshiped. Although throughout the New Testament the existence of unseen evil powers that resist God and try to hold man captive is assumed, the effect of the recognition of God's sole sovereignty was to empty them of power and significance, so that for the Christian man it was only a short step to the questioning of their existence. Christianity itself was therefore one of the major factors in putting an end to the ancient world view in which the unseen world was constantly obtruding itself upon the attention of man and had to be taken into account in all his concerns — in business, in the waging of war, in travel, in the determination of political policies, in securing fruitfulness either in the field, the flock, or the family, and even in his minor interests. It was not the intention of the Christian faith to secularize vast areas of life but only to relate all human affairs and concerns to the will and purpose of one sovereign God; however, it was perhaps inevitable that with the death of the ancient gods and demons, there should arise the modern concept of the world as a region empty of deity. The man of the ancient world had to choose between many gods or One; the man of the modern world has to choose between one God or none.

This world empty of God infringes upon the life of our pupils at many points. Avery Dulles, in his autobiographical *A Testimonial to Grace,* in which he tells how he, the son of a distinguished Protestant home, became a Jesuit priest, describes the effect of his educational experience in a New England prep school. No teacher was guilty of disseminating a positive atheistic doctrine, but the effect of his studies upon him was to make him an atheist. In all his subjects it was assumed that God was not a reality to be taken into account in human existence. History was a purely human sequence of influences and events with which God had nothing to do. The world presented to his mind was a world in which man was alone. So, also, much of modern drama and literature presents to the mind a picture of human beings trying to find some vestige of meaning in a world that is empty of God. There are unseen powers at work in it, but they are entirely psychological, forces that intrude upon the surface of life from the depths of man's unconscious. The artist in words does not invent a world, but, rather, he reflects the world he knows. We have, then, the strange contradiction that although ninety-three per cent of the population take the existence of God for granted, the testimony of our literature is that most of them live their lives day by day in a world in which there are only human forces and presences. This is the kind of world that seems to determine most of the conversations that the child hears. He does not hear anyone speak against God or deny God's existence, but most of what he hears is witness to that empty world in which there seems to be no God. His home may have in it between Sunday and Sunday not one sign that God is a living reality in the lives of these people all about him, a reality with whom they have to reckon moment by moment. Even such a small thing as grace at meals may take on a very great significance in this situation as an acknowledgment of God in what otherwise seems to be a completely secularized home.

From another angle we might with equal truth describe the modern situation as one in which the powers that ancient man conceived in personal terms as gods and demons are still at work in an impersonal form, still with their ancient cunning and force to take man captive and still with all their old destructiveness. Modern man sees his sanity, his ability to play his part in life, the happiness of his marriage, and much else threatened by forces hostile to him that lie buried in his unconscious mind. Where the ancient man went to the exorcist, the modern one goes to the psychiatrist or psychoanalyst to secure his freedom. We have also had sufficient instances in the twentieth century of the way in which a nation can become an idol, and nationalism a fanatical worship of the idol, intolerant of any other faith that seems to interfere. A god is whatever commands the loyalty and devotion of the human soul. With this definition we uncover a multitude of gods, most of them depersonalized and so concealed, all of them actively present in our world, promising great rewards of happiness and prosperity to their worshipers, and competing, sometimes even within the church, against the claims of Jesus Christ. Therefore, to believe in God as a Christian is to make a decision in which one's entire life is at stake, a decision for one God and against all the others. Faith is decision in which one says Yes to God and No to all the false gods. It is this negation which is involved in faith that makes it costly. Where nothing more is asked than that one say Yes to God, the Yes is robbed of all its content by the absence of the No. This is a peculiar danger in a society that welcomes affirmations but is unfriendly to what it calls " negative thinking." The positive has no meaning without its corresponding negative. Israel's Yes to God was genuine only when Israel said No to all the baals. The disciple's Yes to Jesus Christ cost him a radical No! to his own disordered yet fondly cherished self.

THE PERIL OF PROOF

When a teacher meets with a questioning of the existence of God, the temptation is to seek out rational proofs that may set such questionings at rest. If all that we desire is the pupil's, and our own, peace of mind, then such proofs may serve. But if our hope is that the pupil may eventually come to a genuinely Christian faith in God, we shall not be so eager to furnish him with proofs. It should weigh heavily in our minds that not one of the prophets or apostles deals in proofs; rather, what they offer to their fellow men is witness. Proofs are calculated only to produce an intellectual assurance of the fact of God, while witness is a personal testimony to what one knows of God — a testimony that points the way for others to enter upon the same relationship. The peril of the proofs is multiple: they may convince an adolescent mind and then in later years prove so deficient that the entire structure that has been built upon them will be cast aside as resting upon an untenable basis; or again the faith in God's existence that rests upon them may be taken to be the Christian faith in God and so become an obstacle to the formation of any but this shallow intellectual belief; or again the assurance so provided may become the foundation on which some one or more of the false beliefs in God that have been described is made to rest. What men think they have arrived at by reasonable argument is likely to resist any witness that the Scriptures can provide.

We need to recognize also that the personal problems that give rise to such questioning are not all of the same character or to be met in the same way. It may be a questioning by the young mind merely of the gods in whom so many people seem to believe and whom they take to be the Christian God, so that the repudiation of them is a sign that this pupil is reaching out in hope that some more adequate faith may be possible, and therefore an unusual opportunity to make clear the distinctive nature of a Christian faith in God. Or it may be a sign simply of a mind that has begun to think for itself, is not content to take anything at second hand but insists upon knowing for itself, and therefore a mind that demands to know what the church has to say for God or it will turn away in disillusionment. Or again, it may be a sign of a conscience burdened and distressed by its guilt before God and trying to escape the distress by persuading itself that God is an illusion about which no sensible person need be troubled. What lies behind the questioning in each particular instance we can know only by sympathetic openness and penetration, but of one thing we can be sure: that by proofs of God we ourselves evade in each instance the necessity of facing and sharing our pupil's grappling with the realities of his human situation.

This denial that we can prove the existence of God or any other element in the Christian faith by rational arguments does not mean that faith is opposed to reason or that our human reason has no place in the Christian life. Faith is not some kind of irrational response to God in which we give up the attempt to understand and simply accept as true certain propositions that are supernaturally implanted in our minds. The demand for understanding of ourselves and of all the realities that impinge upon our life is intrinsic to our natures as human beings. The coming of God to us does not annihilate our human nature but rather brings it to its fulfillment. The demand for understanding becomes not less but rather more intense. Faith does not give us easy answers to the problems of life but on the contrary discloses to us the full depth and complexity of the problems, makes us willing to acknowledge the deficiencies of our answers, and sets us to the task of *thinking* our way through them patiently and deliberately. The Christian protest is only against a superficial form of reasoning that counts nothing true unless it can be proved by rational argument and refuses to recognize the mystery that reaches far beyond our conscious probing in all realms both human and divine.

4.

. . . *The Father Almighty*

One of the qualities of a good teacher is to anticipate the difficulties of the pupils. We may be assured that before they have gone far in life they will come face to face with tragedy, a friend struck down by sickness or accident and crippled for life, some cruel misfortune in their own home, some disaster near at hand that suddenly blots out a number of lives. But, whatever it is, it is likely to set in question either the love or the power of God, or both. If children have any contact at all with the Christian church, they grow up thinking of God in terms of love and power. They hear more of God's love and fatherly care than of anything else. God is the unseen Father, who watches over them, provides for them, and keeps them from harm. And he can do this because he is all-powerful. Bible stories very often emphasize upon the mind of the child the power of God to make things happen or to keep undesirable things from happening. God is in control of the world and can do anything he wants to do. This seems to be what it means to believe in the Father Almighty. Therefore, when tragedy strikes, the mind inevitably asks how this could happen in a world ruled by a God of love who is almighty. If God has the power to prevent meaningless suffering, why does he not use it if he loves mankind? The impact of the horrors of war upon many minds is to make them deny that there can be any Father Almighty. It seems to be a sentimental delusion fit only for children who have not yet discovered what kind of place the world is.

The way is prepared for this shipwreck of faith by a failure of Christian teaching to make clear how we understand the power and love of God. That he is the Father in heaven dare not be made to signify just a general fatherliness but has to be understood in the light of what it meant for Jesus Christ to have God as Father. He is the Father of our Lord Jesus Christ, and our Father only as we belong together with Jesus to the same God. But that God was the Father of Jesus Christ did not exclude tragedy from the life of Jesus. He called God "Father" in Gethsemane as he shrank from the horrible destiny that lay before him and on the cross as the nails tore through his hands and feet. Where in all history is there a suffering less deserved or more cruel than that of Jesus in his death? Therefore, a belief in God's Fatherhood that has the right source and starting point, where God is revealed in the cross and resurrection of Jesus Christ, is no sentimental delusion but is a faith that is ready to meet all eventualities in human experience.

So also the word "Almighty" must be understood from this same center. We assume that we know what power is and therefore that we know the meaning of omnipotence. But there are different kinds of power. There is mechanical power that makes things happen by direct control. So much pressure exerted at one point produces a certain effect at another point. Power of control is therefore the power to determine directly what will happen. The weakness of dictators is that they covet this power of the impersonal machine and attempt to perfect it by turning society into a machine and men into mere cogs. Power of this kind raised to the nth degree and attributed to God makes of the world an impersonal realm in which God merely pushes the buttons and things happen. Omnipotence is the exclusive control of the heavenly buttons.

But there is another kind of power with which we are familiar that resides in persons. It operates not by compulsion but by the exertion of a mysterious force that makes the other person want to do certain things. It never treats any human being as a mere thing to be pushed about but so acts upon him that whatever he does he does in freedom. This is the power that a wise parent has over his children, not the mechanical power residing in his strength, his purse, and his ownership of the keys, but a personal power that depends entirely upon the love, understanding, justice, and truthfulness of his dealings with them. This kind of power is in the long run effective in the building of a home and family, and, if effective in the smallest unit of society, why not also in the larger unit, and even in the largest? This inner, hidden power is *real* power, power to make things happen, power to get things done, power to shape a world, power to create a meaningful existence, power to control. Why, then, should we use the image of mechanical power when we think of God and not the image of personal power? This is what we must not do if we are to understand omnipotence as the power of God revealed in the cross and resurrection of Jesus Christ.

THE FATHER OF OUR LORD

We must take with full seriousness, then, the statement attributed to Jesus in John's Gospel: "No man cometh unto the Father except by me." How basic this was to the early church's faith in God as Father is evident from the fact that it is repeated in Matthew's Gospel in a different form. "No one knows the Father, except the Son, and those to whom the Son is pleased to reveal him." It becomes apparent that for the early Christians it was no light matter to know God as Father. This was not an easy confidence in the benevolence of the power behind the world, but on the contrary it was a new relation with God into which men had come through Jesus Christ and by which the meaning of all things in life had been transformed for them. This and this alone was the relation in which they could with full assurance call God "Father" and know themselves to be his children. This new relation with God was possible for them only because it had first been the reality of Jesus' own relation with the Father, and because in his ministry, death, and resurrection his supreme achievement had been to impart to them nothing less than a share in his own life with God. In giving himself to them he took them into his relationship with the Father, so that his Father was their Father and they were sons of God together with him.

It is only when we grasp this uniquely Christian use of the term "Father" for God that the confession begins to have its rightful meaning. When we find that in other religions there are instances of men calling their god "Father," meaning by it merely his headship over all the family of the gods, or that the human race has had its origin in him, or that he rules the world with fatherly benevolence, we may be inclined at first to let the seeming parallel obscure the distinctiveness of the Christian use, seeing in it in every instance nothing more than an analogy drawn from human relations to suggest the nature of God. But its use in the New Testament in depicting the inner relations of the Godhead is something much profounder than this. When Jesus speaks of the Father and the Son and then of children of God, this is not just picture language. It is his way of saying who God is, who he himself is, and who we are, in relationships to each other that are the foundation of all existence.

It should be pointed out that in the Old Testament, God is sometimes, though not often, spoken of as the Father of Israel. More often the likeness of husband and wife is used to describe the intimate relation between God and his people, just as in the New Testament the church is the bride of Christ. But there are instances in which Israel is called God's son, or Israelites God's children, and there are prayers in which Israel calls out to God as Father. This is in direct line with the New Testament use, for it arises out of the most intense consciousness of the personal covenant relation between God and Israel. Israel belongs to God as a son to a father. God has brought Israel into being that in the midst of the world there might be a people in closest fellowship with him, responding to his love with love and to his faithfulness with faithfulness, reflecting his holiness and justice and truth. That this is the relation with God in which all men belong is expressed in the first chapter of Genesis, where man as man is created to be God's representative and partner on earth and to reflect his nature. The prophets look forward eagerly to a day when through Israel all nations will recognize and embrace this as their human destiny. But the story of Israel as it unfolds is the story of a broken relation and of a people missing its destiny. "Sons have I raised up, but they have rebelled against me."

In Jesus Christ the destiny of Israel is fulfilled. He is the Son who responds to the Father with complete love and faithfulness. He is the new Adam, who does not assert his own self-will and so put Eden behind him but who submits his will unconditionally to the will of the Father and so brings Eden back to earth. He is the very likeness and image of the Father, reflecting in his whole being the holiness and love and wisdom of the Father. This is his great work on earth by which he opens the gates of the Kingdom of Heaven, not so much by his words and deeds of themselves but by the fact that from beginning to end he is in himself the Son of the Father and so inaugurates a new era on earth in which all men have the possibility of being restored through him to their true relationship to God, to themselves, and to their fellow men. "Now are we sons of God, and it doth not yet appear what we shall be, but we shall be like him." The note of triumph bursts through when these Christians call God "Father" and themselves "his sons through Christ." This is their redemption in which they rejoice, that in Christ the broken relation between God and man has been decisively healed, so that they no longer merely call him "Father," but he *is* their Father and they *are* his sons, living moment by moment in the light and strength and joy of this restored relation.

"Father" was Jesus' word of address to God in prayer. We hear it in Gethsemane: "Father, if thou be willing, let this cup pass from me." We hear it on the cross: "Father, into thy hands I commend my spirit." The Gospel of John draws the portrait of Jesus faithfully when it depicts him as being moment by moment in such oneness with the Father that all the Father's words and actions were reflected in him as in a mirror. The word he spoke was the word of the Father. In his actions it was God himself who dealt with men. And yet this unity of Jesus with the Father was not a simple unity; it was oneness with him in a personal relation and it was maintained only at a cost. To be the Son of the Father in the midst of a world that was in rebellion against God was to be the One in whom God claimed his rightful place in relation to men and against whom men would vent all their antagonism and hatred toward God. Jesus' faithfulness in his Sonship was to take him to the cross. And we do well to note his warnings to his disciples that to share his relationship with God and to be God's sons, the sons of the Kingdom, must always be a costly life as long as it has to be lived out in a world that is in rebellion against God.

Nowhere is Jesus' mind concerning divine Fatherhood and human sonship made clearer than in the parable of the prodigal. The parable begins with the rupture in the family relationship between the son and the father, not an angry rupture, for all the son wanted was freedom to live his own life. That was all Adam wanted in Eden, freedom from a relation with God that put him under restraint and responsibility. Thus does Jesus understand the predicament of all of us. The drive to self-assertion cuts us apart from the relation with God in which alone we can be ourselves. Free, as a broken self, we soon exhaust the possibilities of our life and waken from the dream that we took to be life to recognize the utter emptiness of our isolated existence. It is when man remembers that he has a Father that he comes to himself. But the Father can mean nothing to him unless he makes a journey. He has to rise and go to his Father, claiming nothing from him as a right, acknowledging that to be accepted as a son is more than he can expect. He has to humble himself completely before the Father. But the wonder is that the Father comes to meet him, embraces him as his son in spite of his unworthiness, receives him as though nothing has ever happened except that he has been away, and restores him to his place in the family. Only as a consequence of this restoration can any man rightly know God as his Father. And it is because the work of Jesus Christ was to restore men to the Father that the first Christians denied that any man could know the Father except through Jesus Christ.

THE WEAKNESS OF GOD

It is strange that when we hear the words " Almighty " or " omnipotent " our minds immediately seize upon the material or mechanical image of power and leave aside the personal. It is an indication of how prone we are to think that the tangible is the real
and the intangible the unreal. An essential part of our education
is to learn to reverse this order and to recognize that the primary
realities of our existence are intangible and that the tangible are
always secondary. The New Testament is full of warnings against
the folly of seeking our security in things that can be seen and
touched and stored in barns (or banks) rather than in the things
that are unseen. Also, in the New Testament, power is constantly associated with the presence of the Holy Spirit. It is in the
power of the Holy Spirit that Jesus does his mighty works, casting out demons, healing the sick, and transforming the lives of
men. The church in The Acts of the Apostles is without power
until the Holy Spirit comes upon it and fills it with the very presence of God. But plainly the power of the Holy Spirit is not material or mechanical power that moves men about as though they
were things. It is the power of God in person, entering into such
closeness of fellowship with men that he can be said to dwell in
them as in temples. However close the relationship, it remains
personal. God speaks and man hears; God gives and man receives;
God commands and man obeys; man prays and God acts.

And yet the inclination of Christians has ever been to conceive
God's power impersonally. Nowhere is this more evident than in
the wooden conception of predestination that seems always to
come first to the mind when that word is pronounced. Since God
is omnipotent, he must control everything that happens in the
world; and since he is omniscient, he must know ahead of time
everything that is going to happen to the end of time. For anything to happen without his willing it would set his omnipotence
in question. Our salvation, therefore, is according to his choice
and planning, and if we are logical, we have to go on to say
that the damnation of others is according to his will and plan.

The logic of this argument is so flawless that it held the minds of Christians captive for many years. To question it seemed to involve one in the denial either of the omnipotence or of the omniscience of God. But behind this whole way of thinking is the false assumption that God's control of the world is basically a mechanical control. It represents him as dealing with men and their destinies as though they were not persons but things. The whole of history is reduced to a puppet show, with God holding all the strings in his hands. Even Jesus is a puppet and not a person. But the unanimous testimony of Scripture is that God has no interest in puppets but only in persons who, because they are free to make decisions, are capable of a personal relation with himself in which they may respond to his love with love and reflect his holiness, justice, and truth.

History in the Old Testament and the New is the life of persons in their relation with God, responding to him or rebelling against him, but whether they like it or not, with their life determined from beginning to end by what God is in relation to them. It was not figurative language when the prophets warned Israel that its life was at stake in the maintaining of the covenant relation with God and that to break the covenant was to die. The Gospel of John expresses the same truth for individuals when it says that in oneness with God through Jesus Christ we have life but that broken apart from the true vine of life we are already dead. God's power in history is power over life and death. It is in his relation with us, and ours with him, that our destinies are determined. Our thinking about predestination must begin, therefore, not with abstract conceptions of omnipotence and omniscience into which we unconsciously read unchristian meanings, but with the nature of God revealed in Jesus Christ. God is a person who deals with us and with all men as persons and not things. God is our Father, who has chosen us to be his sons and to know the fullness of life in loving response to him, so that whatever may befall us in life will be taken up into the unfolding of his purpose for us. God's power is the supreme and ultimate power in the universe because it is what he is to us and what he does through the events of our lives that determines their meaning for us. He always has the last word concerning the significance of what happens to us.

Because God's power is personal and not mechanical, it seems to the mind that thinks only in material terms to be weakness. The men who called up to Jesus on the cross, "Come down and we will believe," were unable to recognize a power of God that was not materially visible. Paul says that the cross was the peculiar stumbling block of his Jewish people because for them God's omnipotence was denied if God's Messiah could be made to die a criminal's death. The cross taught Christians a totally new understanding of God's power. "The weakness of God is stronger than men." A power was present in the person of Jesus Christ upon the cross, in his weakness and helplessness, that could break the power of evil over man once and for all and establish a new era in the life of humanity. The cross was fashioned by men as an instrument with which to silence the voice of Jesus Christ, but the power of God to determine the final issue of events is such that the cross became the pulpit from which Jesus' voice reached most penetratingly across the whole world.

Because God's power is personal, it is hidden and has to be revealed. We create misunderstandings and needless difficulties for faith when we fail to make as clear as the Bible does the hiddenness of God. We are sometimes so anxious to recommend the Christian faith for its reasonableness that we leave the impression that it will always find validation in the outward facts of life. We prove the justice of God by instances of how in a time of trouble everything came out all right for people who just had faith. But what if things go from bad to worse, as they did for the prophet Jeremiah — and for Jesus? And what if dishonest and unprincipled men prosper and keep the upper hand for years? Faith is not rightly faith unless it is a believing where we cannot see. It is based on what God is and not on what we can expect from him in a material way in the immediate future. Satan, in The Book of Job, suggested that Job believed in God not for God's own sake but because of what it was worth to him to be on good terms with God. But when God stripped from Job every visible and tangible evidence of his favor, Job, even in the darkness and incomprehensibleness of his experience, could not let go his hold upon God, for to surrender God would have been for him to surrender life. So also the Israelites in the exile went through years of darkness when it seemed as though they could hope for nothing from God in the future. God was hidden from them. But in Isa., chs. 40 to 66, a prophet proclaimed to them a faith that hoped valiantly when there seemed to be no basis for hope in the human prospect, a hope that based itself wholly upon the nature of God. We need, like that prophet and his Israelites, to learn to walk in darkness, with confidence in God in spite of all the facts that seem to contradict our faith, because to every person, sooner or later, there come such times of darkness when it seems as though the very face of God is hidden and the way into the future completely blocked. We must believe, not because the facts of life seem to prove such faith reasonable but because we are confident that it is God who ultimately gives to all the facts of life their true significance.

The Father with the Son and Holy Spirit

Sufficient has already been said about the impossibility of knowing the Father apart from the Son, Jesus Christ, and it has been suggested that the almighty power of the Father is revealed in the power of the Spirit. But we are so inclined to separate the Persons of the Trinity as though they were apart until we put them together in our minds that it needs perhaps to be emphasized that God the Father is not to be conceived as the one true, basic, original, Creator God, and the Son and the Spirit as somehow secondary, derivative, and subordinate. This is a false separation of the Persons of the Trinity that can have serious consequences. It takes different forms. For some people, "God the Father Almighty, Creator of heaven and earth," is the one God they worship; Jesus is his prophet, and the Spirit merely another way of speaking of his presence. For others, Jesus is God, the only God they need; his living presence with them is the Spirit, at work within a universe that cares as little for him as it cares for us. For yet others, the Spirit is God, a divine Spirit that pervades the universe and dwells in all men, in Jesus more than any other but not uniquely; and " Father " is but one of the many names with which men honor the Spirit. Each of these is really a form of Unitarianism and an abandonment of the Trinitarian faith, put forward usually with the claim that it is a simplification of the Christian's faith in God. Under the guise of a simplification, it presents another faith than that which meets us in the New Testament, a different Father Almighty, a different Jesus Christ, a different Holy Spirit. Only as we see with clarity the distinctiveness of the Christian faith in God as Father, Son, and Holy Spirit and the distinctiveness of the implications of that faith for life are we able to say what difference it makes.

We believe in one God, who is Father, Son, and Holy Spirit. We know him as our Father only as we know him as our Savior, crucified and risen for our sakes, and only as the crucified and risen Lord sends his Spirit, who is also the Spirit of the Father, to take possession of our hearts. It is of no use to stand before the mystery of the universe, looking out on the spectacle of the total life of man in history, and ask, " How, in the light of all we see, can we believe that behind this universe is a Father Almighty? " The claim of the Christian faith is not that the secret of the universe is an open secret requiring only an attentive ear, but a secret revealed in a particular history, the history of Israel, and in a particular person in whom that history comes to its focus, in Jesus Christ. God has spoken in a Word that in the fullness of time was made flesh in Jesus Christ. The Father has spoken to us and come to us in his Son to make known to us the meaning of this mysterious universe and of our life within it. Therefore, to know the Father Almighty we must stand in wonder not just before the mystery of the universe but also before the mystery of Jesus Christ upon his cross. And there, at one and the same time and as one and the same reality, we learn of the Father, whose love for us was so great that he gave up his Son to death that we might be reconciled to him; of the Son of God, who in his oneness with the Father upon the cross, is God's judgment upon our sins and the pioneer of our salvation; and of the Holy Spirit, who is God no longer distant from us but through Jesus Christ present with us and in us to be the source and power of a new life.

5.

. . . *Maker of Heaven and Earth*

For most people who repeat the Apostles' Creed, the words "Maker of heaven and earth" are not so much a confession of faith as the assertion of a fact, the fact that at the beginning of time all things had their origin in a creative act of God. The act belongs to an inconceivably distant past, before there were any human beings on the earth to observe and report it, so that some bright member of the class may pose the problem how the authors of Genesis or anyone else could know about the Creation in order to set down a report of it. Must not any account of the Creation be pure invention? It is most unwise to evade this problem by supposing that the authors of Scripture had the power not only to report events before they happened but also to peer backward into a time when no man was present on the earth and describe what happened then. The Biblical faith in God as Creator of heaven and earth has to do not so much with an event of the past as with a reality of the present. The prophets proclaim that God *is* the Creator and that the world and man *are* his creation. It is God who spreads out the heavens and gives fruitfulness to the earth. It is God who gives life to men and takes it again when he will. "The earth is the Lord's, . . . and they that dwell therein." The cattle on a thousand hills are his. The hope of man for the future lies in the prospect of a new creative act of God. But only by faith can man know the Creator, not by any manner of observation, and, from this knowledge that God *is* the Creator, he arrives at the knowledge expressed in Genesis and elsewhere that God *was* the Creator.

Both in the creed and in Gen. 1:1, the text speaks of the creation of "the heaven and the earth." This is more than just the story of how life began on earth. Rather, what we hear is a confession of faith concerning all reality, the seen and the unseen. The world had its origin in God and has its life from God but nevertheless must be distinguished from God. Man himself has his life both in the seen and the unseen, but in all his life he is God's creature. The more spiritual elements in his being are not divine. God is not to be identified with anything in man or with the ultimate being of the universe. He is the Creator on whom the creation and the creature both depend for their being.

We are concerned, then, not so much with an event in the distant past as with the present reality of the relation of God to the world and man. The goal of our teaching is not to secure the assent of our pupils to the proposition that at the beginning of time God made everything, a proposition that standing by itself may mean nothing to them except a contradiction to what their schoolbooks tell them was the origin of the world and man. Rather, our goal is that they may believe in God as *their* Creator and the world's Creator. Luther gave the doctrine this interpretation in his catechism by phrasing it, "I believe that God made me together with all other creatures." It should be the confession of God's relationship with us and ours with him on which is based our understanding of ourselves and of our world.

The Practical Importance of the Doctrine

"What difference does it make?" the human mind is inclined to ask with each article of doctrine. Are not all these shades of meaning in Christian doctrines a theological hairsplitting that may be amusing to scholars who have time for it but annoying to other people who are interested rather in what happens in life? We must be ready to say what difference truth or falsehood in doctrine makes in life. Belief in God as Creator can be shown to have very great practical importance in determining the approach of the Christian to various aspects of his life in the world.

No person can escape standing in some relation to the world and having some attitude toward the world any more than he can escape a relation to his parents and the members of his family. That relation between the person and the world becomes the background of his consciousness and so of his actions. It is always present and always entering into his understanding of all that happens, with a profound influence upon his judgments and responses. A shock of some kind early in life can create in a child a fear of the world that, if not overcome, can have a distorting and paralyzing effect for years. On the other hand, a confidence in the world as God's creation and as the realm in which he has chosen to unfold his purpose for us as his creatures can overcome such fears and send the person out into the world with an openness toward life no matter what experiences it may bring.

The teacher, then, should be familiar with all the different possibilities of what may be his pupils' relations with the world. They are likely most often to be not simple but complex, the consequence of a variety of influences, and may combine quite contradictory features. Perhaps the strongest influence in shaping the modern youth's thinking concerning the world is natural science. As it meets him in school, he may learn from it to conceive the universe as an entity existing in itself with its own laws, with its origin so far in the past that it seems infinite and with an equally infinite future, that is, unless man invents a way to blast everything to pieces. The phenomena are orderly, proceeding in sequences that man can discover and so predict. By scientific knowledge he attains a power of control over nature, at least sufficient to produce substantial benefits for himself — with certain attendant dangers. But this vast universe which unfolds before his mind seems to roll on its way through millions of years in complete indifference to the fate of man. Man seems little more than a fly-speck upon the surface of time, and yet it is man whose mind seeks to compass it all. Man is so small and yet so great. There may seem too little room in such a world for a Creator. Yet a scientific approach to the world does not need to lead to this conclusion, and for many eminent scientists it does not. Laws, after all, are generalizations concerning the behavior of phenomena that, in spite of all measurement, description, and generalization, retain the mystery of their meaning. The most thoughtful scientist is aware of the limitations of his knowledge and is slow to pronounce on matters beyond the scope of his investigations. But at a more superficial level, negative judgments are sometimes made that claim the authority of " science " and create the impression that the Biblical faith is impossible for modern man. If he is to continue to believe in a Creator, it can only be as a creative spiritual force within the universe and not a Creator of the heaven and the earth.

For others, the problem lies much deeper than the intellect. All of us, perhaps, have had at least a taste of what it is to feel the world standing over against us as a massive, hostile power that seems intent upon our humiliation and defeat. A succession of unhappy experiences can plunge a person into a mood of despondency in which the whole world seems to be against him. Thomas Carlyle, in his *Sartor Resartus,* tells how for a time the universe seemed to him to be a monstrous cruel machine that was bent upon crushing the life out of him. Life said No to him at every turn, and he said No to life. Not until he heard what he called " the everlasting Yea " of the universe to which he could answer Yes with his whole being could he get on with the business of living. Imprisoned in an everlasting Nay, one wastes the energies of his existence in frustration.

Closely related to this impression of a universe hostile to man and perhaps a consequence of it, is the idea that has exerted a widespread influence in the life of man and in the shaping of religions and cultures, that the material world is evil, irremediably evil. For the Greek the only enduring reality was in the ideal world of mind. The actual world of historical happenings was such an unceasing flux that it was useless to try to find meaning in it. Mind was divine, but it was imprisoned in a body that was hostile to it, so that its highest joy would be to be set free from the body. So also in Hinduism the world is a place of darkness and pain, where man can never hope to find the fulfillment of his life. To attain the goal of life in oneness with God, he has to escape from the world and from the body. This pessimism about the world and the flesh has invaded the Christian church in various forms: in a monasticism in which one has to flee from the world if he would truly find God, and in a pietism which tries to build a sacred circle of thought and action within the world in which one will be free from worldly contamination. The world is to be approached with distrust as a treacherous place for Christians, so full of sin and sorrow that it is only to be endured in hope of what lies beyond.

A primitive concept of the world that breaks in still among Christians more often than we recognize is that its happenings are controlled by dim impersonal fates. In the ancient world these fates were gods or heavenly powers such as the stars, whose intentions had to be divined in various ways and whose ill will had to be propitiated. The millions of books on astrology that are still sold are an indication of how these superstitions persist. Their last relic is in the customs of touching wood or throwing salt over one's shoulder to ward off bad luck. But often with children, and others than children, such superstitious fears can be very strong. The fear of darkness has linked with it the fear of powers that work in darkness. The only effective liberation from them is faith in the sovereign power of God over all things in his creation.

Yet another relation to the world that is encouraged in many quarters, particularly by a certain kind of religious poetry, is that in which nature is confused with God. The psalmist's exultant declaration that " the heavens declare the glory of God " is taken as an encouragement to seek God in nature, and the joy that is natural to most people in the presence of the beauties and wonders of nature is exalted into an experience of God. There have been areas in religious education in the past where the motto seemed to be " Go to nature to find God." Teachers and preachers have enthused over the possibility of arriving at a genuine faith in God by looking into the heart of a flower or by standing in the midst of impressive mountains. This is an excellent way to produce atheists, or at least to confuse people about what the Christian faith has to say of God. The psalmist who heard the heavens declaring God's glory was a member of a people who knew God not by seeking him in nature but by responding to his personal claim upon them in his Word. The Christian gospel offers man no hope of knowing God except through Jesus Christ. The youth in desperate need of God who follows the instruction to seek God in nature is in for bitter disillusionment. Nature is God's creation to be rejoiced in, not his chosen means of revealing himself to man.

Not only can no human being escape adopting some attitude toward the world, based upon some belief concerning its meaning, but also no Christian teacher can escape expressing and encouraging some one attitude and belief, or perhaps more than one. It is not uncommon to find a compromise between differing beliefs or even a combination of contradictory beliefs. A teacher should begin, therefore, by asking himself what conception of God's relation to the world underlies his teaching.

CREATOR AND CREATION IN THE GOSPEL

The story of creation holds such a commanding position at the opening of the Old Testament, and God is addressed as Creator so often by prophets and psalmists, that the impression has sometimes prevailed that this is a peculiarly Old Testament doctrine in which the New Testament has little interest. Marcion, in the second century A.D., set the Creator God of the Old Testament in opposition to the Redeemer God of the New Testament, alleging that these were two different gods. He held the Creator God responsible for all the evils of the world. But a more careful examination of the New Testament shows that the relation between God and the world everywhere presupposed in the New Testament is that of Creator and creation. The new beginning in the life of the world, which is effected in the life, death, and resurrection of Jesus, is a new creation, that is, a new creative act of

God corresponding to the first creative act by which the heaven and the earth were made. Jesus Christ is the second Adam, and the Christian is a new creature descended from him. But the Christian looks forward to yet another creative act of God which will bring God's purpose to its consummation in a new heaven and a new earth. Thus, in the New Testament, God's dealings with the world and man from the beginning to the end of history are represented as those of a Creator with his creation.

But the New Testament does not merely repeat what the Old Testament says concerning the Creator. At its center, where it speaks of Jesus Christ, the New Testament has certain things to say about Creator and creation that are unheard of in the Old Testament. Just as the new creation is through Jesus Christ, so also the original creation was through the Word of God, which is Christ's inmost nature. " By faith we understand that the world was created by the word of God." " All things were made through him, and without him was not anything made that was made." " In him all things were created, in heaven and on earth, visible and invisible, . . . all things were created through him and for him." In these statements three New Testament authors are insisting that in Jesus Christ the purpose of the Creator with his creation is revealed. We must begin with Him and not with Genesis if we would rightly understand the relation between God and the world. This is not, as it might seem at first sight, a speculative projection of Jesus Christ back into the days of creation in order to glorify his divine powers, but rather follows directly from the church's faith that in Jesus' person God and man are reconciled, so that in him and in him alone is revealed the true relation between God and the world. Apart from Jesus Christ we see only a world that has missed its destiny, only a mankind that resists the Creator and so distorts the creation, and we ourselves are part of that distorted creation. We recognize ourselves in Adam, who, by his self-will, brought enmity between himself and his Creator. But in Jesus Christ the enmity is overcome. He is our flesh and blood, creature together with us, sharing with us even our death. His life is part of our history: he belongs to our world.

But in him the world, our world, is no longer estranged from God by sin; in him it is a world in which God is loved and obeyed, in which man perfectly reflects God's glory and is perfectly at one with God. And this is our own true life and destiny, our own true relation with God, our own true world! If we would know the Creator, we must first see his creator hand at work in Jesus Christ shaping for us a new world and a new humanity. And if we would know the meaning of the creation and of our life as creatures, again we have to start with him in whom creation and creature are healed of their distortions and are known as they truly are. What this means for us we shall see more clearly as we spell out the implications of the doctrine of creation.

THE DIFFERENCE THAT IT MAKES

That God is Creator of heaven and earth means before all else that God is not to be confused with any thing or any power within his creation. Nothing in heaven or earth, and that means also in man or in human culture, is God. God transcends all things seen and unseen. God is God and man is man. The two stand in a most intimate relation, so that all of man's life is determined by his relation with God and God's with him. But it is a relation between Creator and creature that is confused and destroyed when the creature begins to think of himself as in some way divine by nature, or when he conceives his god as residing somewhere within the creation itself. Because in Israel life was known to depend wholly upon the covenant relation between God and man, and this relation was intensely personal, there was an emphatic prohibition, unknown in any other nation, of the worship of any thing or power or person in heaven or earth as though it were divine. There was a distance between Creator and creation, that there might be a relation between Creator and creation. The dissolving of the distance would be the dissolving of the relation. The constant warning of the prophets to Israel was that if Israel followed the example of its neighbors and gave its worship to divinities within the creation — stars, or trees, or rocks, or powers of fruitfulness in nature itself, or kings who symbolized the nation's life — it would destroy the covenant relation with God on which its life and health depended.

Most men, both in ancient and modern times, have felt the Hebrew faith to be too intolerant and austere. They have sought a power or presence to worship closer to them and more intimately a part of their existence, a divinity more comfortably near. The frequency with which we speak of things that give us joy as "divine" may suggest how strong this inclination is: the sublime in music and art or the beauty of nature. And some scatter the adjective "divine" even more freely. This is not a harmless exaggeration of speech; it is a form of pantheism for which the world itself and man within it are endowed with divinity. There is a spark of divinity in every man to correspond to the divinity in nature, we say. But for a Christian, God is not a substance of which sparks can be scattered about in nature and in man; God is a person who stands in a personal relation with man, the presence and power of whose Spirit may reside in man but with whom no man is ever likely to confuse himself. To be indwelt by God's Spirit is to be possessed by a Spirit of love and truth and justice and mercy, before whose presence man confesses his lovelessness and falsity and injustice and unforgivingness. We try to conceal this painful gulf between God and ourselves when we endow ourselves with a potential divinity or identify the spiritual values of our national culture or of our civilization with the divine. We want to be on more familiar terms with God — without the cost in personal responsibility. We want to be something other than creatures utterly dependent on their Creator.

The starkness with which the Hebrew preserved the distinction between God and man, particularly in the face of a Greek world that found the divine in man's reason, makes all the more amazing the Christian faith, born in the midst of the Jewish people: that, in a man who had grown up in one of their own Palestinian towns, God himself was present and dwelt bodily. This seemed to be a blasphemous confusion of man with God, the worshiping of a creature in place of the Creator. It was either blasphemy — or truth, the most revolutionary truth yet known to man. But in this faith there was no sentimental mingling of the human and divine into one. Christians, like the Jews before them, had no inclination to attribute divinity to man or to anything in the creation. The gulf between creature and Creator remained. But all was changed for them, because in Jesus Christ, the God in whom all things and all men have their life was present in our world and in our flesh and lifted our life and the life of our world up into oneness with himself.

God is praised at many points in Scripture as the Creator who brings into being that which was not. He creates from nothing. When Hebrews and Christians spoke thus of God, they had in mind not just the original creation of the world but also the birth of Israel, a band of slaves in Egypt transformed into a nation with a great and enduring destiny, and the birth of the church in which a handful of disciples became a world-conquering church. God is not limited by what seem to be the calculable possibilities of the human situation. The future may seem completely dark, as it did for Israel in exile, and as it does for everyone at times, but the darkness comes from reckoning only on the forces within our creaturely existence. We forget that the creation and the creature have a Creator, and that the Creator is the primary factor in every situation. The song of Hannah and the Magnificat of Mary both sing of how he lays the mighty in the dust and lifts up the heads of those who seemed to have no hope. The world remains his world even when it is most in revolt against him. Man has freedom for his words and deeds, but the final word and the final deed is always God's. There are two ways of reading the first story of creation, one that sees God as shaping the heaven and the earth from an already existing watery mass; the other, which is a *creatio ex nihilo,* in which at first there is only God and at God's command the heaven and the earth come into being, stage by stage, and take their shape. The peculiar force of the second is that it emphasizes the dependence of the entire creation upon God for its very existence and exalts the power and freedom of God in relation to all things in the creation.

The freedom of God within his own creation is limited when the possibility of miracle is denied. Faith does not demand of us that we accept all miracles reported in Scripture as actual happenings. There is a border line of superstition on the periphery of Scripture where men think to magnify the power of God or the power of a man of God by attributing to him the power to work miracles. Elisha can make an iron ax head float, and dishonest people drop dead when Peter accuses them of their sin. But when men become so sure that they know from their present experience what can happen and what cannot happen in this world, and deny to God any initiative in action, any freedom to intervene in the life of man, they are the victims of their own blindness. The central miracle of all time is the intervention of God in Jesus Christ, an event that cannot be explained from anything that came before, totally unexpected and unique. To deny miracle in principle is to deny the present active power of God in his creation. Faith in the Creator means life in constant expectation of God's creative action. The world is not a dead impersonal machine grinding on its way according to its inexorable laws. It is God's creation, and, as such, an orderly creation, but the drama of its life arises from its relation with its Creator. The history of the world is not just the story of man upon earth but the story of an unceasing dialogue between God and man. Blot God out and the drama has lost the initiator of its action. God acts in history because as Creator he does not cease at any moment to love and care for his creation. That there should be special acts of God at special moments does not surprise us if our eyes have been opened to recognize God's continual action in his personal relation with us as his creatures.

God's continual action is his providence. The creation is never without its Creator. We must insist on the distinction between creation and Creator, but we must not cut the creation apart from its Creator. Even when man by his sin denies his Creator and

lives as though there were no God, he is not wholly cut apart
from his Creator. From God's side the relation remains. In fact,
man is kept from destroying himself in his self-destructive sin
only because, hidden from him, God continues to guide and sus-
tain him. God loves every thing that he has made and continues
to love man even in the bitterness of man's rebellion. This loving
providence of God overrules our evil so that it is made to serve
his victory, but frequently, in men's minds, it is reduced to an
overshadowing care that supplies their daily needs and protects
them from harm. It is conceived as a divine activity quite separate
from all other divine activities. God will provide! God will protect! To believe in Providence is to trust God never to let you lack
your daily bread or come to harm! Does not the psalmist say that
those who trust in the Lord will not lack any good thing and
that a thousand may fall at our side and ten thousand at our right
hand but the evil will not come near us? We dare not forget,
however, that it was an Israel that had suffered the most devastat-
ing catastrophes that composed and sang these psalms. And we
sing them under the shadow of a cross on which the Son of God
died. Providence for Israel and for Jesus Christ did not mean
freedom from want and freedom from harm. Jesus in his temptations put from him the desire for that kind of protection. In his
oneness with God he had all the security that he could ask and
all that he needed, the knowledge that no matter what each new
moment should bring forth, whether of joy or pain, God would
be with him in such a way that the experience would be taken up
into his will and made to serve his glory. False promises in the
name of Providence, promises that cannot be made in the name
of the God and Father of Jesus Christ, are a peril to the faith of
any man. And if the promise of God's living and all-transforming
presence is not sufficient for him, then he asks of God what his
Lord could not and did not ask.

The Creator's presence with his creation, his love for his creation, and his joy in his creation are revealed in Jesus Christ. He
chooses to make our creaturely flesh the dwelling place of his
Spirit. Who dare despise the body that God has so honored? The

Christian faith is falsified when well-meaning people create the impression that the world and the flesh belong in closer association with the devil than with God. In Genesis, God does not look with suspicion upon his creation: " God saw every thing that he had made, and, behold, it was very good." Evil was an intrusion into God's good creation. Sin was a distortion of the nature God gave to man, not his original nature. Man is by nature God's man, made to reflect his likeness, and God is not willing to let himself be defeated in his purpose for man and for the world. Evil and chaos have threatened the world from the beginning, and the history of the world is the history of the battle to overcome them. So grim is the struggle that when we look only at the world and ourselves we may despair. But when God sets in our hearts and on our lips the Word in which he makes us his own, lightens our darkness, and unmasks the powers of evil that deceive us, or better, when he takes us prisoner with his Word in Jesus Christ, we become sharers with Christ in his victory over death and hell, and the world becomes the place where, in spite of all its evil, we are at home as members of God's family in his creation.

Salvation, for religions that despise the world as evil, has to be an escape or a deliverance out of the life of the world. But Christian salvation is the consequence of God's invasion and conquest of the life of the world, first in Jesus Christ, and then through the church, which is the body of Christ. In fact, the Christian life is a participation in God's invasion and conquest of the world in hope of the day when God's victory will be complete, the power of evil destroyed, and the creation restored to its true order, reflecting in all its life the glory of its Creator. To believe in the Creator, then, is to rejoice in all that God has made, giving thanks for the abundance of God's gifts to us in all created things, receiving them with openness and trust, reverencing them as God's, even when they are also ours, and using them for God's glory and the welfare of his far-scattered children. To confess God as Creator is to acknowledge that nothing, not even our own children or our own bodies, are our own, that all are God's gifts entrusted to us for a time, but only for a time. This is the basis of our steward-ship, but it is also the source of our freedom from anxiety. We are liberated from the tension and the burden of going through life possessed by persons and things and instead possess them joy-fully in God.

6.

. . . *And in Jesus Christ, His Son*

A problem is created for the teacher by the very order of the creed. The pupil who repeats it says that he believes in the Father Almighty *and* in Jesus Christ his Son *and* in the Holy Spirit. What other impression could he get from this than that one believes first in the Father, then in the Son, and finally in the Holy Spirit? The basic question, then, for him, from which all else proceeds, is whether or not he can believe in God as the Father Almighty. Do I or do I not believe in God? Having settled this question, he expects then to move on to ask himself what it means to believe in Jesus as the Son of God. There are two fatal errors in this: the one, that the pupil should be allowed to think that a Christian belief in God is a possibility except in confrontation with Jesus Christ; the other, that having formed in his mind some conception of God, he tries to combine it in some way with the picture of the man Jesus that he draws from the Gospels, ending up either with a somewhat deified man or a somewhat humanized God — and most likely with serious doubts about the whole project.

Let us face frankly the fact that most people even within the Christian church are accustomed to make the decision whether or not they believe in God on a basis that does not take Jesus Christ intimately into account. This is regarded as a prior question, a decision for or against a religious approach to life and a religious interpretation of reality, and the question " Christian or not Christian " comes only as a second step. This is perhaps why there are so many people who count themselves Christians because they have taken the second step but who have an essentially unchristian conception of God that constantly prevents them from understanding and from giving themselves wholeheartedly to a really Christian faith. Moreover, they are encouraged often by what they meet in the church in thinking that they have first to settle the question of God before they can inquire more deeply into the Christian gospel. Perhaps we try to settle the question for them by giving them rational arguments to prove that there is a God, or we interpret their experiences of life for them to show them that they already believe in God without knowing it, or we invite them to participate in some form of worship with the hope that they will feel God's presence and be convinced. Often we succeed in one or other of these approaches and congratulate ourselves that we have helped them take the first step *toward* a Christian faith. But are they not already in confusion because we have led them to think that they can have a Christian belief in God apart from Jesus Christ? Could not this be the reason why so many church members have a belief in God which is the source of their spiritual assurance but which seems to commit them in no way to put themselves unconditionally at the disposal of the God of infinite mercy and compassion, who meets us and claims us in Jesus Christ? Jesus Christ and the decisions with which Jesus Christ confronts man have been bypassed from the very beginning. A sub-Christian or non-Christian belief in God is a poor starting point for an expedition that hopes to arrive one day at a full Christian faith. A *Christian* decision for or against God is possible only when one has been brought face to face with Jesus Christ by the hearing of the gospel.

There should be no misunderstanding, then, about where Jesus Christ belongs in the creed. As it stands, he is its center, and it is easy enough to see that the articles concerning him occupy more space than any others. But he is not just its center; he is also its beginning and its conclusion. We do not believe at all as Christians until we believe in him. There would be no such creed possible were it not for what happened in a few short years in Palestine over nineteen centuries ago. The church would not exist if he had not lived and spoken and died and risen. It is through him that there is forgiveness of sins, God's free forgiveness of our sins and our free forgiveness of the sins of our fellow men. Death is conquered for us, and we have hope of life everlasting only when we die with him and with him rise into newness of life.

THE MAN JESUS

Our approach to this central article of the creed should ever be one of astonishment. It ought not to surprise us that anyone, young or old, should find it unbelievable and should stumble at it. Most Jews of the first century found it downright blasphemous, and to many intelligent Gentiles it was the height of absurdity, to say that a young Jew in his early thirties, known to his fellow townsmen in Nazareth as the carpenter, who was executed for his revolutionary tendencies after a brief and none too successful ministry in Galilee and Judea, was none other than the Son of God, and as such should be worshiped and obeyed as God himself! The whole history of Israel's religion had been a battle against idolatry, against worshiping any person or thing within the creation as though it were divine. Pagans might bow down and worship men as gods. The Roman emperor became a god at his death, and the king of Egypt was called a son of God and was worshiped as divine. Therefore, the early Christians seemed to their fellow Jews to be falling away into paganism when they gave their worship to Jesus as the Christ. But these Christians, who had the same strict training in a tradition that abhorred idolatry, were insistent upon their monotheism and upon the fact that their worship of Jesus was not the worship of a creature. They too worshiped God alone, the God of Abraham, Isaac, and Jacob, the God who brought Israel out of Egypt, the God of the prophets, but he had come to them in a wholly new way, in the person of Jesus. According to all previous ways of thinking, it was unbelievable. But it was true, and they were willing to stake their lives on the truth of it.

Why are we so rarely astonished at this central assertion of the

Christian gospel? Partly it is because we do not take seriously the full humanity of Jesus and so we dissolve the problem. On the basis of the stories of the miracles in the Gospels, and of other instances of Jesus' possession of supernatural powers, we make him into a supernatural man, so that he ceases to be flesh of our flesh, a man subject to creaturely limitations as we are. But here we are going contrary to what all the authors of the New Testament insist: that Jesus was one of us, born a helpless babe, subject to all the necessities of a growing life, " in all points tempted like as we are," sustained and guided by the word of God in Scripture and by prayer, and with the final clinching proof of his humanity that he died as we do. Neither the miracle stories nor any other traditions concerning Jesus were intended by the New Testament authors to obscure Jesus' humanity. After all, there were other men in Scripture who were reported to have performed miracles, and no one had ever suggested that they were more than human. But when we have made Jesus a supernatural man, it ceases to astonish us that his disciples considered him divine. Unfortunately, he ceases also to be the Jesus in whom the disciples confessed their faith and who had power to reconcile them to God.

Another approach that makes the article easily believable is to interpret the title " Son of God " as expressing only a profound respect for the divine qualities that resided in Jesus' character — and may reside also in a lesser degree in our characters. Jesus is then the ultimate expression of the divine in man. Beyond him, as also beyond us, is the Father Almighty. Did he not pray to the Father and submit himself to him? But the first Christians who worshiped Jesus as God were not worshiping divine qualities in him; nor did they think of themselves as being divine as Jesus was divine though in a lesser degree. They knew themselves sinners in darkness and slavery because of the absence of God from them, and in the company of Jesus they became most acutely aware of their resistance to God, their emptiness, weakness, and poverty of soul. But where they were empty of God, he was full of God; where they resisted God, there was perfect obedience in him, even when it meant his death. From him light shone into their darkness. His oneness with God, which was the source of his power, his love, and his joy, made their own broken relation with God an embarrassment and an agony to them. The will of God in him cut across their wills like a razor-edged sword, and some, like Judas, could not bear it. One thing is certain: neither in Jesus' lifetime nor later had the disciples any inclination to think of themselves as divine. Even when they were most conscious of the Spirit of God, who is the Spirit of divine power and love and holiness and joy, dwelling in them, they were too aware of all that in them still resisted God's Spirit to say of themselves, "We too are divine."

That Jesus is the Christ, that he is God, is a mystery that is hidden from the eyes of men and has to be revealed. Let the teacher beware of dissolving the mystery. Only too often teachers speak of Jesus as the Christ or as divine as though this were a truth which they can communicate to pupils merely by telling them. It was revealed to the disciples, and no further revelation is necessary. Peter and the other disciples may have been blind to it in spite of their closeness to Jesus, so that they came to know it only when God himself broke in upon them in a wholly new way through Jesus, but, for us, it is simply one of the truths concerning Jesus that we accept on the authority of the disciples in the New Testament. This, of course, simplifies our work of teaching, but it is a simplification that substitutes the intellectual or emotional acceptance of a statement about Jesus for a living personal faith in him, a faith that is possible only when the pupil in his present-day existence has come face to face with Jesus and has had to say *for himself* who this is. It is not sufficient that there was a revelation of God in Jesus over nineteen centuries ago; not until there is today for each of us a revelation, which is a coming of God to us in him, can we with integrity confess that this is also *our* faith.

Where, then, do we start? We start where Peter, James, and John started — with the man Jesus, the Jesus who confronts us in the Gospels; not with an attempt to reconstruct out of the Gospels an attractive human figure whom we can idealize as the perfect man, but rather by putting ourselves in the place of the disciples and facing the questions with which the existence of Jesus in their midst confronted them. The man Jesus proclaims to us, as he did to them, the nearness of the Kingdom of God and calls us to repent. The life of the Kingdom, which is life under God's immediate rule in the power of his indwelling Spirit, is a reality in Jesus' own person. The sickness of men is that they live shut out from God, attempting to shape for themselves a satisfactory life out of their own human cultural and religious resources. The sin that destroys them even in their most earnest religiousness is their determination to remain rulers of themselves, masters of their own destinies. Their life has no adequate basis until they are what God created them to be — sons of God, made to reflect his love, his truth, his holiness, his justice, in a relation of unconditional openness to him. Life in God is man's only true, free, joyful life. But it is possible for man only when he has let himself be humbled before God and has recognized that all that he has without God is as nothing. But when he is humbled and lets God be the sovereign of his existence in this unconditional way, then he becomes rich as no other man is rich, the possessor of all that is worth possessing in the whole earth — in God. The earth is no longer a place merely of dangers and uncertainties that threaten his life but is God's world, in which everything, even the most painful experiences, are made to serve God's will. This is the good news of the man Jesus to men. It is bad news to every man who wishes to remain his own ruler and to keep the control of his life in his own hands, and particularly for those who, whether they are conscious of it or not, use their religion and good conduct as a defense for themselves against any more radical claim of God upon them. But, for those who are in despair with their own self-rule and with what they have been able to make of life by their own efforts, it is the best news they ever heard, news of a totally new possibility of life in God. But even when we have, with the disciples, heard this good news and have welcomed it in repentance, he who brings it to us is no more than prophet and teacher.

But now this man Jesus offers us himself and invites us to share with him his ministry. All about us are human beings who do not know the possibilities of life in God that are at their door, so near to them and yet so far from them, and who live in darkness as prisoners of the powers of darkness that lord it over men wherever they are cut off from God. Therefore, the net of the gospel has to be flung out into this dark world to draw men into the life of the Kingdom. There must be not just one but many fishermen, heralds of the Kingdom, themselves open to the same Spirit of the living God who was so powerfully present in Jesus and thus able to open to men the possibility of a new wholeness of body and spirit, a new freedom from all the dark powers that enslave them and a new meaningfulness in the living of their days. We accept the invitation. We begin to share his ministry. We taste its triumphs as we see life transformed for men and women by this gospel. And we also taste its cost as men with an entrenched interest in the existing order of things resist what seems to them an inordinate and unreasonable claim on God's behalf. Perhaps, like Judas, we become frightened at the revolutionary implications of the coming of the Kingdom and draw back. But if we do not draw back, we find ourselves in a close relation with Jesus that exposes us to the strange, puzzling reality of his being. He is in every way a man. We know many of the particulars of his human life. And yet the claim he makes upon us is a claim that only God can make, and a decision for or against him is a decision for or against God. He is not just a proclaimer of God's word to us like the prophets; he *is* God's word in his person. He speaks for God not just with his life but with his actions and with his very being. It is God himself who comes to us in him, and when we in response come to him, we have come to none other than the living God.

CHRIST, HIS SON

The teacher may find it frustrating to be told that the goal of teaching is that the pupil may know Jesus as the Christ but that this knowledge cannot be given directly to anyone. At the most decisive point in Christian teaching the teacher has to confess a helplessness and exercise a severe restraint. His task is to be a guide for the pupil into the maze of the Scriptures, that he may find his way to the point in them where he really hears the voice of Jesus Christ for himself. It is easy to get so lost in Scripture that one never comes to that point of decision. It is so easy to read Scripture merely as a religious book that tells us all the right things to believe and to do. Every pupil comes to Scripture with certain false conceptions that keep him from seeing what is there. A large part of teaching is to clear obstacles out of the way and to keep the pupil moving ever deeper into Scripture that he may not stop part way on the journey to his confrontation with Jesus Christ. Our part is to do as Peter did with his brother: bring him to that point of meeting, confident that no person can come face to face with Jesus Christ and ever be the same again. The documents of the New Testament can themselves become obstacles in the way if we fail to understand each of them in its uniqueness and so expect them all to speak in the same tone and in perfect agreement on every detail. The value of literary and historical study of Scripture to the teacher is that it enables him to hear each document in its own setting and in its own way bearing its witness to Jesus Christ. Paul is not John, or John Matthew, or Matthew Mark. Each author has his own background and standpoint, and each has his own audience. He must be allowed to speak without being pressed into some preconceived pattern of what he ought to be saying. Each will tell us who Jesus is for him, but even this does not answer our question for us. They do no more than point into the heart of the mystery where they have found life and into which each person must go alone if there is to be life for him.

We have now to consider the fact that while Jesus was still with the disciples on earth, their faith in him as the Christ, the Son of God, remained broken, uncertain, and confused. The power of God in him that drew from them the confession that he was the Christ led them to expect that at any moment he would inaugurate a universal kingdom in which he would visibly and conclusively establish his authority as Messianic king, so that his death was the defeat of all their hopes. Peter thought that he had burned his bridges and had cast in his lot unconditionally with Jesus, but he was deceived about himself; he had still an avenue of retreat that he was to use in the hour of testing. They all had avenues of retreat. Jesus in his lifetime was not able to get them past the point of no return. Their faith, for all its depth and strength, carrying them as it did into a life of poverty with Jesus and a sharing of his ministry, was still a conditional faith. They miscalculated the strength of the enemy and the extent to which they remained in the grip of the enemy, because self in them had not yet died that they might come alive to God in newness of life. There was something that had to be done for them that could not be done except by the death of Jesus, which by a peculiar but powerful interchange would be their death, and the resurrection of Jesus, which would be their resurrection from the dead.

We too miscalculate the strength of the enemy if we think that we need no more than what the man Jesus does for us, that when God comes to us through him and opens to us the life of his Kingdom, we have arrived at our true faith as Christians and need go no farther. We have a faith indeed, a faith sufficient to make us confess Jesus as the Christ, but it is a faith that is constantly broken and shaken by the forces within the self that resist it. We think perhaps that our spiritual battle has been won when actually God's enemy within us has not yet been flushed out into the open. We do not rightly know either Jesus Christ or ourselves until the cross has done its work with us. *We* are the world that has it in its heart to let the cross be erected on Calvary and to let Jesus, in spite of all he means to us, hang upon it in agony and die. We would never have believed it of ourselves if there had been no cross. The power of evil that wars against God's love and truth has its stronghold not in evil men, scorners of religion and of order in society, but in good men like us, lovers of religion, models of orthodox doctrine, defenders of law and order. It is always in the name of something that seems unquestionably good that we crucify Christ. This is the deceptive power of evil that is unmasked only by the cross: that evil has its power only in that empty place in man's self into which God has not yet come. The only safety against evil is to die wholly to self, that where self has reigned God may reign. Jesus took with him to the cross the burden of our emptiness and imprisonment that we might see in horror that our sin is his death. He died that everything in us that made him die might be crucified with him, and so we might be set free to live our true life in God.

But who is this whose death for our sakes becomes the death of God's enemy in us and so our life? Who has power over life and death and to bring life out of death? Who can this be who calls us to go through death to life? The disciples were not left long with these questions tearing them apart. Early the third day after the crucifixion Jesus was known to them with all concealment of his divine nature and power cast aside. He was with them as the living and triumphant presence of God himself. The risen Lord was not a disembodied spirit of the man Jesus. He was the unveiling to the disciples of the divine glory, so that they knew that it was none other than God himself who had been with them in the human life of Jesus, had loved them and chosen them and given himself to them, and when he could overcome their ultimate resistance in no other way, had died for them. The risen Lord came only to men who had died with him when he died for them on the cross, and his coming to them was the decisive coming of God to them to abide with them and by his abiding presence with them to be the foundation of a new people of God, a new humanity, a new world.

How, then, can we know the Christ, the Son of God? There is no road to the knowledge of him in whom we are created anew except by way of the cross. Christian baptism for Paul was an outward sign of man's going down into death with Christ that he might come up on the other side of the cross into a new life in which Christ reigns triumphant. It is in that new life in which the reign of Christ is none other than the reign of God that we have full confidence to confess that Jesus is the Christ, the Son of God, and to mean by that that he is to us no less than God himself.

DEIFICATION OR INCARNATION

There is one problem that is likely to arise for the teacher that we have not as yet considered. The idea is widespread today and arises spontaneously in many minds that the church's doctrine of the divinity of Jesus is actually the deification of a man. It goes something like this. In himself Jesus was no more than a very wonderful religious teacher who opened to men a way of life higher and better than any man had ever known before. He gave men a new understanding of God and of themselves and of the meaning of life. But he never claimed to be anything more than a prophet and teacher. Higher claims for him have been read back into the stories by a later era. But he attached his disciples to himself with a deep love and loyalty, and when his ministry was cut abruptly short by the fear of the Jewish and Roman authorities that he was a revolutionist, the disciples could not let the cross be the last word about their master. In their overwrought and grief-stricken condition after his death, they had visions of him that encouraged them to ascribe to him a divine nature and to offer to him worship as to a god. Their visions assured them that he was not dead but lived on in the heavenly regions.

To support this explanation, it is usually pointed out that the deification of a man is not an unusual happening in the phenomena of religion. Buddha, who insisted that he was only human, later became the object of worship to millions of Buddhists. The Roman emperors, as they died, became gods of the Roman state. These we regard as instances of superstition. Why, then, should we not regard the Christian claims concerning Jesus as the product of Christian superstition?

It is true that in the earliest tradition Jesus never claims to be God. It is unthinkable that he should do so, because then his divinity would be not a mystery revealed only to faith but rather a fact concerning him that could be communicated directly by flesh and blood. For Jesus to have announced himself as God would have been to have made himself an idol. A corollary of this is the fact that the worship of the man Jesus among Christians is a form of idolatry that ought not to be encouraged, as it often is. It is also true that higher claims for Jesus have been read back into the record as, for instance, in John's Gospel where, in contrast to the Synoptics, the author has Jesus apply to himself attributes of divinity. But it is not necessary to conclude from this that Jesus considered himself merely a prophet and teacher. It is doubtful that he ever claimed openly to be the Messiah, but it is certain that for him the "Last Days" that Israel had long expected, when God's Kingdom would be established among men, had already begun, and the promises of God to Israel were being fulfilled in his ministry. If we interpret the baptism and temptations of Jesus as visionary experiences, similar to those of Isaiah and Paul, and therefore to be known only from Jesus' own account of them, they say to us that at his baptism he was conscious of standing in a unique relation to God as God's Son and of having before him a unique mission as the Suffering Servant of God, who would bear and so bear away the sins of men. His forgiveness of men's sins was blasphemy to his fellow Jews, since only God could forgive sins. His demand upon men to deny themselves utterly and follow him asked of them what only God could ask. For any man to ask this of his fellow men would be for him to be a tyrant who would rob them of their freedom. A decision for or against him and his gospel was a decision for or against God. And when at the Last Supper he offered *himself* to the disciples in the bread and wine as the inexhaustible source of life for them in all the time to come, it is clear that by this he meant not just himself as the man of Galilee but the infinite and unsearchable resources of the God with whom he knew himself one. The divinity of Jesus was hidden in his lifetime and only brokenly revealed, but these hints suggest that Jesus was not unconscious of the mystery of his own being and that the author of John's Gospel, when at a later time he put such higher claims for Jesus in Jesus' own mouth, was doing no violence to the original reality but rather was only drawing aside the curtain that had temporarily concealed who Jesus was. His portrayal of the unbroken oneness of Jesus with the Father is the picture of Jesus that comes to us from every segment of the New Testament tradition.

Again, it is false to represent the disciples as thinking to honor their dead master by raising him to the dignity of a God. This might be comprehensible with Romans, Greeks, or Egyptians, but not with Jews. Long centuries of training had made them abhor such practices. God must ever be God alone, and no created thing or person must ever be permitted to share his worship. What is striking is that the disciples were confident of their faithfulness to that strict tradition. They worshiped the God of Israel in him. Paul, in his rabbinic days, reacted as a faithful Jew to the Christian testimony concerning Jesus. It was blasphemy especially foul and obvious. How could men be such fools? Therefore, it was against all of Paul's natural inclinations that he was forced by his vision of the risen Lord to acknowledge him as the one true revelation of God. This, then, was no sentimental enthusiasm of disciples for a beloved teacher. Rather, the evidence is that a reality met them in him that they were slow to recognize in its true nature but that they were forced eventually to confess to be the reality of the living God himself, meeting them in judgment and in mercy and opening to mankind an unbelievable new future. Therefore, in their interpretation of what had happened, there is no suggestion of a process of deifying a man but rather the constant assertion of the opposite, that in Jesus, God became man and dwelt in our human nature, not that men might have another god to worship, but that men through Jesus might come to know their only true life as a life indwelt by God.

7.

. . . Our Lord

The question may be asked why in the creed we make a triple confession concerning Jesus: that he is Christ, God's Son, and our Lord. All three are in danger of becoming merely titles of respect for Jesus with no specific content except the recognition of his divinity. The New Testament has yet other titles for Jesus that do not occur in the creed: Servant of God, Savior, our great High Priest, the Word, the Son of Man, the Lamb of God; each of them expresses some aspect of his nature and work. Why, then, are these three chosen and what is the special significance of each?

The title "Christ" points backward into the Old Testament and into the life of Israel and acknowledges that Jesus in his ministry, death, and resurrection is the fulfillment of God's promises to Israel. It binds him together with the Old Testament as the One on whom the hopes of Israel were set, and it binds the Old Testament together with him as the record of the mercy and severity of God that were to come to their climax in him. In demonstrating this relation of Jesus to the Old Testament, it is a mistake for a teacher merely to hunt out references to the Christ, or Messiah, in various passages in order to show that the coming of the Christ was predicted long before Jesus' birth. We need to be warned that Jesus in many respects refused to be the kind of Messiah that the Jewish people were expecting on the basis of the Old Testament. He was to be a king, like David of old, who would be distinguished not only by great wisdom but also by his power to establish an earthly kingdom and subdue the Gentile nations to his rule. According to John the Baptist, he would bring all men to judgment, destroying the wicked and establishing an eternal Kingdom for the faithful. Jesus' failure to fit any of the patterns of Messiah (Christ) in the minds of the men of his time (including his own disciples) was a major element in the perplexity of men concerning him.

If we would understand the promise of the Old Testament fulfilled in Jesus, we must look beyond the few passages that speak of a Messiah. The whole Old Testament embodies the promise, for the whole Old Testament has to do with a relationship of God to Israel and of Israel to God in which the possibility of what might be was infinitely beyond the actuality of the relation at any given time. Israel was called to be a nation in covenant with God, responding to God's love with a loving obedience and reflecting in its life the very nature of God, his mercy, his truth, his justice, his holiness. This personal relation with God had in it the promise of blessedness, because in it man would be alive to God and alive and responsive to his fellow man. In so far as it was realized in Israel, men entered upon their true life in God, and their songs of thankful joy that keep recurring, not only in the psalms but elsewhere, are their testimony that in fellowship with God man becomes what he was created to be. But from the beginning the covenant relation was broken. Man used his freedom not for loving obedience but rather for proud self-assertion, trying to find a satisfying life in independence of God. The story of Israel is the story of hope deferred and promise unfulfilled because of a stubborn unwillingness to have its life from God alone. The man who was created to reflect God's holiness, justice, mercy, and truth, became unjust, unmerciful, false, and unclean. All of Israel's troubles and disasters were recognized by the prophets as having their origin in the rupture of the covenant relation, and the only hope for the future lay in its restoration, the making of a new covenant or the recalling of Israel to its true relation with God. Perhaps against this background we can see more clearly how Jesus fulfilled the promise of God and the hopes of Israel. In him God's call for an Israel that would respond to his love with loving obedience was answered. In him the covenant was kept inviolate. In him there was an Israel that lived moment by moment wholly in dependence upon God. In him there was a man who was in the likeness and image of God, reflecting God's holiness, mercy, truth, and justice. The sin that had cut Israel apart from God was overcome. Therefore, in him a new covenant came into being, a new relation between God and man, which created wholly new possibilities of life for the human race. A new world began. This is what the church was saying when it confessed that Jesus was the Christ, and our teaching of the Old Testament has as its main purpose to lay bare the longing in the heart of mankind that never finds its answer until it finds it in him.

If the title "Christ" points backward, the title "God's Son" might be said to point upward, expressing as it does the relation between God the Father and Jesus Christ. It is possible to get the mind very badly tangled at this point, because we have to assert two things that seem to our ordinary ways of thinking to be contradictory: that God the Father and Jesus Christ are one and yet that there is a personal relation between them, so that we have to speak of both the Father and the Son. The personal relation is clearly evident to us in Jesus' earthly ministry, where he prays to the Father and speaks of him in his teaching as someone *apart* from himself. In Gethsemane he asks the Father to let the cup of suffering pass from him, and then he submits his will to the Father's will. On the cross he commits himself into the Father's hands. Yet in Jesus' relation with the Father there is no separation, as there is for every other man who ever lived, but instead there is perfect oneness. His obedience to the Father's will is perfect, not without a costly and agonized wrestling, but nevertheless so perfect that his will reveals the Father's will. No line of distinction can be drawn between his forgiveness of sin and God's forgiveness: it is the infinite love of God in him that penetrates the sinner's situation, bears the pain and guilt of the sin, and redeems the sinner. His search for God's lost sons is God's search for them. His judgment upon man is God's judgment, so that to submit one's life to his judgment is to have already come under God's last judgment. His mind is God's mind. The life that he possessed is life in fellowship with God, but it is more than that: it is God's own life in which there is no death. He is not just the man who of all men draws closest to God; he is God, who draws close to man, breaking into man's world and man's life from beyond in order to reconcile him to God. In order to express both Jesus' oneness with the Father and his distinction from the Father, we confess that he is God's Son. That must not suggest to us subordination as though he were less than God, but only the personal relation in which Jesus so responds to the Father that the Father reveals himself to us in him and accomplishes our salvation.

The third title, "our Lord," points downward to us and expresses what Jesus Christ is *for us*. He is the Christ and he is God's Son for our sakes, that he may expose and overcome the sin that cuts us apart from God and robs us of our life, but all that he is and all that he says and all that he does counts for nothing so far as we are concerned until he is our Lord. A Lord is a master or sovereign who has absolute power over all that belongs under his rule. The character of our human sin is that in it we assert our right to be masters over our own lives, every man his own lord. The two most penetrating descriptions of sin in the Bible are the picture in Gen., ch. 3, of man's wanting to be his own god with no limitations set upon his will from beyond himself, and Jesus' description of the prodigal son who wanted to get out from under the authority of his father in order to live his own life as he pleased. There is in every one of us a self that from the earliest years asserts its rule not only over the things that belong to our own existence but also over extensive areas of the existence of others. Some of the most popular philosophies of life in America encourage this self-assertion as both natural and right. In our criticism of them we must not give the impression that to be a Christian one must put his own desires and convictions so decisively in the background that he spends his life letting everyone walk over him. Teen-agers who never think and act for themselves but remain completely submissive to their parents' wills are likely to be weaklings for life. But equally true is it that teen-agers who drink in a doctrine that the way to be strong and successful in life is by ruthless though cunning self-assertion, studying how to use even friendship and the most intimate relations in order to extend the area of their own influence and power, will become incapable of any enduring relation either with men or with God. The definition of freedom as the right of every man to do what he likes with his own life and possessions must in the light of the Christian faith be recognized as a definition of the freedom of man to be his own lord, to cut himself apart from God, and to destroy the relations with God and man on which his very life depends.

The uniqueness of Jesus' relation with us is that his authority over us as Lord establishes our freedom to be ourselves rather than destroys it. He makes himself our servant in order to be our Lord. He enters into and bears for us the pain and darkness of our separation from God in order to conquer our sin and bring us captive to the feet of God; but because our captivity is a captivity to God's love, its burden is light. He takes from us the right to determine anything in our own existence by ourselves alone, since we belong wholly to our fellow men in God, but, far from being any deprivation, this is the discovery of our true existence. We begin to live only when we find our life beyond ourselves in God and in our fellow men. Confinement to the narrow walls of self as decreed by self-assertion is confinement to a prison, so that we look out at life only through barred windows, incapable of the relations that unlock the doors to life's meaning. Therefore, we have to die to self in order to come alive to God and to our fellow man. This is the decision with which Jesus Christ confronts us at whatever point his life touches ours. It may be in his words, " Blessed are the meek [i.e., those who have been utterly humbled before God]: for they shall inherit the earth," or, " If any man will come after me, let him deny himself, take up his cross, and follow me." It is implicit in the simple call to discipleship, " Follow me." It is present in any action in which he binds the disciple to himself, in his forgiving of our sins, in his washing of our feet, in his giving of himself to us in the bread and wine of the Last Supper. He gives himself to us in self-effacing love, but when we receive him we find that we have received a Lord who is not content until he possesses us wholly; yet to be possessed by him is to be set free to live. Thus it is that on the cross, where he is crucified by man's blind self-assertion, he batters down the last defenses in us and establishes his right to be our Lord.

"Lord," then, is not a human form of speech that we apply to Jesus to do him honor. *We* do not make him Lord by our loving devotion. He is our Lord because of who and what he is. He is the Lord of our life whether we recognize him as Lord or not — and Lord of all mankind. This is important, because many Christians think that while Jesus is *their* Lord, he is not the Lord of other men who belong to other faiths or to no faith at all. The whole enterprise of Christian missions is at stake here. If it is true that in Jesus alone is revealed the sovereignty of God over our human life in which we are set free to be ourselves, then we owe it to all men to let them know what has been achieved for them in Jesus Christ. This is only one of many implications of his Lordship at which we need to look, but it indicates the importance of the distinction between a Lordship that we as Christians attribute to Jesus and a Lordship that he possesses over us because of the presence in him of both a oneness with God and a oneness with us. He is our Lord because, although he is one of us, sharing our life to the full and knowing even our death from the inside, he is also one with God, bringing the fullness of the life of God into the midst of our human situation. He is what no other is, and does what no other does. And what he is and what he does is for our sakes, that our life may be brought to its fulfillment. That he is "our Lord" is God's doing and not ours, and what he is he is eternally. He did not establish his right to be our Lord on the cross and then die leaving us only the memory of him. He conquered death and was known to his disciples as their living Lord to whom all authority belongs in heaven and in earth.

Authority Hidden and Revealed

The disciples of Jesus were conscious of a unique authority in his words and person long before they understood its full nature and source. They said that he spoke with authority and not as the scribes, by which they meant that whereas the scribes based their teachings on time-honored interpretations of the Jewish Scriptures, Jesus' teachings were a word directly from God for man. It was disturbing to his religious contemporaries that sometimes he claimed for his words an authority transcending the authority of Scripture: "You have heard it said of old . . . but I say unto you." Also in his dealings with men and women there is a masterfulness in his handling of the situations. Whether it is the lawyer whose shallow religiousness he exposed in the parable of the good Samaritan, or Simon the Pharisee whom he accused of being loveless because he was blind to his own need of God's mercy, or his own beloved Simon Peter who was unwittingly playing Satan's part in tempting Jesus to take some other way than that of the Suffering Servant, with each man Jesus is in control, reading him like an open book. So also in the trial scenes Jesus says little, and yet he dominates every scene as though he were the judge and all his accusers were on trial before him. Sometimes Jesus is pictured as so humble and gentle that he claimed no authority for himself, asking only that he might serve men, but this is false. Everyone who came in contact with him seems to have felt the claim of a colossal authority in him. From those who wanted to be his disciples he asked that the Kingdom should take precedence over family and possessions, and he turned away volunteers who wanted to compromise at this point because of family and property responsibilities. Such exhorbitant demands kept the number of his disciples small. Also, his repudiation of many elements in the existing religious order of Judaism contained within it a threat to the *status quo* that made his opponents feel his authority. When he cleansed the courts of the Temple he was acting as though he, and not any priest of the Temple, was God's representative. Until we realize that Jesus made his au-

thority felt in these diverse ways, we are unlikely to understand
why his mission aroused such intense fears among the governors
of the community.

It is clear, however, that Jesus never made an open claim to a
place of rule in Judaism. When, following the cleansing of the
Temple courts, he was asked by what authority he acted as he
did, he refused to give a direct answer, but, instead, asked
whether or not his questioners recognized the authority of God
in the ministry of John the Baptist. Their evasion of the question
revealed to him that their concern was only that nothing should
interfere with their own authority. They were not open to an
authority of God that would challenge their religious institutions.
Jesus' authority was the authority of God himself, which could
not be asserted openly and directly like human authorities but
had to be recognized and accepted in faith. Jesus was not willing
to assert an open, direct, compulsive authority that would make
men do and think and say what he wanted them to, and he
warned his disciples against coveting or exercising this kind of
power over their fellow men. Only when by faith men recognized
the authority of God in Jesus' words and deeds and person, and
responded freely, would their obedience be the obedience of
faith that he coveted.

The importance of this consideration becomes evident when we
recognize how prone the church and Christians have been to assert on Jesus' behalf an open, direct, compulsive authority that he
repudiated. Sometimes they have relied on an infallible authority
of the church to guarantee a right solution to all dilemmas, so
that Christians may be in no uncertainty about what is true and
what is false. Then, when the infallibility of any human church
has been set in question, they have asserted the absolute inerrancy
of the Scriptures as the medium by which God has made it possible for us to have the final truth about everything. Both authorities are externally compulsive, dictating to men what they must
believe and do and controlling them by the threat of dire penal-
ties, ostensibly for the glory of God but actually for the glory of
the institution. Both are the consequence of an unwillingness of

Christians to depend upon the hidden personal authority of God himself, substituting for it the seemingly more practical, effective, and definite authority of the Scriptures or the church. And they have the effect, on the one hand of imprisoning Jesus Christ in the church or in the Scriptures so that he is no longer free to be the Lord of all men in his own way, and on the other hand of subjecting men to an authority that, because it is not the personal authority of Jesus Christ, robs them of their freedom and tyrannizes over them. The only absolute authority that we dare recognize is that of God himself, hidden in Jesus Christ and revealed to faith. Both Scriptures and church must take a humbler, yet most essential place, as witnesses each in its own way to Jesus Christ. The witnesses dare not usurp the place and function of the Lord himself. This they are constantly tempted to do.

The Scope of Our Lord's Authority

The aim of Christian teaching has sometimes been thus defined: that the pupil may be led to Jesus Christ as his personal Lord and Savior. Rightly interpreted, this could be directly in line with the earliest Christian confession: Jesus is Lord. But if we compare the meaning of the New Testament confession with the contemporary definition, we shall find significant differences. In the New Testament the emphasis is upon Jesus' sovereignty over all mankind and over the whole creation, then in a special sense over the church which is his body, and finally over individual Christians within the church. The risen Lord is proclaimed King over all, and the day is anticipated when the kingdoms of this world will be brought into submission to him. In contrast to that, most Christians today begin with the individual's relation to his Lord and many never get beyond it. Some confine the authority of Jesus as Lord to the spiritual life of the individual, sharply distinguishing his spiritual life from his economic, political, or social life in the world. The inner and the outer life of man are separated, and the confession of Jesus as Lord is given relevance only for the inner life. The soul has to be surrendered unconditionally

to him, and, once surrendered, the soul is at peace with God and
has the promise of eternal life.

This separation of the inner life from the outer life is not only
unbiblical but also unreal. It belongs to the realism of the Old
Testament, which carries through into the New, that the Israel
that is in covenant with God is a social, political, economic entity.
The relation of man with God is immediately reflected in his relation with those about him. The two relations are inseparable —
as they are also for Jesus, who could not conceive of any man's
being right with God who was wrong with his brother. Thus,
when Amos wanted to know how things stood between Israel
and God, he did not examine the spiritual life of Israel (whatever that would be); nor did he go about asking men if they
were right with God in their souls. He went, rather, into the
market place where men traded, and into the courts where men
were supposed to receive justice, and to the seats of the government where national policies were determined, and to the Temple
courts where religious festivals were in progress, in short, into
the places where the nation lived and breathed. There he found
his evidence of a broken relation with God. There are ways and
means of cultivating the most delightful and peaceful spiritual
feelings, and it is possible for the beauty of religious worship to
be prostituted to this end, the enjoyment of the inner glow con-
cealing from one's sight the ugly contradiction between the actualities of life and the will of God. It is what we *do* that shows us
what we are. Our relation with God is revealed in our relations
with those about us, relations that, whether we like it or not,
are economic, political, and social. If we would know whether
our confession of Jesus as Lord is genuine, we should not ask
how we feel about our relation with him at 11:30 A.M. on Sunday
morning but rather how we have dealt with those whose lives
have touched ours on Thursday when we were in the press of
everyday events.

It is clear to us, then, that to deny Jesus' authority in any area
of our outer life is to say No! to him in our inner life, no matter
what we *feel* toward him. We dare not fall into the hypocritical

position of those who cry "Lord, Lord" and "do not the will of my Father in heaven." The soul, for the Christian, is not a mystic element hidden somewhere in the body but is the self, with its will and understanding, and takes in the entirety of a man's existence. To yield the soul to Christ as Lord is to let one's whole life come under his sovereignty. There must be no compromise concerning the totalitarian character of this sovereignty. In the Old Testament the prophet's demand is for all things in Israel's life to be brought into obedience to Yahweh as Lord. In the New Testament the apostles' demand is that Christians bring not only every action and word but also every thought into obedience to Jesus as Lord, for only where life is under his sovereignty is it redeemed. This insistence, in the early centuries of the church, set Christians frequently in conflict with the customs and laws of the societies in which they lived. They were able to submit to the dictates of their governments only in so far as it did not make them disobedient to their Lord. Their first loyalty was to him. His authority transcended that of the state.

Here there arises a crucial issue for the modern Christian. Many Christians find themselves living in nations that make demands upon their citizens that move steadily in the direction of totalitarianism, and even in our Western democracies it is frequently taken for granted that loyalty to nation takes precedence over all other loyalties. We live in an era of passionate nationalisms, though we usually see it more clearly in other countries than in our own, and we live also in an era when the state has become colossal in its power, limiting more and more the freedom of its citizens and able through modern communications to control their thinking in a large measure. In countries such as Nazi Germany and Communist Russia the claim of a totalitarian government to rule its citizens absolutely has been open and unconcealed, and the conflict with a Christian's loyalty to Christ as Lord has been immediately and painfully evident. In our democracies the conflict is concealed by the peaceful relations between church and state. We tend to assume that, because we assign religion and the state to separate spheres, there is no problem. But because each Christian is a citizen of his nation as well as a member of the church of Jesus Christ, he is confronted by the problem of the relation of these two loyalties to each other within himself. He has his duties to his nation alongside his obligations to his church and to his Lord, and he hopes that the two will never stand in contradiction to each other. But imperceptibly this way of thinking issues in a sealing of one's citizenship and one's Christianity into separate compartments of the mind so that they may never interfere the one with the other. The state must keep its hands off religion, and religion must keep its hands off the state.

But the state does not consist merely of official government agencies; it is the nation in all the expressions of its life, and it impresses its mind upon the individual not so much through its officialdom as through the schools that it controls and through other instruments of culture. Understood in this sense, the state does not keep its hands off religion, but on the contrary presses constantly upon its citizens forms of religion that are most congenial to the national interests. The schools, or at least many of them, are compelled to avoid those passages in world literature and world history that have to do with the Christian faith, but they are free to teach a humanism that is congenial to the national aspirations, even though it is directly contradictory to the Christian understanding of man. Also, there is a constant subtle pressure to make the religious institutions of the nation an expression of the nation's culture and way of life rather than a church that is obedient in every word and thought to its Lord, Jesus Christ. The state inevitably desires in its midst a form of religion on which it can at all times rely for support. This has been true in all ages. In the Old Testament are numerous instances of the state's demanding of its prophets a favorable word, securing it easily from most prophets, but chagrined when a Micaiah or an Amos or a Jeremiah speaks a word from God in contradiction to what seems to be the obvious national interest. We dare not forget that Jesus was crucified because his teaching and his movement seemed to patriotic leaders to threaten the future of the Jewish nation.

If it is true that no nation ever keeps its hands off religion, it is equally true that no truly Christian church can keep its hands off the state. The state is simply one form of the world in which man has his life — the world, which is God's creation, which he loves, and for which Christ died that it might be restored to its true order in relation to God. Jesus Christ is the Redeemer of the whole man, the citizen as well as the churchman, and therefore Lord of the whole man. To remove any area of life from the scope of his rule is to deny that he is Lord over all. Perhaps the most serious and dangerous repudiation of Jesus as Lord is not by so-called secularists but by churchmen who limit Jesus' sovereignty to a spiritual or ecclesiastical realm and assert for themselves a freedom to follow their own inclinations in political, economic, and social matters. It is true that the church dare not act as though it were Lord of the state and competent to direct the life of the state, but neither dare it forget for a moment that the Lord whom it serves is Lord of the state, concerned with all that is happening to man in the life of the state and alone able to speak the word that judges and redeems it. The speaking and the hearing of that word is a matter of life or death for the state. Therefore, only the church that speaks that word of judgment and redemption is really loyal to the state. But so to speak takes courage and discernment.

Every Man's Lord

There is the possibility that when Christians confess Jesus to be "our Lord," they take this to mean only the Lord of Christians. This is what he is *for us,* but for those who stand outside the Christian faith he is merely a Jewish teacher who became the founder of the Christian church. This is distinctly not what the first Christians believed. By the resurrection Jesus was revealed to be the rightful king of all mankind. As Christ he was the fulfillment of the hopes of Israel for a King who would unite all men and nations under his rule. As Son of God, that is, in his oneness with God, the human life of every man was reconciled with God in him and found its true order. He was the new man in whom a new humanity was born, but in this new humanity he was not just one among many or the first of many; rather, he was perpetually the source of the new humanity, on whom it would remain ever dependent for its life. The achievement of Jesus Christ is not that he presents us with a new and better religion than all other religions, but simply that when he becomes our Lord and the Source of our life, he makes us human as he was human, delivering us from all that robs us of our humanity. The source of our inhumanity is always some form of self-centeredness. His work is to break open the hard and stubborn core of self in us and to set God, the God who possessed him wholly in his Spirit, in the place of rule within us. The secret of being human is to have our life no longer in ourselves but in God, since the life that is unconditionally open to God is unconditionally open also toward our fellow man. But it is in Jesus Christ *alone* that this secret is revealed, that only in so far as man is indwelt by God is he able to be man.

It must be said, then, that the life of every man is hidden in Jesus Christ. The Judaism of Jesus' day was in many respects a noble religion, purer by far than most others in its conception of God and man and in the dignity of its worship, but it did not open to man his life in God as Jesus did. So also in other world religions there can be found much that is true and good, but never the secret of how man can alone be truly man. Only when Jesus Christ lives and speaks and dies and rises again does man ever know that to be truly himself he must die to self.

On this basis we must develop the world mission of the church, not on the basis that our Christian religion is superior to all other religions, because in some of its forms it may even at times be inferior; and most certainly not on the basis that we possess a Christian civilization that we want to share with other nations and that may be only a concealed form of religious imperialism.

If all we can offer is what we take to be a new and better religion, we no longer understand the ministry and gospel of Jesus Christ. What he offered to men was the life that was his own in God, in which men would know the joy and wholeness of being themselves in God. If we ourselves have received him and know that joy and wholeness, we cannot bear that any man in any nation should be without the life in God that is hidden for him in Jesus Christ waiting to be revealed.

8.

. . . *Conceived by the Holy Ghost,*
Born of the Virgin Mary

The primary intent of the two articles that have to do with the birth of Jesus is somewhat concealed, a fact that in the past has led to more than a little confusion at this point. They have seemed to be mainly concerned with the virgin birth, "conceived by the Holy Ghost" denying that Jesus had a human father, and "born of the Virgin Mary" asserting that Mary was a virgin when Jesus was born. But so to read the articles is to let a secondary negative meaning displace the primary positive one. Their first concern is not to deny the participation of a human father in the birth of Jesus but rather to make the double assertion that Jesus had the source of his life wholly in God, being uniquely born of God, and that at the same time he shared with us the manner of our human birth, being born of Mary. If we have any doubt whether this is where the emphasis lies, then we should read with care the birth stories in Matthew and Luke on which these articles are based, and observe how powerfully they preserve this double recognition, holding the divine and human nature of Jesus in perfect balance: born of God, yet born the helpless babe of Mary.

In the early church, just as today, there were two constant tendencies: to lose sight of Jesus' humanity in affirming his divinity and to lose sight of his divinity in affirming his humanity. The birth stories guard against both errors. They assert that Jesus was uniquely born of God, not as other men are born of God at some time in the course of their life through their receiving of the

Holy Spirit, but from the first moment of his earthly life in the womb of Mary. Whereas in us there is a self that must be overcome, not just once but ever afresh to the end of our days, by the power of the Holy Spirit, the self of Jesus was from the beginning responsive and obedient to the Spirit. Where our relation to God is a broken one long before we are conscious of it since we are born into a humanity that is estranged from God, his relation to God is one of unbroken oneness. This is the sinlessness of Jesus that is asserted everywhere in the New Testament, the perfectness of his relation with God, so that in him the very nature of God is reflected. The cleft between man and God that in us is the source of all our misery and helplessness was absent in him. His perfectness was not, as is sometimes thought, a supernatural inerrancy, as though the child Jesus could never make a mistake in arithmetic or misstate a fact or live a normal human life in a home with his brothers and sisters. In the Synoptic Gospels and the Gospel of John, Jesus is one with the Father through the indwelling of the Holy Spirit. "Conceived by the Holy Ghost" asserts that this was the nature of his being from the first moment of his earthly existence. But the New Testament goes farther than this and asserts that he was one with the Father before ever the worlds began to be.

The birth stories put equal emphasis upon the human origin and nature of Jesus. He is born the child of a young Jewish woman in very humble circumstances. She is distinguished only by the simplicity of her faith and by the fact that she of all women was chosen of God to be the mother of our Lord. All four of the Gospels emphasize some aspect of her humanity. None of them shows any tendency to make her an object of adoration. They report the existence of a large family of at least five brothers and two sisters. None of these is found among Jesus' disciples during his lifetime, although Mary was present at the cross, apparently estranged from her family, and James, the brother of Jesus, became prominent later in the Jerusalem church. Jesus at one point speaks of a prophet's being without honor among his own kinfolk, and there is one passage that suggests that his family thought him to be out of his mind. Also, when a woman in the crowd cried out, "Blessed is the womb that bore you, and the breasts that gave you suck," Jesus answered, "Blessed rather is he who knows the will of God and does it." Parallel with this saying is that of Jesus when his mother and brothers came to see him where he was teaching. Instead of going out to them at once, Jesus looked round at his hearers and said, "You are my mother and my sisters and my brothers if you do the will of my Father in heaven." The fact that the early church preserved the memory of incidents such as these shows its determination to resist any tendency to give undue honor to Mary or to the human family of Jesus. No greater honor need be Mary's than to be the mother of Jesus. The Gospel of Luke dwells particularly upon the human aspect of Jesus' birth, the pathetic situation of the strangers in Bethlehem, the stable where Jesus was born, the carefulness of the parents to do for him all that was prescribed in the Jewish law, Jesus' subordination as a child to his parents, his growth like any other child in body and mind and in his relations both with God and men. Frequently Christians have been reluctant to go as far as Luke goes in describing the full humanity of Jesus lest they should set his divinity in question. But, like Luke, they should know that any assertion of Jesus' divinity that casts the slightest suspicion upon his human nature, that is, upon his sharing of our human life, embodies somewhere within it a false conception of divinity.

Why can we not be satisfied with this positive meaning of the articles and leave aside the negative doctrine of the virgin birth? What difference does it make to us whether or not Jesus had a human father? If we respond in faith to God as he meets us in the words of Jesus, in the person of Jesus, in the death and resurrection of Jesus, and in the gospel as proclaimed by the early church, why need we commit ourselves to any statement concerning the manner of Jesus' birth? Surely what matters is his life and mission, his person and work, his power to forgive us our sins and to open to us the life of his Kingdom, our reconciliation with God in him and through him. The gospel is good news concerning what God has done for us in Jesus Christ. Every word of it is in some way good news. But where is the good news in this negative assertion that Jesus had no human father? Is it, then, essential to the gospel? How could it be essential when two Gospels, Mark's and John's, make no mention of it, and the great apostle Paul has nothing to say of it in any of his letters? Shall we, then, be content to confess with John that the Word became flesh, that is, God became man, in Jesus Christ?

Perhaps when our mind runs in this channel we are in rather unseemly haste to get rid of the doctrine of the virgin birth. This haste may have different sources: our contact with Christians who make the virgin birth the key doctrine of the Christian faith, a kind of test doctrine; our reaction against the cult of the Virgin Mary in the Roman Church and in the high-church sections of Protestantism; our observation that in some passages in the New Testament, Joseph is spoken of as the father of Jesus; our suspicion that the story of Mary's virginity arose not as a factual report from Mary herself but as the church drew out the implications of the doctrine of the incarnation. These are very real factors in the thinking of Christians and cannot be ignored. Our recognition of them should help us to understand why many Christians see no need even to discuss the virgin birth. But we cannot lightly brush aside a doctrine that is so closely associated with the central doctrine of the incarnation, that comes to expression in two of our four Gospels (after all, the Sermon on the Mount occurs only in these two Gospels and is not mentioned by Mark, John, or Paul), that is incorporated in the Apostles' Creed and has for centuries retained its place in the teaching of the church. We need to understand what it means before we can either affirm or deny it. The denial of it can all too easily become also in some degree a denial of the incarnation. And the affirmation of it is indeed in many instances an affirmation that contains within it elements that go contrary to a really Christian understanding of God and man. A doctrine that has led so many people astray *both* in the affirmation and in the denial of it has a right to be treated by us with respect and interest.

THE INCARNATION

One of the tragedies of the Christmas season usually is that, in our engrossment with all the charming details of the story of Jesus' birth and our enjoyment of Christmas music and Christmas legends, we fail to ask what happened at Bethlehem. Matthew and Luke tell what happened: that a Savior was born who would save his people from their sins, that the King was come to earth who would establish God's Kingdom in the midst of men, that the day of Jesus' birth was the long-expected day when God would keep his promise to Israel and would come to it to create a wholly new era in the life of the world. But somehow this remains for us merely an element in the beautiful stories and music and decorations that are appropriate to Christmas, all of which we lay carefully away for the remainder of the year. Perhaps we need to preach Christmas sermons and to teach Christmas lessons in midsummer in order to detach the event of Jesus' birth from its customary festive setting and to see its significance for the whole of our human existence. Or we may need only to turn more often to John's Gospel, where all the familiar stories are left aside that the event itself may appear with greater clarity: the Word was made flesh and dwelt among us. John has already in the Prologue made clear that the Word is God himself in that form of his being in which as Light and Life he seeks to impart himself to men and so to overcome the darkness and death in which they live. To receive him in his Word is to be born of his Spirit, so that, being indwelt by God, men know themselves children of God. But men have ever loved darkness more than light and have rejected the Word of God. The birth of Jesus was therefore God's unbelievable act of love toward us that, in order to break through the barrier of our human resistance to him, his Word became a man like us, still the very Word of God and yet flesh of our flesh, a human person born into a human family and experiencing all that we experience from birth to death. In Jesus, there was lived a life on earth that was wholly indwelt by God. In him, in the midst of human history, darkness and death were conquered by the Life and Light of God; there was peace and perfect oneness between God and man. Therefore, this event is the center point of human history, the point where God is revealed in his relation with man and man is revealed in his relation with God, but, more than that, the event in which God comes to our humanity in Jesus Christ and where we as human beings come to God in Jesus Christ. He is our peace, our reconciliation, our way of access to God.

The incarnation should shake us loose out of all our customary ways of thinking of God. This is not how we or our pupils ordinarily think of God. God is for us an eternal Spirit, a loving and holy Father in heaven, who has his existence somewhere beyond the world and beyond us. We believe in him — up there. We pray to him — up there. And he remains for us — up there, at a safe distance from us. But the incarnation abolishes this safe distance, or rather it exposes this distance that we maintain between ourselves and God as our separation from God and our resistance to him. What God wills is not distance and separation but the closest communion in which our entire life would be a life with him as children with a Father. We are the ones who will the distance and the separation, that we may remain free from God, free to have our life in some measure without God. We want our God at a safe distance, that he may not interfere too much with our ordering of the world and our sovereignty in our own lives. In Jesus Christ the distance between God and man is closed, abolished, and God has his dwelling place in this man among men. To this end Jesus lived and died: that, once and for all, men might know that God wills to have his dwelling place *in them, in our humanity, in us.* He is the Son of God, that there may be many sons of God. He is the image of the Father, that all men through him may be restored to their true nature in the likeness of God. The love that is God's nature dwells in him, that through him it may take possession of all men. He is the new Adam, the new man, not just that men may believe in him and honor him as God's new man — at a distance, but that men through him may know themselves new men together with him, God's new men through whom the life of all mankind may be renewed and transformed.

Far too often the effect of the doctrine of the incarnation for Christians is the opposite to what it should be. They acknowledge that God became man in Jesus, and thereupon remove Jesus to the same distance from themselves at which they have always kept God. They seal God within the person of Jesus, so that God cannot get through the humanity of Jesus into their own humanity. They build a barrier between Jesus and themselves across which they worship him, but it does not occur to them that the God who indwelt the human life of Jesus wills to indwell their human life now. They spend large sums for the erection of beautiful churches as temples for God, but they do not grasp what is set before their minds in the fact of Jesus Christ — that where God chooses to have his temple is in *man*, not just in Jesus but through him in all men.

Jesus is what he is not for his own sake but for our sakes. God became man in him for love of us. Therefore, Jesus is not willing to be alone in his relation with the Father but reaches out to draw all men with him into the same relation. He is willing to go to any length to take us with him. When we blindly resist this fulfillment of our life in God, seeing in it a threat to our existence instead of the promise of our only true existence, he accepts us in spite of our blindness and hostility and takes upon himself, as though it were his own, the burden and the pain of our resistance to God. He will do anything to overcome our stubborn imprisonment in self, that we may find with him the joy and freedom of self-fulfillment in fellowship with God. It is his own life in God that he is determined should be ours. And when there is no other way to break our confidence in self, to reveal to us that hidden in the unconquered self is an enmity toward God that is our deadliest enemy, and to make us sure that the love of God that is his life is the ultimate power in the events of this world, he goes willingly to the cross. Jesus binds us to him in spite of ourselves that we may share with him his life in God. And it is only when we let ourselves be bound together with him and when his Spirit, which is the Spirit of the Father and the love of the Father, is shed abroad in our hearts that we begin to understand the incarnation. It is when we have been born of the Spirit, that is, have received God in his Spirit, the living God, to be the sovereign center and wellspring of our existence, that it has meaning for us to speak of Jesus as conceived and born of the Holy Spirit. We are acutely conscious, then, of the brokenness and incompleteness of our relation with God. We remain to the end of our days members of a humanity that resists its destiny and has ever afresh to be humbled and conquered for God. But in Jesus Christ there is no trace of any such conflict or incompleteness. There is a radical difference between his relation with God and our sharing in his relation. Therefore, when we say that he is born of God we are asserting the completeness and unbrokenness of his relation with God. Could it be better expressed than in the words of the creed "conceived by the Holy Ghost"?

There are two ways of evading the truth of the incarnation. The one makes its appeal to us under the guise of humility: Jesus is the divine Lord, but we are only human; therefore, what was possible for him is not possible for us. His selfless love is not practicable for us who live in a competitive society. His forgiving an infinite number of times and forgiving even enemies simply will not work in our kind of world. Jesus thus is removed to a plane above us where his words no longer apply directly to the situations of our human life. The Sermon on the Mount is set aside as intended for an ideal world and not for the kind of world in which we live. But this is actually a denial of Jesus' humanity, that he was flesh of our flesh. The Sermon on the Mount is a practicable ethic only for a society that through Jesus Christ has entered upon a wholly new relation with God, what we might call the new society or the new humanity of the incarnation.

The other way of evading the truth of the incarnation, which has been followed in much popular and widely circulated religious literature, is to make the incarnation only the supreme example of what is true of all men. Certainly God was present in Jesus just as he is present in all men. Hidden within every man is the divine Spirit or the divine Mind. In Jesus there was an unusual consciousness and realization of this intrinsic divinity of the human self, so that he is able to help us become conscious of what we are. The purpose of religion is to bring out the hidden and unrealized divinity in every man. This way of thinking has a singular appeal in our American scene. The humanism of Emerson and others prepared the way for it a century ago. Groups such as Christian Science and Unity have their doctrine centered in it, but it has also had eloquent spokesmen within all our churches. What doctrine could be more congenial to a man-centered faith? But it stands in sharpest conflict with a God-centered faith in which the sickness of man is recognized as his willful separation of himself from God and the remedy for his sickness a reconciliation with God that demands of him that he die to self that he may come alive to God. The man who already has an intrinsic divinity within himself and is thereby assured of his own immortality has an impregnable defense against the claim of the gospel that he should die with Christ that he may live with him. Moreover, he is likely to find the real doctrine of the incarnation not only uninteresting but incomprehensible.

The Virgin Birth

It should be clear by now that the virgin birth has its importance only in relation to the incarnation. When it is lifted out of the secondary place that it occupies both in the creed and in the Scriptures and is erected into a primary doctrine of the faith, violence is done to the structure of the faith itself. When it is made the touchstone to determine whether or not a man is really a Christian, faith ceases to be understood as a response of the whole being of a man to God's offer of himself in Jesus Christ and becomes an intellectual and emotional acceptance of a series of propositions based on Scripture. The mere denial that Jesus had a human father is not an act of faith. So far as the " fact " is concerned, we no longer have satisfactory historical evidence on which to base either a denial or an affirmation. We have only the testimony of the early church, which is embedded in its total witness to the divine and human nature of Jesus. Therefore, when men reject this testimony of the early church, it cannot be because they know that Joseph was the father of Jesus but only because the story of the virgin birth sounds to them like a superstitious myth invented by the church to emphasize the divine origin of Jesus. But frequently they go on from this to dismiss also the incarnation as another superstitious myth, a mythical way of saying that Jesus was the bearer of a decisive revelation from God to man. For this reason, we must always ask what it is that is being rejected, since many persons who think they are dismissing only the virgin birth are actually dismissing from consideration the whole New Testament doctrine of the incarnation.

There is need also to distinguish between the virgin birth in the New Testament and Apostles' Creed and in various Roman and Protestant interpretations of it. Some current interpretations we not only may but rather must reject in faithfulness to the Scriptures. The Roman doctrine of the perpetual virginity of Mary requires the explaining away of Jesus' brothers and sisters as cousins, which has no basis in the text, and, what is more serious, it embodies the assumption that to be sinless Jesus had to be born of a woman who never knew a normal marriage relation with a man. Perfection, sinlessness, or sainthood is regarded as impossible for human beings involved in the ordinary situations of life but possible in a life apart. The world is evil and has to be left behind. Sin is transmitted from generation to generation in the act of procreation. Therefore, Mary, to be a sinless mother of a sinless Jesus, had to be immaculately conceived. The meaning of the incarnation itself seems here to have been forgotten. Sin is no longer seen as the deep cleft in the self of *all* men that cuts them apart from God, and Jesus is no longer seen as the one in whom *alone* the cleft is bridged and man is restored to his true life in God.

Protestantism is capable of producing equally unacceptable interpretations. Many Protestants, while reacting against the Roman conception of Mary, hold to the Roman idea of sin's being transmitted in the act of procreation, so that the virgin birth was necessary for Jesus to be sinless. They take this concept of physical transmission to be the doctrine of original sin. But sin, according to the Scriptures, is not a physical contamination: it is an act of the self as it asserts itself against God. The doctrine of original sin merely emphasizes the solidarity of the human race in sin and the inescapableness of sin. We are born into a humanity in which we are involved in a massive rebellion against God long before we are conscious of it. As we have already seen, Jesus' sinlessness is the expression of his perfect oneness with God. Dare we say that he could not have been one with God if he had had a human father as well as a human mother? Why should a father involve him in human sinfulness any more than a mother? It is also within Protestantism that one sometimes hears the virgin birth interpreted as necessary to the atonement. Because Jesus was born with a divine instead of a human father, the blood in his veins was divine blood and therefore had divine value to purchase our salvation! But to attribute divinity to blood is a return to primitive animism in which impersonal substance can be divine. And to suggest that there was a marriage relation between the Holy Spirit and Mary is to be guilty of a crudity of which there is no trace in the New Testament story. In comparison with such Roman and Protestant interpretations, the Gospels are most restrained, asserting only that, just as the miracle of the resurrection stood at the point of Jesus' exit from the world, so the miracle of the virgin birth stood at the point of his entrance into our human life. Both miracles alike were intended to bear witness that Jesus came from God and returned to God.

9.

. . . *Suffered Under Pontius Pilate*

To the teacher who has been accustomed to focus his attention mainly on the life and teaching of Jesus it may seem that the Apostles' Creed omits this all-important and central element of the New Testament story. It goes directly from " born of the Virgin Mary " to " suffered under Pontius Pilate." It seems to jump from Jesus' birth to his death, leaving out the life that was lived in between. However great the importance of Jesus' death, was not his ministry, with its proclamation of the gospel of the Kingdom, its gathering of the disciples and its revolutionary impact upon the life of Judaism, the starting point of the whole Christian movement? How can we understand the meaning of Jesus' death unless we know something of what he was like in his life? But perhaps we are assuming too quickly that " suffered under Pontius Pilate " refers only to the sufferings of the cross. Jesus' entire ministry was " under Pontius Pilate," and from beginning to end it was a ministry of suffering. All his suffering was not at the hands of Pontius Pilate. The Roman governor had his share in it, but if we look at the whole story, we find that both friends and enemies made their contributions.

Sometimes the story of Jesus' ministry is told as though at first in Galilee he met with great success, vast throngs surrounding him and welcoming his gospel, so that it seemed as though he would carry everything before him, until his rejection at Jerusalem came as a crushing disappointment. We do well to remember that Jesus began his ministry under the shadow of the arrest and imprisonment of John the Baptist, whose sharp prophetic words were disturbing to the authorities. It had always been dangerous in earlier years in Israel for a prophet to speak his word from God that set all the existing order in question. Jesus had been closely associated with John, and he must have known that his own message to the nation was to be more radically revolutionary than anything John had said. Moreover, he intended to speak it, not in the more remote region of the wilderness of Jordan, but in the synagogues and homes of Galilee, in the streets and villages, and on the beaches beside the sea. Could he expect the authorities whose chief interest lay in preserving the existing order to be better disposed toward him than they had been toward John? Also, there is evidence that Jesus was familiar with the Servant passages in Isa., chs. 40 to 66, which portray the Servant of the Word of God as having to endure persecution and suffering at the hands of men in order to bear his witness faithfully, and as winning his victory for God only by his death. The fact that some of the words that Jesus heard from God at his baptism are found in Isa. 42:1, and that in his first sermon in his home synagogue in Nazareth he used the Servant's description of his mission in Isa. 61:1 f. to define his own mission, suggests that from the very first Jesus was conscious of what was likely to be the cost of fulfilling his destiny. He undoubtedly did what he recommended that others should do — never to begin any venture without first sitting down and counting the cost.

There were crowds pressing upon Jesus in the early days of his ministry, but he does not seem to have set any great store by them. His parable of the sower, which describes the response of various classes of people to his message, reveals his sober evaluation of the fickle crowd. Some were so preoccupied with other things that his words lay only on the surface of their minds and were soon snatched away. Some were so shallow that they were capable only of a brief enthusiasm that faded as soon as difficulties had to be faced. Others who took his message more in earnest came to nothing because of their engrossment in pleasures, possessions, and the anxiety that is inseparable from the pleasures and possessions, the fear of losing them. Also, it is clear that as soon as Jesus began preaching and teaching in Galilee, he found himself faced with sharp antagonisms. It was not difficult for the congregations in the synagogues to perceive that Jesus was not following the accepted traditions of the rabbis. He was not orthodox. His sermon in the Nazareth synagogue is represented as ending in a riot, some of the worshipers being so angry with him that his life was momentarily in danger. This hostility of his home community is reflected also in his saying that a prophet is not without honor except in his own country and among his own kinfolk. But it was not only in Nazareth that there was opposition. Jesus' earliest teaching in Capernaum aroused resentment, and we hear of religious leaders taking counsel together concerning what should be done about this dangerous new doctrine. Increasingly Jesus turned his back on the synagogue and the orthodox community and spent his time ministering to the " publicans and sinners," which describes that large segment of the Jewish community which was in some way or other alienated or excluded from the religious fellowship of the synagogue. The welcome they gave him would not enhance his prestige or popularity in the synagogue.

Judged by the number of converts, the Galilean ministry ended in failure. From all his work in the towns and villages Jesus had only a handful of disciples. There is no record later of a church in Galilee. It is significant that upon leaving Galilee to go up to Jerusalem, Jesus pronounced a judgment upon the towns where he had ministered for having been blind to their opportunity. Clearly he counted himself rejected by them. But so also was he rejected in Jerusalem. It is likely that he visited Jerusalem and Judah more than once and had a more extensive ministry there than just the last few days of his life (a fact preserved in the Johannine tradition but not in the Synoptic), but at the center of the nation's life he met the sharpest antagonism. He made a few disciples here and there, but so far as the nation was concerned he was battering his head against a blank wall. What this meant to Jesus is lost upon our minds when we think of him as an evangelist who went here and there making converts and concerning himself only with individuals. Jesus' mission, like that of the prophets before him, was a mission to Israel, a call to the whole people of God to return to God in repentance, to renew their covenant relation with him, and to take up their destiny as his Servant-people through whom the whole world might one day know the blessing of possessing its true life in God. Jesus confined his mission to "the lost sheep of the house of Israel," and his going up to Jerusalem has to be understood as the climax of his mission to the nation. He came to claim Israel for its God and to bring it to the fulfillment of its destiny. But Israel would not have him. Looking out over the city of Jerusalem from the Mount of Olives, he wept for his people: "O Jerusalem, Jerusalem, that stonest the prophets that are sent unto thee; how often would I have gathered thy children as a hen gathers her brood, but you would not!" Who can measure the pain of that rejection?

But at least Jesus had his disciples, an intimate group who were ready to give up everything for his sake and go with him anywhere! There were not only the twelve men who were continually with him but also a larger group of men and women of which we hear occasionally and of which there is evidence in the seventy and in the one hundred and twenty who gathered in the upper room after the resurrection. Even this larger number is only a handful as representing the harvest of Jesus' entire mission, but it was surely sufficient to provide Jesus with a measure of satisfaction. But we dare not forget the picture these disciples give of themselves in the Gospels. In Jesus' lifetime they continually misunderstood him, so that on one occasion Jesus said to them, "You know not what spirit you are of." One of them who was trained by Jesus to share his ministry betrayed him to his death. Simon Peter, the boldest among them and always the leader, had so little understanding of what Jesus was facing that he tempted him to turn aside from his dangerous path and, when Jesus was standing before his judges to be condemned, denied with an oath that he even knew him lest he too should be condemned. We need to remember also that the disciples' failure to understand Jesus did not end with his death. Some of them continued in the Jerusalem church a tradition that threatened to smother the new faith in its old Jewish garments until Paul more boldly cut it free. Jesus suffered not only from the hatred of his enemies but also from the incomprehension and wavering faith of his friends. We do not grasp the greatness of his burden until we see how fearfully alone he was. This explains his gratitude to Mary, who poured precious ointment on his feet a few nights before he died; it was a sign to him of her understanding that death might overtake him at any moment.

This general survey of the course of Jesus' ministry shows how appropriate it is that it should appear in the creed under the rubric "suffered under Pontius Pilate." But we have not yet probed below the surface to discover the meaning of that suffering.

The Necessity of the Suffering

It is a source of frustration to many teachers that the Gospels provide them with so few biographical details about Jesus. Sometimes, unwisely, they try to fill in imaginatively what has been omitted: a boyhood of Jesus with experiences in the carpenter shop or a description of his home life and his education. It is legitimate to draw upon what is known of Jewish life in the home and synagogue of Jesus' day to re-create the setting of his life, and we may assume that he worked for some years as a carpenter in Nazareth. Also we need to use a controlled imagination to bring to life the incidents that are narrated in the Gospels, lifting them off the flat surface of the page and letting Jesus' encounters with men and women become real encounters with real people. But we shall refrain from trying to construct biographies of Jesus if we once understand why the Gospel writers left out so many of the human details that would be of fascinating interest to us and limited their story almost wholly to the ministry, death, and resurrection of Jesus. They were not concerned to make the story of Jesus' life interesting and enjoyable to later generations. They were not writing a biography. They were bearing witness to a revelation of God, a mighty work of God, that had actually taken place in their midst and on which depended the whole future of mankind. The climax of the shattering, life-transforming revelation was in the death and resurrection of Jesus, so that these took up a major portion of the story and were described in fuller detail than any other elements in it, but they were the climax of a ministry and the crucifixion was the outcome of a teaching, so that the ministry and teaching of Jesus were essential. But nothing belonged in the story that did not in some way serve the revelation. The accounts of Jesus' birth were not told as biographical details but as witness to who he was. Jesus was remembered in the church not as an interesting person of the past about whom we ought to know, but as the One in whom God had acted for man's salvation and whose story had to be retold that through him God might continue to reveal himself to men and to open to them the life that is possible only in him. It is only when we have some other interest in Jesus than this that the scarcity of biographical materials in the Gospels becomes frustrating.

To some teachers it may be an additional source of difficulty that Jesus' ministry was one of suffering and failure. We live in a land where it is shameful to be a failure, and there is unstinted admiration for whoever achieves success, whether it is in business, sports, politics, piano-playing, or a religious vocation. How, then, is Jesus to be an object of admiration if his ministry must be portrayed as something quite other than what we recognize as a success? More than that, are we not in danger of creating in the minds of children and young people an image of Jesus as a poor, sad, beaten person? Instead of the man of sorrows, Jesus may become for them the sorrowful man. This must not happen. The full extent of Jesus' suffering and failure must be brought out, and then, against this dark background, the tremendousness of his joy and of his triumph. His progress from failure to failure was for him a triumphal march at the end of which he reached his victory upon the cross. John's Gospel, in which the hour of Jesus' glory is his crucifixion, makes this clear, but it is true also in the other Gospels that what seems outwardly to be the story of one defeat after the other is actually the unfolding of a consistent redemptive purpose that nothing can defeat. This is the secret of Jesus' ministry: that what looked outwardly like defeat and failure was actually the path to certain victory in what he came to do. The victory was hidden, but it was real, and it was for the joy of it that Jesus endured the cross. Joy and not sadness was the keynote of Jesus' ministry. He likened the life of the Kingdom to a continual marriage feast, the most joyful occasion in Jewish life. He was criticized by pious people who thought a prophet or a teacher of religion should be continually fasting and holding himself aloof from such pleasures as a substantial meal with his friends. Because Jesus did not fit their image of the sad religionist, they called him a " winebibber and a gluttonous man." But Jesus had only scorn for men who made an outward show of religiousness. For him, the central reality was God's sovereign presence comprehending all things in man's existence and bringing life to its only true fulfillment. He proclaimed the Kingdom with such confidence because life under God's rule in the power of God's Spirit was already his own life. His joy was the joy of having God's purpose for the world and for man realized in his own obedience. The goal of life was reached in him. He knew the fullness of life in God in which there was no emptiness or death. And in that joyful oneness with God he was certain that, no matter what road of suffering or darkness he had to go, it would all make its contribution to God's great victory.

But why had there to be a ministry of suffering? Why could not God's purpose be achieved in some less painful way? There are two halves to the answer that must be given. First, to be one with God, obedient to his will and purpose in the midst of a humanity that is estranged from God, blind to God's purpose and intent upon the assertion of its own several wills and purposes, is to be caught between forces that are moving in opposite directions and so to be torn asunder. Mystical and otherworldly religions promise men oneness with God without this conflict by teaching them ways in which to shut out the world or to escape from the world. They give the world up for lost and attain their own blissful union with God beyond the world. But the God of the prophets and of Jesus is not interested in communion with man apart from his life in the world. When a man responds to *this* God, he has to respond not with some mystic, spiritual part of him but with the whole of his existence. There is no giving up of the world for lost, because God is not willing to let the world he made be lost. He is willing to go to any length that it may be found and restored and saved from self-destruction. Therefore, its salvation has to take place in history, and history is where he intends his purpose for his world to triumph. But his only way to bring his purpose to triumph is through men, men who will catch a vision of his purpose for the world and let their wills be conformed to his will, men who will be *his* men, his representatives, his spokesmen, the servants of his Word in the midst of mankind.

Israel was the Servant of the Word, a people marked out by God to live in oneness with him that, through them, he might one day overcome the resistance of men and make all mankind his family. The price of that destiny for Israel was an ever-renewed position of estrangement among the nations and a suffering at their hands such as no other nation has ever endured, a price that Israel continues to pay. But the reward has been that out of Israel have come benefits for mankind such as have come from no other nation. The source of Israel's suffering was the clash between the will of Israel's God and the will of the world. In Judaism, however, a way was found to minimize the clash, the way of legalism. God's will was so interpreted that it was spun out into a network of laws and regulations for the government of life, and he who strictly held himself to these laws and regulations was assured that he was at one with God. The law became a way for Israel to be righteous with God rather than the means whereby the will of God could take command of Israel's life and make Israel his servant in the conquest of mankind. Therefore, that God's purpose might not fail, there arose in Israel a Servant of the Word who let himself be bound so completely by the will of God and gave himself so completely to God's redemptive purpose for all mankind that his life became the point in the history of the world where most completely the conflict between God and man was laid bare. His life and his death were the judgment of God upon all human life, for in him was stripped away from man all concealment of the enmity of his heart toward the will of God. Therefore, it could not be otherwise than that to be the Servant of the Word would be to suffer. Suffering was the cost that had to be paid by the One who in faithfulness to God would incarnate the Word that has to judge and crush and destroy man's rebellious self before it is able to create in him a new and redeemed self.

There is a second half to the answer. If the first half is that Jesus had to suffer in order to be *one with God* in the midst of a humanity alienated from God, the second half is that Jesus had to suffer in order to be *one with a humanity* that was lost in its blind rebellion against God. Jesus does not give up mankind for lost and turn his back upon us that he may enjoy undisturbed his oneness with God. He is not willing to be one with God without us. He lets himself be so bound together with us in our lostness, our alienation from God, our darkness without God, our self-destroying sin, that it is as though it were all his own. This is the love of Christ for us before which we can only stand in awe and wonder — and in gratitude that he did not let himself be repulsed by the stupidity and blindness and selfishness and hatefulness of humanity but looked past these to the broken, helpless, imprisoned self of man. He loved the lost world and gave himself without reserve that the lost might be found, that a world that was broken by its alienation from God might be made whole. But this giving of himself could be accomplished only by an identification of himself with man in the depth of his predicament. He had to lay his own soul open to the agony of the human situation. Sin has in it a bitter poison because the soul that has cut itself apart from God knows only the crushing absence of life, the darkness of infinite emptiness. Jesus' penetration of man's situation meant a tasting of that poison and an experiencing of the hatefulness and horror of sin within himself. This is what Paul means when he says that he who knew no sin was made sin for us. He put himself in our place and experienced in himself the full weight of our burden of condemnation and separation from God. "Substitution" in its original meaning is not a theory of some kind of legal transference of guilt in a heavenly court from us to Jesus, but rather it describes what Jesus did both in his ministry and in his death. He took the burden of our sin and guilt upon him as though it belonged to him. Because of his love for us and his hatred of all that separated us from our true life in God, he made himself one with us that he might make us one with God.

This element is already evident in Jesus' baptism. Why would he submit himself to a baptism that was an outward sign of repentance for sin and cleansing from sin? It has been interpreted by some as proof that Jesus recognized himself to be a sinner like all other men. But it is in keeping with all else in his ministry that he felt the sin of Israel and the sin of man bearing down upon him with such crushing weight that more than any other he welcomed John's baptism as a promise of forgiveness and cleansing. His ministry throughout was marked by a penetration of the situation of individuals, so that he seemed to read them from the inside. He understood them better than they understood themselves. "He knew what was in man." But this was gained only at a price, the price of putting himself in their place. Anyone who has dared to cross the border into the life of another man in order to lift some burden of guilt or sorrow knows that there can be no sharing of help unless there is a willingness to share the pain of the burden. Jesus took upon himself the whole burden and agony of human sin that by bearing it he might bear it away and destroy its power to hold man enslaved. Therefore, there was no way for him to do what he came into the world to do except by a ministry of suffering. His purpose was to save his people from their sins, to gather up the sins and griefs and cares that were destroying men, to tear them out of their hearts even though it meant taking them into his own heart, that they might be lost in the infinite depths of God's forgiveness. That was what had to be done, and he would do it. It is right, then, to say that he chose to suffer. The suffering that came to him was not an accident or a misfortune that he might have avoided. It was the cost of being what it was his destiny to be: the Man who in the midst of history would be both one with God and one with man so that in him God and man would be reconciled.

THE FELLOWSHIP OF HIS SUFFERINGS

There are some uncomfortable consequences of the preceding definition of Jesus' ministry. We have said that he was not willing to be alone in the joy and strength of his oneness with God. He chose others to be with him and to share his joy. He gave himself to them, that his life should be theirs. And after his resurrection he poured forth the very Spirit of God, who was the secret of his love and power, to be the secret center of their existence too. To belong to him in the church, which was his body, was to be taken not only into his life with God but also into his ministry for God. His church was called to be the servant of the Word in dependence upon him. And even in his lifetime he made it very plain that to share his ministry would be to share his sufferings. How could it be otherwise if, as we have seen, the suffering of the servant was the consequence of the integrity of his relation with God and the completeness of his identification with man? The church is truly his church, his body, only in so far as it is a fellowship that yields itself unconditionally to the will of God no matter how sharply that may bring it into conflict with the world's will, and that lays itself open to the world, not holding itself apart from it in spiritual superiority but identifying itself with it in all humility.

All the sufferings of the Servant were not borne under Pontius Pilate. For Paul, it was the highest privilege of his ministry, which was ever the ministry of the living Lord in him, that he should be counted worthy to know " the fellowship of Jesus' sufferings."

Suffering for the sake of the gospel was for him not something to be endured but rather an occasion for rejoicing, a sign that in him God was at work marching to victory over his enemies. It has to be faced frankly, then, that there is no way for the church to be the church, or for a Christian to be a Christian, without suffering. In a land where Christians form a majority and no one dares speak evil of the church, there is danger that this fact will be concealed. The church may have to suffer in other lands but not in ours. Here there is no cost in suffering to pay for being a Christian. Here the world has been tamed and no longer shows its teeth at God. There can be no greater delusion than this, and the propagation of it among young Christians lulls them into a blind and paralyzing complacency. If there is no cost in suffering for us to be Christians or to be the church, we had best look carefully to see in what degree two things have happened: that we have evaded the conflict between God and the world by some form of compromise between God's will and the world's will, and that we have made of the church a spiritual community in which we create for ourselves a protected life apart from the agonies and dilemmas of the world's life. A sign that the first has happened is that we no longer have in Christ the joy and power of an unconditional oneness with God, and the indubitable sign of the second is that the ordinary Christian finds himself helpless and speechless when confronted with a person who confesses honestly his unbelief or his agony of guilt. The world that hates God and uses every possible means to evade his totalitarian claim upon it is still with us, perhaps closer to us than we know. We dare not be deceived by the sophisticated forms of its expression, nor by the subtlety of its devices. We had best begin by recognizing its presence in ourselves, and then we shall have eyes to see it beyond ourselves. It is the same blind, foolish, self-destroying world that it was in Jesus' day, and God in his love for it has no other way to reach it and redeem it except through men and women who will let themselves be chosen in Christ to have their existence in the world for God and for their fellow men no matter what it may cost in suffering.

UNDER PONTIUS PILATE

It may seem strange that a Roman governor should be named in the Christian creed. Pilate would long since have been forgotten had he not been thus remembered by Christians. The mention of his name has more than one significance. It points to the fact that Jesus' ministry and death actually happened in history in a particular place at a particular time. Thus it resists the tendency to detach Jesus from concrete history and make him an ideal figure suspended above all time. His history was an integral part of our human history. He was condemned to death by the Roman governor.

Perhaps we need to put ourselves in the situation of those who first formulated this creed if we are to understand Pilate's presence in it. They were Christians of the second century A.D. who were suffering for their faith under Roman governors in various parts of the Empire. Two centuries later they were to conquer the Empire that had tried to crush them, but that was as yet far ahead. They were confessing their faith in the midst of persecutions and often in peril of their lives. Therefore, Pilate in the creed was the symbol of a Roman power and authority that dared to set itself above the power and authority of God that they acknowledged in Jesus. The Empire through Pilate could make Jesus suffer and could crucify him, but it could not keep him from being the Son of God with power, the Lord of all mankind, ruling the world from his unseen throne and destined one day to judge the world. If this is true, then there was a note of defiance in the confession when the Roman Christians said " suffered under Pontius Pilate." The world has its victories for a time, and then in God's good time Christ has *his* victory.

10.

. . . *Crucified, Dead, Buried, Descended Into Hell*

It is strange that the creed heaps up four terms to emphasize the death of Jesus. They are like hammer blows, driving home upon our minds the fact of Jesus' death as though this were the crucial point at which there dare not be any misunderstanding. The first depicts the manner of his dying — crucified, executed as a criminal is executed. The modern parallel would be the hangman's noose or the electric chair: the most shameful death that any man can die. The second is the word that for human beings has in its very sound the note of finality: dead, the negation of life. The third reinforces that negation: the body, from which life has departed, is removed from sight and returned to the earth. The fourth extends the fact of death to the whole self; death was not just a dissolution of the body leaving the soul untouched but was a separation from God that comprehended the whole being of Jesus: *he* died and not just his body. He descended into hell, the world of darkness, where man knows himself shut out from God.

It is the fourth of these assertions that rouses our distrust and troubled questioning. What kind of legend is this, that Jesus descended into hell? We may dismiss it as a curious early explanation of what Jesus was doing between the time he died on Friday and the hour that he rose from the dead on Sunday: that he was in the underworld of hell, or Sheol, where the departed spirits dwelt in the shadows, preaching his gospel to them that they might have the opportunity of eternal life. Or we may, with Calvin, interpret it as a graphic description of the desolation of the soul of Jesus when God was hidden from him in his dark hour and he cried out, "My God, my God, why hast thou forsaken me?" But is this all it says? Death is the blotting out of life, the threat of nothingness. It is not the dissolution of the body that strikes fear into man, nor would most men fear a death that meant extinction. There is another death of which the bodily death is but a symbol, an inner deprivation that man has already known in part and that he cannot endure. It is like the torture of remembering a relationship of love from which one stands excluded. What is hell except the agony of the human spirit that has built a wall between itself and God and so is self-excluded from the only enduring Source of life? Hell is the ultimate defeat of life, the emptiness of meaning that is unendurable. Perhaps, then, "he descended into hell" is meant to say to us that Jesus not only shared with us our death and burial, that strange and troubling ending of our familiar life, but so bound himself into one with man that he knew the agony of man's utmost deprivation of life. Death is the enemy whom he must defeat, this deeper death which lays life waste and has its tyrannous power over man as long as he remains shut in upon himself. Sin is the seed of death, that sin in which a man means only to claim his right to a life of his own, apart from God and in independence of his fellows, but with it ruptures the relationships in which he has his only hope of life. Hell is the existence of the man who is alone with himself with no way of access either to God or to his fellow man. The descent into hell, then, is Christ with man in hell, what no man could expect, what no man could deserve: the love of God reaching across the abyss that sin has made, bearing the pain and darkness of hell with man in order to deliver him into the brightness and joy of life with God. In this sense, the whole ministry of Jesus was a descending into hell, that the power of death might be destroyed and men might live. What it means in connection with his death and burial we can only dimly grasp, but this at least it means: that in his death he conquered death and hell, finishing the battle that he had waged throughout his life.

How he conquered is the mystery of the cross.

We are so familiar with the story of the resurrection that followed close upon the cross, and we speak so freely of "the living Christ," that we never quite look at the fact that Jesus died. Or, if we do, it is just a moment's shadow between his life on earth and his more glorious life as the risen Lord. Perhaps if we acknowledged what is really in our minds, we would have to say that we do not think of him as ever dead. We do not think of anyone as ever dead. The immortal part of them persists untouched by death. But if this is so, then there was no need of a *resurrection* of Jesus, since he was not really dead. What is called the resurrection in the Gospels is merely a series of appearances of the soul of Jesus to his disciples! But this is not the Christian faith. In it there is death and resurrection and not just the persistence of an immortal soul through death. The New Testament takes death with far more seriousness than we do. In fact, throughout the whole of Scripture there is an emphasis upon the mortality of man. It is no accident that, in contrast to the Greeks, who believed so easily in the immortality of man, the Hebrews long insisted that man's life is bounded by his birth and death. The Greek belief was linked with the conviction that man possessed within himself a mind that was a fragment of the divine, so that belief in immortality was intrinsically belief in himself. But, for the Hebrew, God alone was God, and man was mortal. Life was God's gift to man and not an inalienable possession of man within himself. Only in covenant, or fellowship, with God could man have life. Bereft of God, all hope of life for him was gone. Mortal man had nothing in himself that would encourage him to set his confidence upon himself. God alone could be the object of man's confidence. Therefore, Israel resisted every encouragement from the surrounding world to make man immortal. Life is God's gift and God's creation, not man's right. Therefore, death is the end of the life that began at birth, and we have no right to assume that in some automatic way our life goes on. We die, and because Jesus shared our life completely, he died as we die and was buried as we are buried. Not until we grasp this fact securely do we admit the full humanity of Jesus, that he was one with us, not just in his being clothed with our flesh and his experiencing of our temptations, but also in this final decisive mark of our humanity, that he died.

Later we shall see how important it is that we should believe in a resurrection to life that is God's gift rather than in an immortality that we possess within ourselves. For the present our concern is with the death of Jesus. Our refusal to look at his death is coupled with a refusal to take with full seriousness the fact of our own death. We co-operate in a widespread conspiracy to conceal the fact of death. Children must be protected from the frightening knowledge of it as long as possible; and then adults extend the protection to themselves, using every device they can to put far away the thought of death. But is not this in itself a confession of the fear of death, an admission that belief in our own immortality is not able to take from death its sting or to free us from its power? We have no light within ourselves to penetrate the darkness of the mystery that stands at the end of our way, and yet, as long as it remains an impenetrable wall, our life between the bounds of birth and death does not make sense. It is when we acknowledge this darkness in which the prospect of our own death plunges us and when at the cross we find Jesus together with us in the darkness, that the expectation begins to stir in us that with God this fearful fact of death may have some other deeper meaning than the end and dissolution of our life. We have no word or thought or power that conquers death. But at the cross Jesus goes out on our behalf to face the reality of death and to conquer or be conquered.

THE HIDDEN MEANING

The cross and resurrection of Jesus pose for the Christian teacher the most difficult tasks that he will ever have to face. Here he touches the very heart and center of the Christian faith, and from whatever side he approaches, he is made aware that he treads on holy ground, for in these events the Christian church had its birth and from them it draws all its understanding of its life. The church is "the church of God, which he hath purchased with his own blood," and all its life, and the life of Christians in it, is determined by the remembrance of the Lord's death upon the cross. A church that has found a way to be the church without passing through the cross soon betrays in its character and actions that it is something less than the church of God. At the same time, the church is the church of the risen Lord, undismayed by any task and undeterred by any obstacle, because its trust is not in itself but in the power of Him to whom it belongs who passed through death to life.

We need perhaps to remind ourselves how peculiar it is that the death of Jesus should be so central to the Christian gospel. If we were strangers to Christianity reading the New Testament for the first time, we would be struck by the way in which attention is focused on Jesus' dying. From a quarter to a half of each of the Gospels is given to the account of Jesus' death and resurrection, and the remainder is already under its shadow. Paul desires to preach only Christ and him crucified. Then, in the church, the high point of worship is the Eucharist, a perpetual memorial of Jesus' death. What would we think if the biography of some great man were to occupy itself chiefly with how he came to die and we were to find his friends years later solemnly recalling the circumstances of his death? It would seem to us morbid. Our interest in great men is in their life story and in their achievements, not in their deaths. That it is otherwise with Jesus points to the difference between him and even the greatest of men. It is not what he did that is the primary focus of our attention but what God has done and does in him. Our interest is not in the greatness of his achievements or the beauty of his character, though both are evident in the story, but that God meets us in him in a mysterious way that we cannot explain. Confronted with him, in his words and actions, but above all in his death and resurrection, we find ourselves utterly humbled under the judgment of God and yet at the same time not rejected but accepted of God. The cross is, for the church, the place where God reveals himself and in revealing himself reveals us to ourselves and to each other.

The teacher who knows this will never make the mistake of speaking of the cross as though its meaning were immediately self-evident to the human mind. The meaning is hidden in the outward events and has to be revealed to faith. In Paul's day the preaching of the cross was a stumbling block to Jews and foolishness to Greeks, and the power and wisdom of God only to those who were called, that is, only to those whose lives had been laid open to God by their confrontation with Jesus Christ. To the Jew, the death of Jesus upon the cross was proof that he was only a man. To the Greek, it made no sense to say that the death of a Galilean Jew was the turning point in the history of mankind. Both Jew and Greek were reasonable men, and we ought not to be surprised to find them present in any class we teach, unable to see more in the story of the cross than a tragic death, the barely legalized murder of an innocent man. To press upon them such statements as " He died for our sins," " His blood has washed away our sin," " By his cross we are reconciled to God," is likely only to perplex them or to repulse them, or it may extort from them a formal orthodox confession that corresponds to no reality in their lives.

There is encouragement in the New Testament story itself for Christians who are puzzled by what seem extravagant and unreasonable claims about the cross. To Jesus' first disciples, who had been trained to preach his gospel and to share with him in his mission, it was no more than a tragic event at the time it happened. It crushed their hopes of what might yet be achieved by Jesus' ministry and theirs. It was a blank wall that suddenly shut out the future for them. There is no evidence that at first it had any redemptive significance for them. They did not stand below the cross and say " This death is our life " but rather " This death is our defeat." There was for them only darkness, impenetrable darkness, in the event itself until the whole of Jesus' life and death was reinterpreted for them in the light of the resurrection. What sympathy we ought to have, then, with modern disciples for whom the passage from Good Friday to Easter Day is often much more difficult to make than it was for the first disciples!

An unnecessary obstacle to the understanding of the cross is sometimes put in the way of pupils when the ministry and teaching of Jesus are described in such a manner that it is incomprehensible how anyone could take serious offense at him. By emphasizing only Jesus' unselfish helpfulness to others and his depth of spiritual understanding, and ignoring all those points at which Jesus gave offense to good religious people of his day, a teacher does four things: he makes of Jesus an innocuous and unreal ideal figure; he conceals the conflict between the mind of Jesus and the minds of good religious people such as ourselves; he makes the crucifixion seem an act of vicious, criminal-minded men rather than the act of ordinary men; and he destroys the unity that is preserved by all the Gospels between the ministry of Jesus and the cross. The teacher needs to beware of books that, in their endeavor to make Jesus attractive and admirable to children and teen-agers, depict a person who would never have been crucified in any age. This " gentle Jesus, meek and mild " fits only too comfortably into a milieu of anemic religiosity.

We need to make clear, then, that the hiddenness of the cross's meaning has two aspects. It is hidden in the event itself, so that to the merely curious, inquiring mind, however intelligent, the cross cannot be made to disclose a redemptive significance. Only where a bond has already been created between Jesus and ourselves, and our life has begun to be laid open to his life, do we cease to be spectators of the cross and find it rearing itself up within our most intimate existence. But it is hidden also by a certain willful blindness in us. We do not want to see it. We want a faith and worship and a way of life in which there will be no cross. We do not consciously remove it; rather, we have grown up into a form of Christianity from which it has already been removed. The church itself may be of a character that hides from us the cross. Therefore, if the cross is not to remain hidden from our pupils, they must be drawn down off the balcony from which they contemplate the cross to recognize the involvement of their own life in the events, and they must learn, as true Protestants, to let the church and the form of Christianity into which they have been born be set in question by both the gospel and the church that meets them in the person of Jesus Christ.

THE JUDGMENT OF THE WORLD

The New Testament speaks often of the necessity of the cross. Jesus is represented in the Gospels as saying that he *must* die. The understanding of this "must" takes us a long way into the meaning of the cross. It dare not be interpreted in a fatalistic manner as though the events were prearranged by God so that Judas had to betray Jesus and Jesus had to die at just that moment. There are no puppets in the story of the cross but only persons, disturbingly like ourselves, who act in freedom under impulses that we can readily identify. The "must" of Jesus' death, like the "must" of his suffering, was a necessity from within and not imposed upon him from without. It does not contradict in any way the freedom with which he gave himself at each step in obedience to God's will and in Gethsemane chose the way of death when it was the only way in which he could win his final victory.

All the Gospels are agreed concerning the unique oneness of Jesus with the Father, never a static oneness of simple identification but always a personal oneness in which love is responded to by love and God's commands are embraced in implicit obedience. This is the oneness for which God created man in the beginning when he made him in his likeness for fellowship with him and to rule for him in the midst of his creation, and it is the oneness that was intended when God called Israel to a life in covenant with him. But man in his pride and self-will chose for himself a life apart from God, a half life at best, and Israel through the centuries was torn between a life in covenant with God reflecting his holiness, justice, and truth, and a life of broken faith reflecting the characteristics of its neighbors. In Jesus, therefore, the purpose of God for his creation reached its goal. He was both the true Israel keeping covenant with God, and the true man reflecting in his nature the very nature of God. He was the Servant of God, with his life wholly at the disposal of the Word of God, and the Son of Man, the new Adam, the first-born of a new humanity. But to be the true Israel in the midst of an Israel whose order of life was an evasion of its destiny was to be God's judgment upon Israel. He was in himself what Israel was called to be and had stamped deep in its soul as its true calling, and so merely by his existence he constituted the most penetrating rebuke that Israel could ever know. And to be the true man reflecting God's nature was to be the incarnation of God's judgment upon all the perversions of humanity in which men were imprisoned. Thus, at one and the same time, he was the hope of a new Israel, a new humanity, and a new world, and the judgment of God upon an old Israel, an old humanity, and an old world. Two worlds intersected where he stood, and it was his destiny to be the point of intersection embodying in himself both the threat of death and the promise of life.

He was the threat of death to Judaism. Nothing could remain the same if he lived. The Pharisees felt the whole order of their religion shaken by his words and acts. To the priests he was a revolutionist. Judas was undoubtedly a patriot who suddenly realized the radical implications of Jesus' teachings for his nation's future. It was better that one man die than that the nation perish. But the offensiveness of Jesus went deeper still. He was the threat of death to man, because it was man's one true life in God that was reality in him. He had only to be in the midst of men for them to be uncomfortably guilty for being what they were, in their various forms of inhumanity and in their alienation from God and from their fellow men. Both in Jesus' gospel and in his person God laid claim to the whole self of man uncompromisingly. And the self of man in its determination to be free, unwilling to let itself be bound into such oneness with God, struck out blindly at him to rid itself of the peril he seemed to constitute to its existence. The cross, therefore, that seemed to be an easily made decision concerning the man Jesus, was actually a life or

death decision both for Israel and for man, a decision for or
against God, but more, a decision concerning both the destiny of
Israel and the destiny of man. The cross was Israel's No! to the
destiny offered it in Jesus, and it was man's No! to the life of a
new humanity to which Jesus was the open door. They only
wanted to be rid of him that they might continue as they were,
but when they nailed him to the cross, they nailed God with him
to the cross and made it the place where for evermore they and
all humanity with them are brought under the judgment of God.
On the cross is Jesus in the integrity of his oneness with God, saying his Yes! to God on behalf of all mankind. But below the
cross are those who say their No! to God, also on behalf of all
mankind, and man has to choose which is to be his representative.
It is this which makes of the cross the place of ultimate decision
where at last there is no middle ground. Jesus, in his oneness
with God, crucified by man, is the judgment of the world.

But we do not approach the cross as though the decision as to
where we stand had yet to be made. Whether we know it or not,
our decision was made long since and we recognize ourselves, if
not in Judas, then in Peter; if not in the Pharisees or priests, then
in Pilate or the fickle mob. The faces of the men about the cross
are only too familiar: Judas, who only loved his nation a frac-
tion more than he loved his God; Peter, who thought his loyalty to Jesus would stand any test but miscalculated its strength;
the scribes and Pharisees, who were so sure that all God's truth
was comprehended in their interpretations that they could not
endure a word that set in question any of their doctrines or practices; the priests, for whom the existing order in the religious institution was sacrosanct; Pilate, who wanted to play safe and
avoid any disturbance in the community; and the mob of men
and women, who did no thinking for themselves but shouted
loudly the words that propagandists put in their mouths. These
faces trouble us as we see our own faces reflected in them. This
is the way we are. These are the faces of our humanity, just ordinary men, not criminals, not unusually wicked men, but law-
abiding citizens, some of us quite religious, some passionately

loyal to our religious institutions, all of us, or almost all, quite sure that we believe in God; and yet we have it in our hearts to put God from us with this decisiveness when he comes to us and lays claim to our total being. Jesus Christ is God's assault upon the stronghold of our human self. In him God does not just ask for our submission; he receives the submission of the human self, and where that submission is given, man is man so completely and so triumphantly that we can no longer defend the proposition that this broken rebellious self of ours is truly man. Our true humanity is not in Judas, or in Peter, or in the Pharisees, or in any of the others on this side of the cross; our true humanity is there in Jesus, crucified upon the cross.

This is the judgment upon all of us that takes place in the death of Jesus. It is, from one way of thinking, merely one event among all the other events of ancient history, the death of an obscure Galilean. But seen in the context of what God has been doing from the beginning of human history and of his purpose for humanity, it is the tearing away of all concealment and self-deception to reveal how things really stand between God and us. Our judgment upon ourselves and upon our fellow men is very different from this. We have our ways of justifying ourselves with God. We point to the virtue of our conduct, the orthodoxy of our religious beliefs, the faithfulness of our attendance upon religious services, the generosity we have shown to our fellow men in need, or, if our record is not too good in some of these categories, we call the roll of all the damning sins that we have not committed. No human occupation claims our more constant attention than that of giving ourselves a character that will justify us first with those round about us and then with God. But at the cross a radical judgment falls upon us that puts an end to all our petty judging of ourselves and of our fellow men. God reveals to us our true life in oneness with him in Jesus Christ; he offers it to us in him; and we have to acknowledge ourselves to be those who have already in thought, word, and action said No! to him. That is our judgment. And if it remains God's judgment upon us, then we are lost.

MAN RECONCILED WITH GOD

In Jesus' oneness with God, the judgment of God meets us in the cross and makes us sinners, tearing from us every vestige of self-justification. But we could not endure this encounter with the cross were there no mercy in the judgment. Judgment and mercy are ever inseparable in God's dealings with his people in Scripture, even though at times the mercy may be hidden. Judgment is not the fury of an angry God at sin but rather the severity of a loving God who will not let his people destroy themselves in blind resistance to his will without shaking them with his judgments. He sets barriers in their way that they may turn before it is too late and find his way. There is always love behind the judgment, and the judgment when it comes has in it always the hope of redemption yet to come.

To find God's mercy in the cross we shall follow the line that begins at Jesus' baptism with his identification of himself with a sinful, covenant-breaking rebellious Israel. It is hard for us to grasp this element in Jesus' mission because of the individualism of our own thinking and living. We consider ourselves responsible only for ourselves, for our own actions, for our own sins. If we are generous we may take some responsibility for others, but it is not rightly ours. We have to answer to God only for ourselves. We confess to God only the sins that we have committed. But in Israel the relation of God was primarily with the community, and what the community was in its life was the responsibility of all its members. The prophets were concerned not so much that individuals within Israel had broken covenant with God as that Israel as a whole had broken covenant and thus endangered its entire future existence. Dishonesty in the market place, foolish national aspirations among the princes, greediness of landlords, and corruption of worship were the sin of Israel in which all Israelites participated and all Israelites were called to repentance. The prophets who recognized the sin, and who certainly were not guilty of such grossness, nevertheless identified themselves with the nation as guilty before God and threatened with the judgment of God. Never do they speak as righteous men standing above the judgment and thundering down at the sinners below them. They stand always with their people under the crushing judgment. Isaiah cries out, "Woe is me! For I am undone; for I am a man of unclean lips, and I dwell in the midst of a people of unclean lips." Second Isaiah confesses, "We have all become like one who is unclean, and all our righteous deeds are like a polluted garment." Moses is represented as asking God to blot him out of his book if he would not have mercy upon Israel in spite of its sin.

It is in this succession that Jesus stands. In himself and in his warnings of doom he is God's judgment upon Israel, but the weight of the judgment falls upon him. He promises his followers and himself no escape. On the contrary, it is his calling as the Servant of God to bear in himself the burden and the pain of the estrangement of his fellow men from God. He is not willing to enter upon the new age without them. He cannot bear to be cut apart from any man. They belong together with him as children of God no matter how far they may have wandered from their destiny. As *Son* of God he knows himself one with every *child* of God. They are his, even though they may have sinned disgracefully; to do an injury to one of them is to injure him, and to feed or clothe or shelter one of them in trouble is to feed and clothe and shelter him. Jesus' love for man is no puny calculating love that gives itself where it is deserved and where there will be love in return; it is a reaching out to every man to bind him to him and to let himself be bound to him. It is an openness to every man that makes that man know himself accepted in spite of all the reasons for his rejection. This was what the woman in the house of Simon the Pharisee, and Zacchaeus, and a host of others, experienced with such joy in Jesus. They to whom so many doors were closed and who daily felt the condemnation of men of virtue and piety found themselves accepted in some marvelous and unbelievable way by Jesus. And his acceptance of them was somehow God's acceptance of them. His love that found them was God's love finding them. Neither Simon nor any other Pharisee could understand it, and there is so much in us of the Pharisaic defender of religious and moral standards that it is hard for us to understand it too. Was there, then, no word of judgment from Jesus for the sinners? Yes, but indirectly. They had only to be with him in openness and gratitude to judge themselves. His love is in itself sufficient judgment upon the repentant sinner.

But we have yet to trace the line from this sin-bearing to the cross. God's ordering of the world is such that sin is in its inmost nature self-destructive; its hatefulness is that it is the seed of death, being in its essence a denial of life, a rupture of the relationships with God and man in which alone is life. But the death that sin brings is not ever confined to the sinner. Most men would be content if, having sinned, they could bear all the consequences of the sin themselves. It would be to them a kind of balancing of accounts. But the horror of sin is that most often it is someone else who has to bear the consequences of it. The sin of Cain, whatever it was that was the barrier between him and God, had as its consequence the murder of his brother Abel. The folly of parents has its bitter fruits in the children and the grandchildren. This is the hatefulness of sin, that it brings death where we do not want death to come. Its consequence is borne most heavily by whoever has bound himself most closely in love to the sinner.

Had Jesus bound himself to no man, there would have been no cross; nor would there have been a ministry. He could have spent his life as an anchorite in some Transjordanian cave in mystic communion with his God — and died forgotten. It was his identification of himself with Judas and with Peter and with all his fellow Israelites that put his life in danger. If he had never come so close to Judas, he would never have been betrayed by Judas. If he had said, " Let the priests and Pharisees and all their following die in their blindness without a word of warning," he would not have roused their fear and enmity. But that was what he could not do. He could no more deny his oneness with man than he could deny his oneness with God. Just as he belonged to God, so all men belonged to him, bound to him by the fact that it was their life, their own most human life, that was being lived out to the full in him. Because of his oneness with God, he was Man in his wholeness, Man in his perfect freedom to be himself, Man who in losing himself so completely for his brothers found himself. He had to give himself completely in order to be himself. So it was that on the last night of his life Jesus instituted a sacrament in which his disciples would constantly be reminded of his giving of himself to them. This was the central reality of his ministry, not his teaching, not his works of healing and exorcism, but the imparting to men of his own life in God that in it they might come to the fulfillment of themselves. All else that he had said and done would have meaning for them only when every inner barrier of self was broken down and they received God himself in the fullness of his wisdom and power to be their life. Therefore, he took their life with its burden of sin and darkness and death into himself that they might take his life with its wholeness and freedom and joy in God into themselves. This incomprehensible yet actual exchange of life was the heart of his ministry, and it reached its climax in the cross. He endured the humiliation, condemnation, and death that we deserve that all the riches of his own oneness with God might be ours. He died for us. His condemnation is our liberation. His death is our life. By his cross we are reconciled with God.

11.

. . The Third Day He Rose Again
from the Dead

The same fate befalls the resurrection of Jesus as his birth: it becomes so identified with a popular religious or nature festival that its distinctive Christian significance is frequently lost from sight. The happy exultant mood that is abroad — for a day or so — has more connection with the rebirth of nature than with any event in the story of Jesus. The immortality of the soul is more often preached at Easter than the resurrection of Jesus from the dead. But even when the resurrection of Jesus is the theme for the preaching and teaching of the day, it tends to be isolated from its context in the total account of Jesus' ministry and from its yet larger context in the Biblical story as a whole. Moreover, if the resurrection is not discussed at any other time than Easter, or its significance taken into account in the consideration of Jesus' person and ministry, this isolation is complete. Perhaps it is a consequence of this that many Christians treat the resurrection of Jesus as an article of faith that stands alone. They try to understand it by itself, and if they come to the conclusion that they cannot honestly believe it, it does not occur to them that its dismissal carries with it any other essential elements in the New Testament faith. They believe in Jesus but not in his resurrection from the dead. But they need to make clear to themselves what place a Jesus who did not rise from the dead has in a creed that is essentially, and certainly in all it says of Jesus, a confession of faith *in God*. The resurrection does not and cannot stand alone. Its removal makes necessary the writing of another creed that will speak differently in all its articles.

Also, it must be frankly recognized that, looked at by themselves, the stories of Jesus' resurrection sound like curious myths that only completely naïve people would take literally. Not only in the Old Testament but in the religious literature of other nations, there are accounts of heavenly beings who in the form of men appear for the moment on earth. In the Homeric epic a god may clothe himself in human form, now of one man, now of another. Ghost stories are told by superstitious people everywhere, and to such people it is not at all surprising that the spirit of someone who has died in unusual circumstances should return at times and communicate with the living. How is the story of Jesus' being seen in various places by his disciples shortly after his death to be distinguished from a ghost story? A man dies on Friday, and his body, after it has been carefully prepared for burial, is laid in a tomb. A great stone is placed against the door of the tomb. For two days nothing happens, but on the third day, early in the morning, the tomb is found open and empty, and the man whom all had seen dead begins to appear to a number of his friends. He talks with them and explains to them things about his life and death that have been too hard for them to understand. His appearances continue for forty days, and then they cease. Is it not understandable that to some people this is just another story about a ghost, and that, since they consider themselves to have passed beyond the superstitious era in which men believed in ghostly or demonic or angelic appearances of beings from another world, they dismiss the story of Jesus' resurrection as a superstitious myth?

The questioning of the resurrection is also encouraged by the conflicting accounts in the various Gospels. Some locate the chief appearances in Galilee; others, in Jerusalem. They cannot be fitted together to form an orderly sequence of events any more than the two stories of the Creation in Genesis can be adjusted to make a play-by-play account of the Creation. But this has no great weight when we consider that the even wider divergences in the description of Jesus' ministry between the Gospel of John and the Synoptics does not make us doubt either the existence of his ministry or that each in its own way intends to depict the same ministry. And when we grasp more clearly the nature of the resurrection appearances and their significance for faith, we shall be less surprised at the variety of their description.

Perhaps the strongest influence, however, in the nineteenth and twentieth centuries in making the resurrection of Jesus a source of embarrassment rather than a source of assurance to Christians has been the attitude of many distinguished New Testament scholars. They felt compelled to undertake the task of distinguishing in the New Testament records between historical fact and mythical invention. But in their definition of history they had room only for the actions, words, and thoughts *of men,* so that wherever the Scriptures speak of the action of God, this had to be placed in the category of the unhistorical or mythical, with the implication that it was unreal. One of the first casualties in this process was the resurrection of Jesus, although the logical application of the principle called for a complete rewriting of the Biblical story to make both the prophetic faith of the Old Testament and the birth of Christianity the products of the interplay of purely natural forces and influences in the human situation. Not only was there no room for a resurrection in this conception of history but actually there was no room for a living God who can act in history. More recently there has been increasing recognition of the inadequacy of this idea of history and an openness to the Biblical understanding of history as determined in its character and outcome by the relationship of God to man and man to God. The thesis of the Old Testament itself that the initiative in Israel's history was not man's but God's is no longer dismissed by competent scholars; and most of them, no matter how they explain the resurrection appearances, recognize that no sense can be made either of New Testament history or of the New Testament documents until it is acknowledged that an event called the resurrection is at their center. Some are inclined to interpret that event as a revival of the disciples' faith in Jesus, expressing itself in visionary experiences, rather than a resurrection of Jesus from the dead, or as the triumphant aspect of Jesus' death, dawning gradually upon the disciples. But few today would dispute the importance of the resurrection in the shaping of the Christian faith and in the origin of the church. Nevertheless, the influence of earlier scholars continues to make itself felt and may well be a complicating factor in the thinking of the teacher himself and in the situation in which he undertakes to teach the resurrection.

THE EVIDENCE OF THE EVENT

The existence of the Christian church is the primary evidence that Jesus' death was not the final act in his relations with his disciples. The impressive fact is not just that a church came into being in loyalty to him and to his teaching, for we can conceive a mission such as his perpetuating itself among his followers when they recovered from the shock of his violent death, but that a church proclaiming him Messiah and calling him its living Lord came into being: this is proof that something happened to change the attitude and outlook of the disciples. Their own testimony is that any thought they had that Jesus might be the Messiah of Israel was dashed to pieces by his death. His own conviction that he was living in the Last Days when God would establish his Kingdom, a conviction that they had come to share with joy as they saw human lives transformed by the power that was at work in him and in them, had proved to be a delusion. God's Messiah could not die. He would be known, when he appeared, by his power to carry all before him. To them, as to the pre-Christian Paul, the cross was proof that Jesus was just a man. And yet the preaching of the church in its earliest form centers in the proclamation that he whom men have crucified is Lord and Christ. The Messiah has come and has been rejected of men, but God has raised him from the dead and has vindicated him and his gospel as the one true hope of Israel. This was a most provoking and dangerous thing to say of one who had recently been executed by the national authorities as a peril to the state. Those who dared to say it took their lives in their hands to make such a claim. That they believed it is beyond all question, and any suggestion that they were preaching a deception in order to forward their movement assumes a calculated trickery in them that is contrary to all we know of them.

The evidence directly from Paul is most impressive. Here we are dealing not with reports of resurrection experiences that have been handed down across several generations but with the first-hand report of a man who claims that the risen Lord appeared to him and that his experience was the same in its nature as that of the first disciples. It is important also that, before his own experience, Paul was certain that the claim of Jesus' rising from the dead was a lie. The security of his traditional faith and the validity of his conduct as a persecutor of the Christian movement depended upon its being a lie. But what once had seemed so certainly a falsehood became the truth of truths for him. The appearance of the risen Lord to him produced a radical reversal of his convictions and a transformation of his life. It is wrong to assume that Paul knew nothing of Jesus or of his teaching before his conversion. His contacts with Christians and his need to understand the Christian teaching in order to combat it would ensure at least some knowledge. Also, his prominence as a persecutor suggests that he saw more clearly than other rabbis, such as Gamaliel, the danger of the Christian movement to Judaism. An enemy who is an honest thinker sometimes sees more clearly and deeply into the truth of things than a friend. Therefore, it was no disembodied heavenly being who confronted Paul on the Damascus road; it was the Jesus whom he had been persecuting in the person of his followers. And the Jesus, crucified and risen, who became the all-engrossing subject of Paul's gospel and the all-determining power within his life is recognizably the Jesus of the earliest Christian tradition. The resurrection convinced Paul that Jesus was the Christ, the long-expected Messiah of Israel. That Christ should have appeared to him, a Hellenistic Jew of the Dispersion, in contrast to the Palestinian disciples, and long after their experiences, was to him his call to be the missionary of Christ to the Gentiles.

The Last Days had come when God would pour out his Spirit upon all men and all nations would be gathered into one with Israel as a great new people of God. It was the harvest time of God. But first, all men must die with Christ on his cross and be raised with him into a glorious new life in his resurrection. The power of evil, and even the power of death, has been defeated. A new humanity has been born into the world with Christ. The old world, and the old man in us, still continues for a time, but only for a time. The day will come when evil will no longer have any power over man and death itself will be destroyed. But this triumphant faith of Paul's rested firmly on the reality of Jesus' resurrection, so much so that he had to say that if Christ were not risen from the dead, then both his faith and his apostleship were vain.

The paramount importance of the resurrection for the early church is evident in the fact that to be an apostle it was necessary that a Christian should have been one of those who had " seen the Lord." It was not sufficient that he had known and heard and followed Jesus in his lifetime or that he had received the Holy Spirit, who was the Spirit that empowered a man to share in Jesus' ministry. No gifts of teaching or of preaching and no qualities of Christian character qualified him for that office. He had to be one who, like Peter or like Paul, had had the curtain of the flesh drawn aside that he might know with certainty the church's Lord.

One further point of evidence is the structure of the Gospels. Whether they begin with Jesus' ministry, like Mark's, or with his birth, like Matthew's and Luke's, or before the creation of the world, like John's, they all speed toward their climax in the cross and resurrection. For all of them the whole story is told in the light of the resurrection. They would not have known rightly what God was doing in Jesus' birth and in his ministry and death if God had not shown them in the resurrection who he was. The resurrection light and triumph shines all the way back to the birth. Take away the stories of the resurrection and all the light that they cast upon the remainder of the story, and each of the Gospels will seem to lose the cement that holds it together. The light will go out and leave only a rather pitiful deluded Jewish rabbi, with some very wonderful insights into life, trudging briefly along a road that ends abruptly at the cross.

The Context in the Story of Jesus

The resurrection, then, is not to be detached from the total witness of the New Testament concerning Jesus. The claim that he rose from the dead is no more outrageous to man's normal expectation of what should happen in a human life than a whole series of claims: that he was one with God in such a way that God was known in him as he is not known otherwise to man; that in his oneness with God he was sinless in spite of sharing with us every human temptation; that in him a new humanity was born and a new age begun in history; that in him and in his death it was judgment day for the human race; that by dying with him to self we are reborn with him into a new life with God, a life that is imperishable; and finally, that he is what no other person has ever been or ever will be, both truly God and truly man. If the claim that he rose from the dead is disallowed, at once the question must be faced whether it can be separated from all these other claims in which the very essence of historic Christianity comes to expression. Can the resurrection be denied without carrying with it, whether consciously or not, the denial of all the others? In short, the question of the resurrection is not a secondary question but the primary one: Who is this Jesus? If, for us, he is no more than a great heroic and epoch-making figure in the history of religion, one of those spectacularly unusual persons who appear from time to time in the history of the world — like Socrates or Confucius — who see more deeply into things than other men and influence their thinking for centuries afterward, then not only the story of the resurrection but the entire apostolic faith in Jesus on which the church is founded must seem to us the product of imaginative superstition. But if in any part that apostolic faith appeals to us as true, no fanciful product of unbalanced minds but the ordered thinking of men who were certain that they were witnesses of events that were the turning point in the life of all humanity, then we shall be open to understand why they gave to the resurrection such a key importance in their faith.

We do well to remind ourselves that the first disciples and Paul were more intensely conscious of the humanity of Jesus than we can ever be. More than that, to them, as Hebrews, it was infinitely more offensive than it is to us to attribute divinity to any man. During the months that the disciples spent with Jesus sharing in his ministry, they became conscious of a mystery concerning him. A power of God dwelt in him, and a truth of God was present in his words. They could not help but be aware of a uniqueness in him in comparison with themselves and with all persons whom they ever knew. But this does not say that they had any inclination to regard him as divine. Peter's confession goes no farther than an acknowledgment that revelation and redemption from God have met him in Jesus. Who Jesus was remained still a mystery to Peter as to all the rest. The story of the transfiguration raises many problems. Perhaps it was a visionary experience of Jesus (similar to those which occurred at his baptism and in his temptations) in which he communed in spirit with Moses and Elijah to gain strength and confidence concerning his destiny (in the retelling of it, as in the retelling of the story of Paul's vision of Christ, the others who are present become participators in the vision). But as it is incorporated in the Gospels it is not intended to suggest that the disciples saw fully into the depths of the mystery of Jesus' being. The effect of the cross upon them shows how uncertain they still were of their answer to the question of who he was. The cross did not just deepen the mystery but rather for the moment seemed to dissolve it, proving that he was no more than what he had seemed to be. The resurrection both restored the mystery and revealed what had lain concealed within it. It compelled them to say what was blasphemy if it was not the truth: that God was in this man and had been in him from the beginning, offering to them the life of his Kingdom, loving them in his human love of them, judging them in his human judgment of them, and dying for them in his human death for them. It was

God himself who was at their door in him. They had not rightly known who he was, but now they knew him with all the human concealment swept away, so that he was with them, still the Jesus whom they had known, but revealed in the fullness of his divine power and glory.

Our experience as Christians is often like that of the disciples in Jesus' lifetime. We have heard in Jesus' words a word from God that we cannot hear elsewhere. He has opened to us an understanding of ourselves and possibilities of life that we could not have known apart from him. He has bound us to himself so that we love him and can no longer conceive of our life without him. But we are not yet sure within ourselves who he is. We sense the mystery of his person but as yet go no farther. But this is no longer a possible stopping place for any man. The Christian who stops here evades the decisions that are awaiting him in the cross and resurrection of his Lord. He wants to live his life on the nearer side of the cross where he does not have to ask or answer the deeper questions and can content himself that, like the disciples, he is a loyal friend of the human Jesus. But life on the nearer side of the cross with just the human Jesus is no longer a possibility for any man. That is what Paul meant when he said that though we have known Christ after the flesh, we know him in that way no more. There is no way to evade the decision of the cross: to die with Christ to self and to the old world of the unreconciled self, or to live on in that world as friends of Jesus who do not choose to taste either the joys or the responsibilities of being new men in Christ. It is a strange kind of Christianity that refuses to know him either in the fellowship of his sufferings (that is, by dying with him) or in the power of his resurrection (that is, by rising with him into a new life in unconditional openness toward God and man).

THE CONTEXT IN THE BIBLE AS A WHOLE

The basic assumption of the Scriptures apart from which nothing in them makes sense is that there are two realities: God, and the world with man in it, the unseen and the seen, heaven and earth. But these double realities are never known apart from each other but only in relation. They are two, but not like two distant lands or two separated worlds so that a line can be clearly drawn between them. Man himself belongs to both worlds and has his life both in the seen and the unseen. But because he has to concern himself so much with things, he is constantly in danger of distrusting the reality of the unseen and of falling into the delusion that only what he can see and touch and measure is real. Not only God but all that belongs to the unseen begins to seem unreal. But in the Scriptures the opposite is true, and this is why they provide a constant shock to our customary ways of thinking: the unseen is there the primary reality. Where, for us, our knowledge of ourselves and of our world is the realm of relative certainty and knowledge of God is problematical, in Scripture the knowledge of God is the point of certainty and all man's knowledge of himself and of his world problematical. The question mark is set not against God and the unseen but radically against our human life.

In their essence the Scriptures are the story of the inbreaking of that other world and of God into the world of men, not just to make us know that there is a God and an unseen world but to reveal to us that our life and the life of our world are in each moment dependent upon God and the unseen. To be ignorant of God is to be without understanding of ourselves. To be unaware of the unseen is to have a distorted vision of the world that we see with the outer eye. In Genesis, Adam and Eve begin to act as though they were alone within their world and free to do as they please with all things in it, but suddenly a Voice sounds in upon them and events begin to happen to them that make them aware how tragic a mistake it is to fail to take account of their relation with the God whom they cannot see. Jacob, fleeing from an angry brother, lies down to sleep at night in Bethel and in his dream sees heaven opened and a ladder joining earth and heaven. The secret of Israel's life that was to make it Israel was an inability to escape from the unseen. What happened to Moses in his fiery vision of God on the mountainside except that he was made aware of a power of God in the unseen infinitely greater than any power of Pharaoh in the visible world? It was by daring to act upon the premise of the reality of that unseen power that Israel came into being as a nation. The covenant was an acknowledgment that a continuing life for Israel as a nation was possible only in the most intimate relation with this unseen power. The prophets were above all else men with eyes to see the reality of God in the unseen, to hear the voice of God sounding in their ears out of the unseen, and to recognize the hand of God at work in the world about them. Isaiah's vision is typical of the prophets': he sees the Lord exalted in holiness and majesty, and then in the light of God he sees himself and his people and his world very differently from before. For him a light shines out of the heavenly world to reveal the ultimate meaning of what is happening among men.

Jesus, in his gospel of the Kingdom of Heaven, proclaimed the nearness of that heavenly world in which alone this world and this life of ours find completion. In his own person, heaven came to earth, which is another way of saying that his human life was fulfilled by being lived wholly in the presence and by the power of God. Heaven and earth, God and man, were reconciled. The life of the Kingdom was his life, and his mission was to open the door of it to every man. It was as yet hidden to the outward eye of man and had to make its way in the world concealed under the form of the Servant, so that it could be known only to faith, but nevertheless, the power that was at work concealed was sovereign power, and the life of the Kingdom, because it was life in God, was eternal life. God was invading the life of our humanity to overcome the sin that robbed man of the fellowship of his human family and to reveal to man his one true life in oneness with God.

The resurrection of Jesus must be set in line with all these other inbreakings of heaven upon earth. It was not just an appearance of Jesus of Nazareth to his friends. It was a revelation of God like all the other revelations of God to which the Scriptures bear witness. There are remarkable similarities between Moses' vision of

God and Paul's experience of the risen Lord. The term "vision" does not denote a subjective experience but, in these instances, a confrontation with divine reality. And just as the revelation of God in Jesus is the climax of all the revelations that preceded, so the resurrection of Jesus is the climax, the final decisive event, in the inbreaking of the heavenly world upon the human. The power and glory of that world had been concealed by the weakness and mortality of Jesus' human form, but now there was no longer any concealment or any uncertainty as the full majesty of his divine nature was revealed to the faith of the disciples. Seen in this context, the resurrection ceases to stand by itself, a single article of faith to be affirmed or denied by itself. What is at stake here is not just that Jesus rose from the dead on the third day, but that God is sovereign in his creation, that the issues of life or death for individuals, societies, and for all mankind are in his hands, and that he alone has power to bring life where there has been only death. If we have had an idea of history in which there is no room for the resurrection, then it is a history in which there is no room for God, and what we must do is to rethink the meaning of history and of all aspects of the life of man in the light of what is revealed to us in the resurrection.

THE CONSEQUENCES OF THE RESURRECTION

We can just briefly indicate some of the consequences of the resurrection of Jesus for the faith of the church.

So far as the disciples were concerned, there was an end to all uncertainty concerning the identity of Jesus. Nowhere is this more clearly evident than in the fact that where they had formerly preached the gospel of the Kingdom, they now preached Jesus Christ. His person and the divine action of God in him became the content of the gospel. They were not embarrassed to state what seemed so contradictory, that God himself had come to them in him and yet that he had shared with them a fully human life. During his lifetime he had not let them speak of him as the Christ because it could only lead to misunderstandings among a people who expected the Christ to be a conquering king, but now they could use the title freely, since the cross had removed all possibility of misunderstanding the manner either of his kingship or of his conquest.

In the light of the resurrection many things became clear that were confused before. The disciples saw meaning in words and actions of Jesus that had been lost to them at the time. And when they told the story of Jesus, they told it as they now understood it, not narrating incidents and reporting speeches as their eyes and ears had received them at the time but interpreting them in the telling to bring out the meaning that now was plain to them. This is what often confuses readers of the Gospels who expect in them simple memoirs or histories of what was said and done, when what they have in their hands are the records of the testimony of the church to what God did in their midst in Jesus Christ.

The most immediate effect of the resurrection was to weld the disciples into a fellowship of faith under the direct authority of their risen Lord. Peter might be recognized as the leader in the Jerusalem church for a time, and Paul might have pre-eminence in the Gentile church, but all human authorities were subject to the rule of Jesus Christ himself. He was the King and Head of his own church. It was a new body for him that through it he might himself continue and multiply his ministry. It was he, in his word and person, in his death and resurrection, who reconciled men to God, the church providing the bridge to men over which he passed.

The Christians were not content, however, to claim for their Lord an authority only over his church. The resurrection had revealed to them that he was the rightful Lord of all mankind, the King before whom one day all kings must bow. If it was true that in him alone was life and light for men, then it would be robbing men to let them remain ignorant of him and outside his rule. All the disciples do not seem to have grasped equally this implication of his resurrection. It took a Paul to bring it fully into the open, though Stephen and the Hellenists undoubtedly preceded him in its recognition. But it was from this source that the world mission of the church was born. It was a fantastic claim: that all mankind should one day bow in humility before this Jesus, the carpenter from Nazareth, who had been revealed to them as the one and only Mediator between God and men. A church that in its sweet reasonableness ceases to make these fantastic claims concerning Jesus has already lost the motive of world mission, but not only of world mission; it has lost the motive to be a church that is a mission to any man, either near or far.

There were also far-reaching ethical implications. The Christian life was life in fellowship with a living Lord. To be in fellowship with him was to share his life, to die with him to self and come alive in the service of one's fellows, to be indwelt by the love of God that was infinitely forgiving, to be set free from anxiety about possessions and also from the fear of evil spirits that wrought so much havoc in men's lives, and then in freedom from anxiety and fear to have the kind of understanding of other men that opened ever new relationships. Life in fellowship with the risen Lord was not a mystical otherworldly life, because it was achieved not by a retreat from the world to commune with him but by his invasion of our common world to give himself to us where we are and to transform our common life into the life of his Kingdom.

Finally, the resurrection was a triumph over death, not for Jesus alone but for all who were joined to him in faith. It revealed God's power to bring life out of death. It revealed in Jesus a life of oneness with God that death could not destroy. Therefore, the receiving of that life from him and the sharing of it with him must be an entrance upon eternal life. His death is thus the conquest of death for all men and his resurrection the foundation of a boundless hope that in fellowship with him we shall be made like him and shall share with him a life that is eternal.

12.

. . . *He Ascended Into Heaven*
and Sitteth at the Right Hand
of God the Father Almighty

It may almost be taken for granted that the picture language in which the doctrine of the ascension is expressed will have conveyed to people, young and old, a false conception of what happened after the resurrection. The article in the creed seems to say that after Jesus had appeared to his disciples, he went away from this world into heaven, where he has remained distant from us ever since. Sunday schools have been known to use a series of slides to depict the ascension, the first showing Jesus hovering in the air just above the heads of his disciples, the second and third showing him smaller and smaller as he ascends in the air, and the fourth representing him as a tiny figure disappearing into the clouds in the sky. The visual aid was quite effective in impressing upon the minds of children a false and confusing conception of a spiritual reality. It taught them that Jesus had by a form of levitation left this world behind and transferred his presence to a heaven that is located spatially somewhere above the bright blue sky beyond the clouds.

This naïve conception can persist surprisingly among adults, especially if they are prisoners of the misconception that every statement of the Biblical authors must be interpreted as a bald and literal assertion of fact, with no allowance for the problem that is posed when divine realities and events have to be described in human language. Some years ago, in a story of Jesus for use in church schools, the author faced the problem of describing the ascension in simple language for junior children in such a way as

159

to create no misconception. He wrote, therefore, that the disciples stood looking up into the sky where Jesus "seemed" to have gone. But there were ministers who took offense at this word "seemed," alleging that it cast doubt upon the whole doctrine of the ascension. When questioned, they made it clear that for them the ascension was a literal bodily movement upward until a heaven above the blue of the sky was reached. But even the child of today can no longer accept the ancient three-story universe with heaven above, the earth in the middle, and hell beneath the earth. He knows that the universe consists of worlds beyond worlds for millions of millions of miles. That he does not try to locate heaven in space does not mean that he denies the existence of an unseen world. But this difference in conception requires a reinterpretation of what is meant by the ascension.

The Biblical authors are forced constantly to use the language of time and space to depict a reality or an event that by its nature is beyond all the limitations of time and space. They frequently speak of God's "coming" to his people although they would acknowledge that he is everywhere. That he has to come does not mean that he has been absent. It is a way of expressing the difference between a state of life in which a man is in distress because God is hidden from him and a state of life in which he rejoices because God's presence with him is revealed. Men are also described as "coming" to God, a movement in the human spirit as it responds to God. The psalmist speaks of being in the depths and of crying out to God in the heights, but we would not expect to be able to measure the distance between him and God. It is like the distance between two human persons who may be worlds apart although they are sitting side by side. So also the familiar Biblical image of the throne in heaven depicts God's sovereignty over all things in heaven and earth, and to be at the right hand of God is to be in a relation to God that is like that of a prime minister in relation to a king, to be his representative in action and to exercise his power. "Ascending" and "descending" are used to describe movement and relation between the heavenly and the earthly world. In the second chapter of The Acts, the Spirit of God "descends" upon the church, but the same event may be described as a receiving of the Spirit or a being born of the Spirit. The resistance to God in man is overcome, and God is given his rightful place as the ruling center of man's life.

What, then, does the ascension mean? First we must remind ourselves where heaven is. It is the unseen world where God dwells in the fullness of his power and glory. But that world is not distant; rather, it overshadows and interpenetrates this world at every moment. Jesus' proclamation of the nearness of the Kingdom of Heaven was meant to overcome the false conception that God was distant from his world and from man and only at some future date would be known in his nearness, a conception that led men into hopeless misunderstandings both of God and of themselves. In Jesus' person, heaven was already touching earth and was at one with it. We have said earlier that the Kingdom of Heaven was the present reality of Jesus' earthly life and that he was so one with God that he lived on earth the life of heaven. This was concealed in his mortal, human life among men and in his death, but it was revealed in his resurrection. How, then, can there be any meaning in an ascension into heaven if he was already one with God, living with him the life of heaven? Moreover, the promise of the risen Lord to his disciples was, "Lo, I am with you always, even to the end of the age," so that his ascension could not mean his departure from them to dwell at a distance from them.

There is a further difficulty that appears in the New Testament account that seems to locate the ascension at the end of the forty days of the resurrection appearances. It was a considerable time later that the appearance of Christ to Paul took place. Paul recognizes that, apart from this one instance, the appearances had long since ceased — he had the experience "as of one born out of due season"—but insists that Christ's appearance to him belongs together with the earlier appearances. This creates a difficulty only if the ascension is interpreted as a removal of Christ to a distance at which he could no longer be known as he was known to Paul.

The ascension seems to play no part in the thought of Paul.

The exaltation of the risen Lord is one with the resurrection. In raising him from the dead, God " installed him as the Son of God with power " to rule over the creation until the end of time, until every knee shall bow to him. Therefore, the references to the ascension, which are remarkably few in the Gospels and The Acts, have sometimes been regarded as merely providing a bridge in the thinking of the early Christians, from that phase of Christ's activity among them in which he was visible to them, to the later phase when he was still active though unseen. Instead of speaking of a continuing presence in a different form, they spoke of a movement from one realm to another and so created the possibility of serious misunderstanding. This is at least a warning to teachers to have a special care what ideas they convey when they speak of the ascension.

THE CONTEXT IN THE STORY OF JESUS

Again, as with the resurrection, the ascension must be considered not alone but in the total context of the church's story of Jesus. We are accustomed to thinking of that story as beginning with the birth of Jesus, but not so the early church. For it, the story began in heaven. Jesus' oneness with the Father and his Sonship did not begin on earth but before there was an earth. He was with God in all eternity. He was the Word through whom God called the world into being. He was the Word through whom in history God let his light shine into the darkness of men and called for a people to live in fellowship with him. Then in the fullness of time he " sent " his Son from heaven: the Word became flesh. The coming of Jesus Christ was therefore a " descent " from heaven, a coming down in humility into the lowly form of man, and his death and resurrection were a triumphant return to the Father, having accomplished the task for which he was sent. But this is not to be the last act in his progress. The decisive victory over evil and the emancipation of mankind have been achieved, but not so has the final victory. The new age has begun with the coming of Jesus Christ, but the old age in which

sin and evil have their power still continues, so that the life of the
Christian is a movement from the old age to the new. He must be
ever putting off the old man and dying to the old world that he
may put on the new man and come alive in the new world. But
it shall not always be so. Finally there must come the day of full
redemption when death and hell shall be destroyed and God shall
be all in all. In that day the same Jesus, in whose fellowship we
have the foretaste of our redemption but who is hidden from us
for a time, will return to judge the quick and the dead and to
reign with his own upon the earth. In the next chapter we shall
consider the significance of the future perspective; here it is important only to see that the ascension marks the end of one stage
in God's redemption of mankind, begins another, and points forward to a consummation at the end of history. In this context we
can understand why Christians would speak of an ascension.

The whole scheme of which the ascension is a part — pre-existence, incarnation, resurrection, ascension, second coming — is
strange today to many Christians. We live, and have been living
for some time, in a historically minded age that tends to equate
what can be established by historical evidence with the real and to
regard the concepts of this scheme as mythological interpretations
of historical experience. Jesus, then, is for us primarily a historical
person whose life began when he was born at Bethlehem and
ended when he died on Calvary. His *real* existence in history was
between the years 1 and 30, but, since so little is known of any
period in his life except that of his ministry, his history extends
over a span perhaps only of one year, perhaps of three. There was
a powerful memory of him after this time among his followers
and an influence that was to extend ever farther across the world,
but we are reluctant to speak of him as existing after his death as
a living person. We are even more reluctant to speak of him as
existing before his birth. If the resurrection is a stumbling block to
modern man, then a pre-existence of Christ seems even more fantastic and incredible.

Yet the early church believed firmly in both the resurrection
and the pre-existence of Jesus Christ. He existed before he was

born and after he was dead! Thus stated, it suggests the existence of a Jesus of Nazareth in the unseen before there was one in the visible world and a Jesus of Nazareth somewhere again in the unseen after his life on earth. But this is not at all what the church intended to say. We shall not understand this as long as our thinking takes the Jesus of history as its starting point. The starting point for the early church was the risen Lord, in whom was disclosed to them the secret of who had been in their midst in Jesus of Nazareth. The question we must pose is the question round which the whole of the thought of the New Testament turns: Who is this Jesus? There are different levels in the answers given. On the surface level, Jesus can be identified as the carpenter of Nazareth, but no one was sufficiently interested in this aspect of Jesus' existence to leave behind a coherent description. Still on the visible surface level, he can be described as the herald of the Kingdom of God, the prophet of salvation and doom, the rebel against the existing order in religion, the healer, the exorcist. But even this did not go deep enough. The disciples were conscious of deeper levels in his person, where strange and disturbing forces were concealed. There was a mystery about him that eluded them. What was he really in the depths of his being? Not until he had died and risen did they give the answer, and even then it was not given all at once. They found themselves compelled to say that it was God himself who met them in him, not some secondary divine power but God the Creator, the God of Israel. At the heart of his being he was one with God. Or again, they had to say that, whereas all the prophets had spoken the word of God, he *was* that word in every aspect of his person, so that, no matter what he did or what happened to him, God spoke to them through him, and speaking, came to them. This was the reality of his being: the Word of God in which the very mind of God is uttered. Therefore, as the Word, he was with God in creation, and it was through him that God called Israel again and again into covenant with him.

Against this background we begin to grasp that it was not fanciful speculation when the church spoke of the pre-existence of

Christ as the Word or as the Son of God with the Father. It was
a confession of their faith in the God who met them and redeemed them in Jesus Christ. They could not rightly state the full
reality of the being of Jesus Christ without speaking both of his
pre-existence and his postexistence. Once we realize what the
church was saying here, we shall not try to visualize what is
meant by the " descent " of the Son of God, or the Word of God,
into the flesh, and we shall put far from our minds any crude conception of a Jesus of Nazareth waiting somewhere in heaven to be
born in Mary's womb. But so also we shall not try to visualize an
" ascent " into heaven in which he who had been known among
men as Jesus of Nazareth was exalted to the right hand of the
Father to be worshiped henceforth as King of Kings and Lord of
Lords.

An End and a Beginning

The ascension, then, is not to be conceived as a movement from
one place to another but rather from one form of manifestation to
another. It is not a " going away " of Jesus but a going from one
way of being known to men to another quite different way of being known. In his earthly life and in his resurrection appearances
Jesus was known directly to his disciples, face to face, person to
person. Paul never ceased to insist upon the directness with which
he had known the risen Lord. But there came a point in time at
which Jesus ceased to be known directly and was henceforth
known only through the remembered witness of those who had
had that direct and immediate relation with him. In both periods,
the direct and the indirect, he was known only by revelation,
that is, by the Spirit of God opening the eyes and hearts of the
disciples to know him by faith. Personal contact (flesh and blood)
was not sufficient to make him known. Thousands who had personal contact with him saw in him only an attractive, or offensive, Jewish preacher. Nor was the remembered witness of his
disciples sufficient of itself: the word of witness was effective only
when God's Spirit spoke through it to reveal Jesus as Christ and
Lord. The ascension is the early church's way of saying that the

time of direct knowledge of Jesus came to an end, and the time of indirect knowledge of him began. In this latter time, even the disciple who had been with Jesus during his ministry and had known him in his risen power could no longer know him in that way but was dependent upon the remembered witness, his own and that of his fellow disciples. This did not mean that Jesus had become remote from them. He was present with them still, as he had promised, and his presence was the living center of their existence both as individuals and as a fellowship, so that they could say with Paul that Christ lived in them. But this realization of his presence was dependent now upon their constant calling to mind of what had been revealed to them in the former time. Jesus had not gone away from them, but he had gone from an immediate relation with them to a mediate one, from the immediacy of the resurrection experiences to the mediacy of a situation in which they as disciples would differ from each other sharply concerning the mind of their Lord, and could settle their dispute only by recalling what he had been to them. He was hidden from them now in a way that he had not been hidden before, hidden as God has always been hidden, so that he has ever to be revealed.

The ascension, as the dividing line between these two times, takes on a very great importance for the church, and the failure to distinguish what it says has serious consequences. Beyond the ascension lies the period of the church in which we have our life. We have not the opportunity of meeting Jesus face to face or of hearing him preach and teach. We are not witnesses of the resurrection. That does not mean that we cannot know him as our living Lord, or that there is any hindrance to our receiving from him the life in God that he so freely gives, or that he cannot take us into his ministry and into fellowship with him as he did his first disciples. But all of this is ours only through the witness of those who knew him in the time before there was a church. It was for us that John wrote concerning the resurrection, " Blessed are those who have not seen and yet believe," that is, by their faith have shared in the knowledge of the risen Lord with those who saw him.

The church, then, is dependent for its very life upon a testimony that comes to it from that primary time of Christ's revealing of himself, and that testimony has an authority for it that is the authority of God himself, God revealed in Jesus Christ. The earliest church could hear by word of mouth the remembered witness of the apostles. But as the apostles died, their witness was preserved in a tradition that eventually was set down in writing in various places and in varied forms. Not always were the remembrances preserved in the same words in churches far removed from each other. It is inevitable that as stories are told and retold for many years, there should be changes and additions. In new situations there had to be radical changes in the telling in order to convey the same meaning. Sometimes there were changes that the church eventually recognized as a perversion of the witness and a concealment of the gospel and excluded from its tradition. But always there was a consciousness that the church depended for its very life upon the preservation of the true tradition, and this it was that finally brought into being the New Testament Scriptures. They were not sufficient of themselves to give to anyone a knowledge of Jesus Christ, just as his earthly presence had not been sufficient. The witness in them had to become the living witness of the Christian fellowship, the power of the Spirit in the midst of the church giving life to the words of the Spirit in the gospel.

What happens when this line which is drawn by the ascension is forgotten? It has been forgotten more than once in the past and in some quarters is in danger of being forgotten today. The consequence is a merging of the time of Christ's direct revealing of himself with the time of the church. It is not difficult to see how it happens. If Jesus Christ really lives again in the life of his church, and if its ministry is in truth *his* ministry, its gospel *his* gospel, its power to forgive and heal *his* power to forgive and heal, its judgment *his* judgment, then ought one not to speak of God's revelation in the church as a direct extension of his revelation in Jesus? Will not the total revelation of God be found not just in the tradition embodied in the Scriptures but also in the living tradition of the church from the time of the closing of the canon of the Scriptures to the present day? Is it not too narrow a view that the authoritative revelation belongs in Scripture alone and not also in the rich and meaningful life of the church of the ages with its Lord? Have we not a revelation of God in our time to add to the revelation of God in that earlier time? How powerful these arguments have been is evidenced not only by the fact that the Roman and Eastern churches have claimed for their tradition a place and an authority in unbroken continuity with the tradition embodied in the Scriptures, but also that in many quarters in Protestantism there has been an ever-renewed attempt to validate a continuing revelation to the church or a revelation to the natural man alongside the revelation of the Scriptures.

The question we have to face, then, is this: Has man, either outside or inside the church, any way of knowing God except through Jesus Christ, and has he any way of knowing Jesus Christ except through the testimony of those first witnesses to which we have access only through the New Testament? This seems to bring man into a narrow pass, too narrow for his liking, for it offers him no opportunity to validate the insights of his own reason or the perceptions of his own conscience or the spiritual dignity of his own religious institutions or the values of his own civilization. But perhaps this narrow pass is the place where alone man takes God seriously. Perhaps the New Testament authors understood better than we do what must happen if all things, really all, are to be brought into subjection to Jesus Christ that in him they may find their freedom. The ascension, therefore, brackets this authoritative time of revelation and marks it off from all that comes afterward. It may seem outrageous to claim that the criterion of truth and of life for all time is to be found in history between the coming of Jesus from the Father and his going to the Father, between his descent and his ascension; yet this is the claim of the New Testament, and the authority of Scripture in the church depends upon the validity of this claim. Wherever it has been set aside to give freer scope to the authority of the church as an institution, or of the human reason and conscience, the Scriptures have receded in importance, and however much honor is paid to them, the ultimate word of authority has been found elsewhere. But when man or some human institution has the ultimate word of authority, Jesus Christ is no longer absolute Lord in his own church. The unique authority of Scripture is important, therefore, not for the sake of Scripture or with the purpose of exalting Scripture, but simply that Jesus Christ, who is known only through Scripture, may have the place and power that belong to him both in the church and in the world. For this reason, the ascension plays an essential part in the exalting of Jesus Christ not just once but always.

13.

. . . *From Thence He Shall Come to Judge the Quick and the Dead*

Our churches tend to go to two opposite extremes on the subject of the Second Coming of Christ and the Last Judgment: either they focus men's thoughts at this point to the neglect of other essential elements of the faith, or they let it recede so far into the background that it practically disappears from sight. There are churches where no sermon is complete without some reference to the Second Coming or to Judgment Day, but there are others where neither a Second Coming nor a Judgment Day seems to be anticipated. The latter is far more frequently found than the former. Unfortunately, the Second Coming of Christ has tended to be monopolized by a type of piety that finds a peculiar fascination in speculating about the future of the world. The books of Daniel and Revelation become the chief books of Scripture in which, if one knows the code, one can discover not only the chief events between now and the end of the world but even the very date of the world's end. The believer lives then in hope of that day when Christ will return to take the true believers (that is, perhaps, those who hold the right doctrine of the Second Coming) with him into his Kingdom and to destroy all the wicked and the unbelievers. The fruit of such a faith is so visibly an arrogant, narrow, and self-righteous complacency, coupled frequently with an indifference and irresponsibility about the social, political, and economic implications of the Christian gospel, that it brings the doctrine of the Second Coming into disrepute.

On the other hand, where the Second Coming and the Last

Judgment are disregarded, the consequences are equally serious. The dimension of Biblical faith that makes it intensely concerned not only with the present but also with the future is lost. Men cease to expect their future from Jesus Christ and come to regard it as essentially in their own hands. Man must make his own future for good or for ill, they say. It is sufficient for them to give attention to the tasks and opportunities that confront them in the present, and, moreover, gazing into the future is likely only to distract them from present responsibilities. But since man cannot live without hope, without some prospect for the future, the abandonment of the Christian hope leads to the substitution of some form of secular hope: a belief in the progress of human society toward utopia, a belief in the future of one's nation, or perhaps only the engrossment of the individual in his own career and the careers of his children.

A very real factor for many people in their attitude to the Second Coming of Christ is an embarrassment that the early church expected its Lord to return almost immediately to finish what he had begun, to bring history to an end, and to establish an eternal Kingdom. The expectation of the first Christians was disappointed, and whenever it has been renewed in the history of the church and Christians have waited breathlessly for the Last Day, the same has been true. Ought we not by now to have learned from these successive disappointments that the early Christians made a mistake? But it was not only the early Christians who made a mistake! The evidence seems to indicate that it was Jesus himself who made the mistake, promising his followers that shortly the world would reach its end and God's Kingdom would come visibly among men with the Messianic King reigning over all. Certainly Jesus warned them not to think that they could predict when that day would be. Not even he himself knew the day or the hour. But they were to live in constant readiness for its coming; they were to pray for its coming; they were to herald its coming in their preaching and teaching; and they were to live as though it had already come. Were all these elements in the program of Jesus with his disciples based on the mistaken premise

that the end of the world was at hand, so that for Christians who
have ceased to be interested in the end of the world such teachings have no significance? Must we either return in a literal and
naïve way to the expectation of the early Christians, or abandon
entirely this aspect of the apostolic faith? These questions demand consideration.

The distaste of many American Christians for the subject of
eschatology (the doctrine of the last things) was evident at the
time of the Evanston Assembly of the World Council of
Churches in 1954. It seemed to them a waste of time to have
lengthy discussions of the Christian hope. For them, the future
was not at all problematical, as it was and is for European Christians. It was the European, for whom there seemed no longer to
be any practicable way forward into the future, who found the
subject of " hope " most relevant. The American, as long as he remained confident in the power of his science, or his political institutions, or his way of life, or his churches, to master the future,
saw no reason to give it his serious attention. In a relatively new
land where the present moment is constantly engrossing, people
have little interest in looking either backward or forward very
far. For this reason, there has long been a resistance not only to
eschatology but also to historical study in general, and only recently have our churches begun to show an interest in their own
history. There is still a reluctance in many quarters to introduce
church history into the church school curriculum. Why spend
time looking backward when there are so many present problems
worth discussing? So, also, why give attention to the end of history when the tasks at hand require all our care?

The fact that the present neglect of eschatology is paralleled by
a corresponding neglect of history is particularly significant when
we note the intense concern of the Biblical faith with *both* history
and eschatology. Faith, in both Old Testament and New, constantly looks backward without any sign of neglecting the present. In fact, it is for the sake of the present that it looks backward
and forward. There is a consciousness that what man is and does
in the present is shaped by his understanding of the past and his

expectation of the future. Memory and hope are essential to his being.

The importance of memory to an individual's present existence is not hard to demonstrate. Memory is the accumulation of all the experiences of the past and the judgments based upon them that form the background against which we interpret what we see and hear and experience in the present. A man who has lost his memory becomes as helpless as a babe because all that happens is incomprehensible to him. He has no context within which to interpret his perceptions. The past is thus the depth beneath the present moment. The history of Israel is Israel's memory of what God has been to it in the past. The history of the church is the church's memory of itself, the depth of life out of which it understands itself and thinks and acts. Take away its memory and it is crippled for present thought and action.

Equally important is the anticipation of the future. Without hope we become paralyzed for present action. A man whose future has been blotted out has no longer any motive for living in the present. When Israel in exile seemed no longer to have any distinctive future before it, the life nerve of the nation was cut. So, also, in the modern world, the threat of the atomic destruction of civilization creates a mood of despair and casts a dark shadow over the present. But even more so, when confidence in the onward and upward progress of mankind, which has been a secular substitute for the Christian hope for many Christians, is shaken by such events as we have experienced in the last half century, the moral and spiritual consequences are very serious. In some it produces a spirit of irresponsibility; in others, an anxiety that makes life difficult to endure. But for all it makes the question most immediately relevant: What has the Christian faith to say concerning man's future?

THE NEW TESTAMENT HOPE AGAINST
THE OLD TESTAMENT BACKGROUND

Enough has been said already about the application of the language of movement to divine realities to guard against the Second Coming of Christ being interpreted merely as the physical return of the person Jesus from a distant heaven to this earth. The thought is not of a reincarnation of Jesus to have a second life and ministry among men in history, but of an end of history when the purpose of God for man in history will reach its final victory and consummation. The first Christians had begun to live in a new world, the Kingdom of God proclaimed by Jesus and incarnated in his person. The new world, in which a new humanity endowed by God's Spirit was possible, was reality in him and through him in them, but it was a new world in the midst of an old world that was still imprisoned by sin and death. It was invading the old world but with a battle yet to be fought and won. The decisive battle that gave promise and assurance of a final victory had already been fought and won by Jesus Christ. But the Christian had to recognize and confess that not only round about him but also within him the old world of sin and darkness still continued. He was on his way from the old world to the new, his journey marked by a continuous series of repentances or turnings from the bondage of self in the world of darkness to the freedom of love in the world of light. Moreover, he was reminded daily by the world's hostility to his faith that the kingdoms of this world had not yet been conquered by the Kingdom of his Lord. How long could this conflict of the two worlds last? To the early Christians, it seemed impossible that the day of victory could be far distant. Surely it would come in their lifetime. In one of his letters, Paul could advise Christians against marrying since the time remaining to them would be so short. Then, as the years passed and the end did not come, there was a necessary shift in viewpoint *but no abandonment of the hope.* The important thing was not *when* the goal of history would be reached but that the goal had been revealed in Jesus Christ and was known to Christians, so that all their life had its meaning as movement toward that goal. The goal for the individual Christian was Jesus Christ, and his hope was for a transformation of his nature, stage by stage, until he would be made like Christ himself to reflect the very nature of God. But the goal for mankind was the same. God's purpose revealed in Jesus was that there should be a humanity that would be the family of God's children responding to him in perfect love and holiness and living with each other in perfect understanding and justice. The resurrection of Jesus was the revelation of the presence of that new world in the midst of time in one man. The Second Coming would be the triumph of that new world at the end of time, not just in one man but in all who had come to have their life by faith in that one man.

It was impossible to separate the idea of judgment from the perfect coming of that new world. The new world of God, wherever it breaks in upon men, is the judgment of the old. Here we must think of judgment in Old Testament terms, not as a legal procedure in which a heavenly judge pronounces sentence of condemnation or acquittal upon a prisoner, but as an event in which God's mind or judgment concerning man is revealed. The judgments of God upon Israel proclaimed by the prophets are punishments for sin, but their primary function in God's gracious dealing with Israel is in tearing away all concealment and revealing how things really stand between Israel and God. It is in this sense that the death of Jesus is the judgment of the world, striking the blindness from men's eyes and laying bare to them the enmity toward God that is poisoning their existence. Sin, because it is not just error or wrongdoing or missing the mark but the rebellion of the human self against God, has to be revealed, and is revealed only when man is brought before God. It is the presence of God in love and holiness and truth that alone makes us conscious of our lovelessness, unholiness, and falsity. Therefore, the presence of the Kingdom in the person of Jesus made him at one and the same time both the salvation of God for man and the judgment of God upon man. He could not be the promise of life without being at the same time the threat of death to those who loved dark-

ness more than light. This being the double reality of which
Christians were already conscious in Jesus, it was inevitable that
as they looked forward to the day when the new world that they
knew in Jesus would have its final victory, they should see it not
only as the day of final salvation but also as the day of final judgment when the secrets of all men would be revealed and all life
would lie open before the presence of God. For Christians, this
would be no fearful day, for they had already faced their judgment in Jesus Christ and had been humbled under his judgment;
not only so, but they had learned to live bringing all things to the
test of his mind concerning them. The Judge of all the earth was
no unknown God, but was the God whose mind had been revealed in Jesus Christ.

The intense eschatological expectation of Jesus and of the early
church is best understood against its Old Testament background,
where it can be seen in its total context as an essential element in
Israel's faith. Seen by itself, it becomes a curious — and mistaken
— belief that shortly the world will come to an end and a new
world will be established in which there will be no evil, a belief
that has little relevance to the life we know. But it was highly relevant to the immediate problems of Israel's existence when Second
Isaiah proclaimed to a despairing Israel in exile that God was
coming at any moment to transform defeat into victory, to raise
a dying people into life, and to create a future where there seemed
to be no future. The prophet's people were being destroyed
within themselves from lack of hope. He restored their hope by
his unshaken confidence that God was about to open a new day
before them. What he actually said may sound foolish when we
read it today. He had visions of God returning to take up his
dwelling place in Jerusalem and of God's glory being visible to
the whole earth. The wealth of the nations would be at the service
of Israel, and Israel would be a nation of priests and prophets in-
structing mankind in the true worship and service of God. These
things did not happen, but was the prophet mistaken in his faith?
God did give Israel a new future, not in the way the prophet en-

visaged, yet nevertheless a reality and the fulfillment of the prophet's hope, for his concern was not with wealth or power for Israel but that God through Israel might carry forward his purpose of redemption for mankind.

Why was the prophet so certain about the future? Was it just a wild surmise or speculation? Or was his confidence rooted in what he knew of God? He tells us plainly that it is God's word that determines the future, the word revealed to Israel in which God discloses his purpose for his creation. God cannot be unfaithful to his word or he would be untrue within himself. Looking into Israel's past, the prophet could see the unfolding of God's purpose, the shaping of a great people from an insignificant beginning with one man, the deliverance of this people from what seemed like certain death in Egypt, God's fashioning of them to be the Servant of his Word among men in spite of their blindness and stubbornness, and, in the midst of disasters that would have wiped out most nations, the keeping alive of a remnant that would not let go its destiny. It was only by God's mercy and power that there had continued to be an Israel, and if now for half a century he might seem to have cast off his people, this was but a time of preparation for a new stage in their destiny that was about to begin. His faith in the future was based firmly upon his faith in God and in the purpose of God that could not fail. God did not create the world to be a chaos, and he did not choose and discipline Israel to let it be destroyed. The sin of Israel and the resistance of mankind might hold back the fulfillment of God's purpose and postpone the day of his victory, but they could not defeat his purpose. The sovereignty of God in his creation demanded a day when his will would be actually sovereign in the lives of men. His sovereignty might be hidden and resisted now, but one day it would be revealed and all men would find their peace and joy in obedience to God. Therefore, Israel's eschatological hope, which carried the nation through periods of darkness and despair and made it unconquerable as long as it held fast to the conviction that God's purpose would yet be fulfilled through it, was rooted in its faith in God as Creator of the world and Lord of history. Their God bound past, present, and future into one.

It was this faith which first made men conscious of a life that is in movement toward a goal. It was in Isreal that the conviction came to birth that God is doing something great and marvelous among men, a work that takes time and that demands of men that they leave much that they value in their past behind them to venture out into an unknown future in hope of " a city which hath foundations." The life of ancient Egypt through the centuries is static, the highest point being reached early in its development, while the life of Israel is dynamic, the nation never being allowed to rest for long in one condition. Israel is a people in movement toward a goal, and it is this because of its relationship with God. What we must grasp is that this is the origin of history. The first historians of the human race were Israelites, setting down the record of the past in order to see more plainly in it the nature of God's dealings with his people. The Greeks, who came much later with their history writing, had no conception of a movement in events and in the lives of men toward a goal, but saw only a continuous rotation of human experiences in circles, so that man was ever coming back where he began. Eschatology, then, in Israel was no fanciful speculation about the future, but was the expression of a faith that a wise and loving purpose of God compasses the whole creation. It may be hidden in the present moment, but it can be seen by looking to the past, and its projection into the future is of the very essence of faith. Faith is by its very nature a pilgrimage into an unknown future but toward a known goal.

Against this background the eschatology of Jesus and the early Christians takes on new meaning. The intensity of their consciousness of God's new world breaking in upon them with its marvelous fullness of life made them eager and impatient for its perfect coming. Their taste of victory made them hungry for the final victory. The revelation of the goal of man's history in Jesus made them so certain of the final destination of man that they saw it looming directly on the horizon. Who are we to talk of their "delusion" when we so rarely share the intensity of their faith? That the expected day did not arrive in their lifetime was no crushing disaster. The important thing was that they lived with their entire existence concentrated toward that goal, asking for nothing of the future except that it should be a realization of the purpose of God for mankind revealed in Jesus Christ.

The Present in the Light of the Future

The ascension and the Second Coming are like two brackets that delimit and define the time in which we live. God's glory was revealed to a chosen few in Jesus in his life and death and resurrection and will be revealed to all men in the final redemption, but it is hidden now and known only in its hiddenness to faith. We walk by faith and not by sight, in remembrance of the events in which it was given to certain men to see and hear and touch the Word of life and in expectation of the day when we shall know as we are known, but not demanding of God or of ourselves other than the broken knowledge that alone is possible in our time. We live in the time of broken knowledge when even a Paul can see only as in a burnished mirror dimly. To forget this is on the one hand to pretend to knowledge that it is not possible for us to possess, a dishonesty that is an enemy of faith, and on the other hand to plague ourselves with a straining after an impossible completeness instead of living thankfully on the crumbs of genuine knowlege that God gives us day by day. There is great comfort in this for the honest teacher who each time he undertakes to teach the Christian faith is made painfully aware how incomplete is his own knowledge. Far from being a reason for abandoning the task, this consciousness of incompleteness is one of the essential qualifications of the Christian teacher. It is the person who mistakes his few crumbs of knowledge for the whole loaf and thinks he knows what he does not know who endangers Christian truth when he undertakes to teach.

Also, the time in which we live is a time between two victories but in itself a time of conflict when it may often seem as though the cause of God were lost. Two worlds contend for mastery, the old world and the new, and the line of battle runs, not, as some would like to think, clearly marked between the church and the world, but through the very center of the life of the church and of the world and through the existence of every man. An unwary church can let itself become, like Simon Peter, an instrument of Satan. An unwary Christian can let his very zeal for the church as an institution and his desire to preserve it unchanged for future generations become an obstacle to the coming of the Kingdom in the midst of the church. Or again, the church may offer prematurely a peace and respite from the struggle of life so that it becomes an encouragement to escape from the strain and bruises of the conflict. The church has then the atmosphere of a placid garden rather than that of an army in training for a battle. The final battle will not be lost, but this one in which we are now engaged *can* be lost. The promise to the church that the gates of hell will not prevail against it is a guarantee of final victory but not of victory always in the time between. There is no basis for false confidence. A weak, confused, and flabby church can be destroyed. The question that this puts to educators in the church is whether the program of education in which they have a part is preparation for life on a battle line where the future of mankind is at stake or for life in a garden where there are no very serious decisions to be made.

A Christian eschatology is the enemy of all utopianism, frequently a besetting weakness of teen-agers. They become impatient with a world that cannot make up its mind between justice and injustice, truth and falsehood, right and wrong, and with a church that seems to them to be always compromising its own gospel by its acts and attitudes. There should be some way to make the Kingdom of God come down to earth tomorrow, and the church, if it is to be worthy of the name of Jesus Christ, should have done with all half-truths and half-solutions. Sometimes young people become so impatient of the church that they can no longer bring themselves to stay within it. This impatience lays those whom it infects open to plausible schemes, of which there is no scarcity, for the establishment of God's Kingdom on earth tomorrow, and it may also send them from one church to the other searching for the one in which there is no compromise of principles. But if they knew the nature of the time in which they live, they would know that there are no perfect Christians, no perfect or nearly perfect churches, no ideal societies; nor will there be within the span of history. If they would know the truth of this, they have only to be honest with themselves and acknowledge what they are within themselves as Christians, as members of the church, and as members of society.

God does not expect perfection of us or of the church or of our human society in time. Until the end we remain a people on our way, burdened with sin and unbelief and ever reaching out, hungering and thirsting for the righteousness of God. But God does expect of us a faith that is a holding to him alone, a trusting no longer in ourselves but in him, an openness to his grace and truth, an eagerness for his gifts. To the very end we shall find nothing in ourselves on which to base our trust but only emptiness and poverty and ever-renewed blindness and resistance to God. It may distress us to find only these " filthy rags of our own righteousnesses " in us in spite of all our earnestness as Christians, until we know that this is all that God lets us see lest we should begin to trust in something in ourselves rather than in him. That this is what we see means that we see ourselves under the judgment of Jesus Christ, so that the Day of Judgment is anticipated for us and is already past. There is no other judge but Jesus Christ, and his judgment is not like any human judgment that we have ever known. He does not keep accounts with us, weighing sins against virtues and virtues against sins and striking a balance. There is no life that we can ever live that is safe against his condemnation. Nothing we can do can assure us of his approval. He asks one thing of us, whoever we are and whatever our life has been: that we receive our life from him, that we let him be our life, that we let ourselves be mastered by his love, his generosity, his truth. The only sin that damns and damns irretrievably, no matter how moral or religious we may be, is that we will not have the gift he offers, the gift of God himself, to be our life. And perhaps what makes men loath to lay themselves so open to God is that there is no way, when once a man has let God in upon him, to keep his heart and life closed tight against a single man of any race or class or color, since they too are God's.

14.

. . . *I Believe in the Holy Spirit*

The Holy Spirit is God. That needs to be said plainly and grasped firmly, because the failure to take it fully in earnest leads to many false conceptions of the Holy Spirit. The Holy Spirit is the Spirit of God the Father Almighty, Creator of heaven and earth, who was revealed in the fullness of his nature and power in the person of Jesus Christ, and who now claims our human existence as his chosen and rightful dwelling place. The Holy Spirit is God in that form of his being in which he is able to be the life-giving center of countless human lives. Not a vague divine something that breathes through the universe; not just a name for the more exalted and more often hidden reaches of the human spirit; but God the Father, whose rebellious children we are, and God the Son, whose inmost Spirit is laid bare to us in his life and death and resurrection, coming to us to be with us in this unbelievable closeness, to be a light shining not beyond us but within us, to be a wellspring of life at the heart of our being: that is the Holy Spirit. Therefore, all that we have said of God the Father and all that we have said of Jesus Christ reveals to us who the Holy Spirit is.

At the very outset we are confronted by the puzzling fact that the Holy Spirit, who in the Scriptures denotes God's most immediate personal presence with man and in man, seems to be the most elusive and indefinite of realities for Christians in the church. The Holy Spirit is mentioned from time to time in Scripture readings, prayers, and sermons. Hymns are sung in which the worshiper entreats the Holy Spirit to fill him with his presence. But it is doubtful if many of the worshipers expect anything to happen. They are not consciously asking God, in the purifying fire of his holiness, in the redemptive power of his love, in the utterly humbling majesty of his sovereignty, to take possession of their inmost being and to be moment by moment the all-determining will within their wills. Yet that is what we ask when we pray for the coming of the Holy Spirit to us. The New Testament speaks of " receiving " or " being born of " or " being in " the Spirit. The Spirit may be in the man or the man may be in the Spirit. But these terms cease to be confusing when we realize that they describe the personal relationship between God and man. To receive the Spirit is to know ourselves no longer alone, worshiping a God who is at a distance, but to have God with us so that no thought or word or action can be apart from him. To be born of the Spirit is to die to a world and a life in which God has counted for little or nothing and to come alive in a new relationship with God that makes all things and all experiences new in their meaning for us. To be in the Spirit or to have the Spirit in us is not a mystic absorption in God that might lead us to confuse ourselves with God but a communion with him in which our separation from him, which is both our sin and our helplessness, is overcome and we live no longer in the poverty of our own wisdom and strength but with access to the infinite resources of God. The descent of the Spirit upon the church is everywhere in the New Testament a mark of the openness of the church to God, its availability for his purposes and its willingness to have all things in its life determined by him.

The Holy Spirit, then, according to the New Testament, is the actuality of God's sovereign presence breaking in upon the lives of individuals and invading the world through the church. What does it mean, then, that in the life of the church and in the lives of individual Christians this is the point of greatest vagueness and uncertainty? Surely it can only mean that at the point where God intends to come closest to them they hold him at such a distance that he is no more than a cloud upon the horizon. But why would Christians hold God at a distance? The answer lies in the power of the drive to self-sovereignty in every human being, Christian and non-Christian. Early and late we guard our right to determine our own existence. Our thoughts must be *our* thoughts, our words *our* words, our actions *our* actions. To have them determined from beyond ourselves threatens our integrity. But there is more than integrity involved; there is also the desire for mastery that is never satisfied with the mastery of ourselves but always seeks to extend its area into other lives. Most conflicts in the home arise from the meeting in one intimate area of two or more wills that are set upon mastery. So, also, in the church many of the problems that are most distressing are the product of competing human sovereignties, each of which considers the church a fit area for its expression. When we trace to their origin some of the most prevalent weaknesses and perversions in the life of the church, we find them anchored in the determination of certain human wills that it should be thus. Man likes to rule even within the church. But if he is to rule, either in the church or in the world or in his home or in his own existence, he has to hold God at arm's length — believing in him, worshiping him, serving him in specific ways, but reserving to himself the right to say where God shall rule and where he himself shall rule. What he dare not do is to receive him as a living power and presence in the Holy Spirit. That would be the end to all self-sovereignty. There would no longer be any possibility of drawing a line beyond which God's sovereignty would not extend, no longer any area large or small in which he could assert himself as having the final word. The vagueness that most Christians feel about the Holy Spirit is therefore a form of unconscious self-defense against the threat of the Spirit to their self-mastery.

This brings out rather sharply the importance of the doctrine of the Trinity as a description of what it means to believe in God as Christians. We do not really believe in God the Father or in Jesus Christ in the Christian sense of believing until we receive God as the Spirit. Yet this does not assert the existence of any other God than the Father of our Lord, who is known to us in his presence with man in Jesus Christ. We are monotheists who believe in one

God alone, but we have to say three separate words in order to confess our faith in him. We confess him as our Father and the Father of all men to whom our world belongs, because in Jesus Christ our only true life has been revealed to us as the life of children with the Father in his world. We confess him as our Lord and Savior in Jesus Christ, because only in utter dependence upon him can we have our life as children of God. We confess him as the life-giving Spirit, because through Jesus Christ he is not just known to us at a distance but comes into the midst of our lives to be our God and to deal with us as his children in all our life's experience.

THE CONSEQUENCES FOR CHRISTIAN KNOWLEDGE

The doctrine of the Holy Spirit becomes crucially important for the Christian teacher, first when it confronts him with the radical decision that is involved in his own relation with God, and then when he begins to take seriously that there is no way for us to know God without receiving him into our total existence as the God that he is, coming under his absolute authority and having our life determined henceforward by his living presence. All our thoughts about him as a Father in heaven, the Creator and Sustainer of the universe, who calls us his children, are ultimately empty and fruitless thoughts until the Father is himself with us in his Spirit, so that, when we say " Father " in prayer, we are speaking to someone who is there for us and not absent in some far-off heaven. We have fellowship with the Father through the Spirit whom he sends into our hearts, and only his presence in the Spirit enables us to know the reality of being his children. So also, all our thoughts about Jesus Christ remain thoughts about a person who lived and died long ago and about events that took place long ago in a very different world from ours, so that, no matter how we try to think of him as present, a great gulf separates him from us until he breathes his Spirit into our midst and we become bound together with him and with each other in the one Spirit. We have fellowship with Jesus Christ when his Spirit rules in us and in all our relationships with others, and it is only when we have found our freedom in living under the rule of his Spirit that we can in sincerity call him " Lord." In short, we cannot know God at all except in a personal relationship with him in which he manifests himself as God and we respond to him as our God. We cannot know him in detachment.

The implications of this for Christian teaching are far-reaching. Much of the teaching of the church school is done in the setting of a Christianity that speaks of God's presence and of the Holy Spirit but does not expect God actually to " come " in his Spirit and does not expect the human beings who compose the Christian congregation to be possessed and mastered by God's Spirit. The task of the teacher is defined as the inculcating of Christian conceptions — of God, of Jesus, perhaps even of the Spirit, and of life in general. The pupil must be given some knowledge of the Bible and must be familiar with the events of Jesus' life and the nature of his teachings. The relation of all of these to the problems of conduct in the present must also be considered. But the point seems never to be reached at which the pupil is confronted with a radical decision in relation to God in which his total existence is involved. He is learning *about* the Christian faith, a reasonably harmless occupation in comparison with that other kind of learning in which he might come to know God and to have his knowledge of himself and his world transformed by his knowledge of God. It is this which is the source of a peculiar distress of the Christian teacher, who seems to himself to be teaching all that he ought to teach but is haunted by a suspicion that all his teaching is somehow irrelevant, or at least remote from the actualities of the pupils' lives. All the true conceptions that they have learned from him seem to make little difference in the shape and quality of their daily living. He has reached their minds, perhaps he has even captured the interest of their minds, with his explanations of the Christian faith, but there is a barrier that he has not penetrated between their minds and their selves, that strange mysterious hidden center within them where life itself is determined.

There is a theory abroad, of which the teacher should beware, that comforts him in this distress by assuring him that there are two necessary steps in Christian knowledge, the first in which only the mind is reached with information, truths, and principles, and the second in which the Holy Spirit comes into action applying and bringing alive the truth in relation to life. First one must know about God, and then he will be able to enter into a personal relation with God. First one must receive the Christian doctrines with his mind, and then it becomes possible that he may also believe them with his heart. This seems to be an eminently reasonable theory, and it has a strong appeal for the teacher, since it enables him to have a good conscience even though he has gone no farther than the communication of information, truths, and principles. He has done the necessary preparatory work and in humility can leave the second stage to the operation of the Holy Spirit. In some instances this means that the second stage is left to chance and the pupil comes away from his church school training with no inkling that the primary intent of Christian learning is that he may know God in immediate and living personal encounter. All that he has learned is essentially dead and fruitless knowledge, because in it God has not come to him and taken possession of his life. There are instances, however, where the second stage is cared for by " decision days " and by periodic evangelistic appeals for the pupil's conversion. Education is not expected to be decisive but only to give him right ideas or correct doctrines that are then infused with life by his conversion. This order of things at least recognizes that God cannot be rightly known without a decision of faith that involves one's whole existence, but it reduces education to a process of indoctrination with which the Holy Spirit has nothing to do and it establishes two kinds of Christian knowledge, one that reaches only to the mind and the other that comprehends the self. Whatever form this theory takes, it becomes a prolific source of dullness in the church school, removing all decisiveness from the content of the teaching and postponing the pupil's radical confrontation with God and so with himself and with his world until some other time.

There is an informational aspect to all teaching. There are facts of history and geography that the pupil must know if he is to understand anything about the Bible or the church. But the truth with which the Bible is concerned and with which we are concerned in Christian teaching cannot be adequately expressed in concepts or grasped by the mind as abstract principles. It has its primary reality in a personal relationship between God and man that by its nature is inseparable from man's relation with his fellow man. It is a truth that is a life in fellowship with God and man and can be comprehended only from within the fellowship. The unfolding of the truth is therefore the discovery of our life in two dimensions — with God and with our fellow man. Christian truth is never at any moment a truth apart from us to be contemplated from a distance but is the truth of our existence. There is no truth of God that is not also the truth in which man is revealed to himself. This is what brings tension and excitement into Christian teaching both for the teacher and for pupils: to know the truth is to be set free to live, and to be ignorant of the truth is to be shut out from some aspect of one's own true life. Teaching is, therefore, a matter of life or death.

This personal involvement of the pupil in Christian learning can be illustrated from the study of the Bible. At first the stories in the Bible — Adam and Eve in conversation with God in Eden, Elijah struggling with prophets of Baal, Simon Peter tempting his Lord to unfaithfulness, or Jesus healing and casting out demons — call up before the pupil's mind strange and puzzling figures in another world, so distant and so different that there seems to be no connection between them and him. But as the modern pupil looks more closely into the ancient story, there comes a growing sense of recognition, and he finds himself drawn into the story until it becomes a story about himself. He is Adam and Elijah and Simon Peter. He is the sick man in need of a physician, the man possessed by demons who needs the liberation of a sovereign word. But when he finds himself in Scripture, he never finds himself alone but always in confrontation with the living God. The Biblical story of God's dealings with Israel, the Old

Israel and the New, and with individuals within Israel, becomes the story of God's dealings with him and with his people in the modern world. The Bible becomes not a library of religious antiquities but a contemporary revelation in which the meaning of his life today is disclosed to him — but only when there is an openness in him to God the Holy Spirit, an eagerness and expectation that God should be to him what he was to the prophets and apostles and to his people in his first revealing of himself. The God of the Scriptures is not our God merely by our reading of him and our thinking of him; he has to "come" to us as the living God who he is and take the place that belongs to him in our existence. We have to know him as the Spirit, and only when we so know him do we have in our own relationship with God the basis for understanding all that is written in Scripture concerning God's relation with his people and theirs with him.

The Goal of Christian Teaching

The doctrines of the incarnation and the Holy Spirit throw light upon each other. In Jesus Christ, God and man are revealed in their oneness with each other. God is revealed as most truly God when he dwells in man, his power and glory hidden and yet present, humbling men under the judgment of his holiness, love, and truth, and receiving them into fellowship with himself when they let themselves be humbled. The incarnation is unique and unrepeatable. There is one Jesus Christ in whom God judges and redeems the world. God's presence in him is a oneness with him so complete that we have to say that he was God. But there is another aspect of the incarnation: the decisive revelation of what it means to be man. Jesus was our flesh; he was one of us. But more than that, as man he was what we were intended to be. In him we see humanity fulfilled. But the secret of its fulfillment is the completeness with which he is indwelt by God. He is what he is in the unconditional openness of his being on the one hand toward the Father and on the other toward his human brother. His life was a life in God and for the brother. A life in oneself and for oneself, cut off from God and from the brother, would be the essence of inhumanity, not life but death. This was already foreshadowed in the life of Israel, where to be in fellowship, or covenant, with God was life and to break the covenant was death. Man is so made that he is not man, not himself, except in fellowship with God. He is not rightly " I " until he is an " I " to God's " Thou " and a " Thou " to God's " I." He was made to reflect God's nature, and his failure to do this because of his determination to have a life of his own apart from God is not just rebellion against God but also the willful destruction of his own humanity, the loss of himself. For the lost to be found is for the broken self of man to be made whole by his restoration to his true relationship with God. Man is himself only when he has the source and center of his life in God, but that means: only when into the emptiness and hollowness of the self he knows comes the very life and light and strength of God. That was the gift that Jesus brought to men in giving himself to them. He gave to them the life and light and strength of God that were the reality of his being and were his to give. He gave them God to make them men. During his lifetime men had this life-transforming fellowship with God in fellowship with Jesus. But after his death and resurrection they knew it only through the mediation of the Spirit. The risen Lord was able then to send his Spirit into their hearts that their broken, dying, darkened selves might find their wholeness and their life and light in God. To be born of the Spirit is therefore to become one of the new race of men of whom the Adam, or first-born, is Jesus Christ and who have their life-center no longer in themselves but in God.

There is a close relation between this doctrine and the central Pauline and Protestant doctrine of justification by faith alone. Paul was experienced in all the ways by which man seeks to justify himself with God, that is, to make himself acceptable to God, to give himself a good conscience before God. His confidence in the correctness of his beliefs and in the exemplary virtue of his conduct, on which he had been able to pride himself as a Pharisee, he recognized as a self-righteousness with which he had been content and which had hidden from him the righteousness of God. The gift of the risen Lord to him was a life in God that he could never otherwise have known. The righteousness of God, which is a name for that glorious life which God gives to man when he gives him himself, was his in spite of all unrighteousness and unworthiness that still belonged to him, not through anything he did but simply when he ceased his own perverse endeavors and let God do for him through Jesus Christ what needed to be done. Faith was Paul's recognition of the futility of the best that he could do to justify himself with God, the death in him of all inclination to trust any longer in himself, the confession of his emptiness and helplessness apart from God, and the laying open of his entire being to be possessed by God. It was through Jesus Christ that God brought him into the narrow pass where this faith became possible. Jesus Christ was God's fiery judgment upon all in which he had trusted heretofore. But Jesus Christ was also God's act of gracious acceptance whereby Paul knew himself taken into an unbelievable fellowship with God. Therefore, the present reality of God in which Paul's life was centered and out of which he lived was called by him the Spirit of Christ, the Spirit of the Lord, or the Spirit of the Father. To be justified by faith was to have one's life no longer in a ceaseless struggle to be acceptable to a distant God but rather in a relationship of openness and trust with a God who dwells not just with man but in man in the power of his Spirit.

This background and the establishment of these parallels is necessary to our understanding of the goal of Christian teaching. We do not always clearly visualize our goal, but consciously or unconsciously we have a goal, and what it is exerts a powerful influence upon all we do. It creates the very atmosphere we and our pupils breathe. Sometimes the goal is nothing more than the preservation into the future of the church that already exists. No thought is needed; no critical evaluations are permitted; the teacher has only to shape the rising generation in the express image of the one that already exists. Few Christians in the present day are likely to be so enraptured with themselves as that, and yet there are approximations to it. More frequently the goal will be " to make good Christians," with the hope that these good Christians of the future will be better Christians than any we have known in past or present. The difficulty arises in the definition of what constitutes a Christian. The definition varies widely in different areas of the church. Perhaps most teachers would define a good Christian as one who believes in Jesus Christ and in his church, who supports the church in its worship and its several ventures, and who in his private life is honest, truthful, responsible, and considerate of others. To some, this is too lax a standard: a Christian must accept unquestioningly all Christian doctrines, must put his church before all other interests, and in his conduct must hold himself apart from all worldly pleasures and associations. To others, however, both these definitions demand too much, the main thing in a Christian being not his beliefs or his relation with the church but the quality of his character. But what may pass unnoticed is that all these definitions have one thing in common: they assume they can define a Christian and can then get on with the task of making Christians. At one end of the scale there emerge schemes for character development and at the other end programs for the effective indoctrination of youth in rigid codes of belief and conduct, with various shadings in between. We are making good Christians of one kind or the other. The approach appeals to practical-minded people because it seems to pose a practicable goal.

But if a Christian is to be defined not by the correctness of his beliefs and conduct or by the superior quality of his character but by the openness of his life to the Spirit of God and by his willingness to put his trust wholly in what God has done and does for him in Jesus Christ, then all these definitions of the goal of Christian teaching fall to the ground. Their practicality is the practicality of the religion of the Pharisee, and they are more calculated in all their forms, both liberal and conservative, to produce a race of men whose trust is in themselves than they are to bring into being a new race of men who confess themselves to be nothing before God that God may be everything to them.

They are modern forms of legalism, and like all legalistic religion, they establish the righteousness, or sovereignty, of men rather than the righteousness, or sovereignty, of God. Where Jesus offended unforgivably the good religious people of his time was when with such boldness he swept away their right to repose their confidence where they did — in human religiousness and virtue. He ridiculed the piety and morality of the Pharisee that led him to confuse his self-approval with God's approval of him. He would not let men speak of any man as good. He pictured even the most virtuous men as bankrupts before God, so far in debt to him for their sins that they had no hope except in his forgiveness.

The goal of Christian teaching is that there may be Christians on this earth today and tomorrow, in fellowship with God and with each other as the church of God, and offering themselves to Jesus Christ as a body through which he may continue his invasion of the world. But we understand our goal only when we understand the nature of the Christian man in the light of the entire Christian gospel. The goal is revealed in Jesus Christ and nowhere else, and it has to be revealed to us in him not just once but many times. For unconsciously we do what all Christians before us have done and adjust our definition of a Christian to bring it closer to ourselves and to relax the tension between it and what we are. The claims of self revive in us to contest the sovereignty of God's Spirit, and we exchange life in the Spirit for a less demanding life according to some respectable code of what it takes to be a Christian. The purest doctrine is in constant danger of becoming a legalistic orthodoxy on which we depend for our salvation. The highest standards of Christian living are in equal danger of becoming a legalistic moral code by which we justify ourselves. So it is that we must live, daily praying, " Come, Holy Spirit," and we must then point the way, for those who depend upon us for their instruction, toward the life that is lived in joyful hope of God's coming in the power of his Spirit.

15.

. . . *The Holy Catholic Church,*
the Communion of Saints

The church belongs in the creed only in so far as it is truly the church of God and the instrument of his action, inseparable from him just as his word is inseparable from him. When God speaks his word to man, man hears in that word the call to become God's man and the servant of God's word, the channel through which it may be heard by other men. From beginning to end of Scripture, there is never a word of God without a people of God living under the judgment and by the promise of that word and by their very existence bearing witness to the reality of God before all men. Therefore, the church belongs in the creed in which we confess our faith in God, and we do not believe in God the Father, God the Son, and God the Holy Spirit unless we believe also in the church. But strangely, the church, which belongs so essentially in the creed, has in the past century had great difficulty in getting into the curriculum of Christian teaching. Not long ago there were few Protestant churches that gave any space to the church and its history in their educational programs. The situation has improved greatly in recent years, but there are still many quarters in which there is resistance, and the source of the resistance is adherence to a creed that differs from the Apostles' Creed in this: there is no place in it for the church.

We must be careful to distinguish between loyalty to the church, or enthusiasm for it or even love for it, and belief in it as an article of faith in close and inseparable association with our belief in God. The high percentage of our population that constitutes the membership of the churches and the large attendances at many churches might seem to us to denote a widespread belief in the church. But a closer acquaintance with the membership yields a less heartening result. Evaluation of the church as an excellent spiritual influence in one's own community, well worthy of generous support, is not inconsistent with a refusal to have anything to do with the establishment of the church in Japan or India, and in the refusal is implicit a repudiation of the holy catholic church. So also an intense devotion to Presbyterianism or Anglicanism or Lutheranism may be little more than a sentimental loyalty to one's own religious family, coexistent with an unbelief in the holy catholic church, an unbelief that shows itself in an indifference concerning Christians in other traditions. Or if we questioned the members of a church concerning their attachment to it and they were honest in their answers, we might find a wide variety of reasons why they are there — from the attractiveness of the nursery, past the beauty of the music to the qualities of the minister's personality, with rarely an assertion that they are in the church because they believe in the church as an indispensable expression of the Christian faith. They believe in God; they believe in Christianity; but they prefer to say that they *belong to* the church rather than that they believe in it. "Belonging" suggests a relationship that can be dissolved, but "believing" means an inner binding and an irretrievable commitment. One belongs to service clubs, political and cultural organizations, and all manner of human societies. As long as the church is merely a human organization for moral and spiritual purposes to which one belongs, it has no place either in the creed or in the curriculum of the church school. But when it is defined as "holy" to mark it as God's church, and when it is understood as God's provision for the carrying forward of his redemptive purpose for the world, its omission is a warning sign that the apostolic faith has begun to give way to some other faith.

There are a number of factors that have been involved in the exclusion or passing over of the subject of the church in Christian education. The strongest has been the deeply rooted conviction that nothing except the Bible should be studied in the church school: the time available is so short and the Bible as the one means of knowing God is so much more important to the pupil than all else that it should have all the attention. But the Bible itself forces upon our notice the subject of the church, and the history of the church is the history of the interpretation of the Bible, the story of what has happened in the world as a consequence of the ongoing influence of events that are recorded in the Bible. The wide use of international uniform lessons has also contributed to the situation, since, in order to be acceptable in all denominations, they have been kept free of allusions to the history of the church. The Bible seemed to be the common point of meeting and the interpretation of the church a subject on which no one would agree. It was not noticed that the Bible itself becomes innocuous when we leave aside all subjects on which we disagree. A third factor is the tendency to regard Christianity as a point of view to be adopted rather than a life to be lived in fellowship with God and man within the church. Individualism has been a powerful force in our environment, and it is not surprising that men should think of the Christian faith in individualistic terms. According to this viewpoint, each man has his own faith, and his way of life is his own concern. His education in the Christian faith is a process of thinking out his own point of view and arriving at his own basis for living. The faith of the individual is primary and his relationship to some church quite secondary. In fact, if he has a really Christian point of view and basis for living, he may find it more congenial to live the Christian life outside the church. He does not need the church. All these factors have played their part in creating a Christian education that is much more inclined to be an education in Christianity in general than an education for a life of Christian discipleship within the fellowship of the church.

The Divine Origin of the Church

The inclusion of the church in the creed and the insistence of the creed upon its holiness lends to the church a dignity that sets it apart from all other human associations. It is this uniqueness and separateness which has tended to be lost from sight even among Christians who are most loyal to their church. It is essential, therefore, that we see with clarity why the gospel demands a church and what it is in the origin and nature of the church that sets it in the creed in sequence with Father, Son, and Holy Spirit.

There is a church not because at a certain time in history men decided that there should be a church and have found it advantageous ever since to preserve the church in being, but because a church was necessary to the unfolding of God's purpose in the midst of men. The existence of the church is rooted in the relationship of God to his creation. The creation is his creation, made to reflect his glory, and mankind his sons and daughters, made to have their life in fellowship with him. But this true destiny of the world and man has been tragically lost and broken, and would be lost forever had not God in love for his creation intervened in the midst of the human tragedy to open to man a way of recovery and return. God was not willing that his cause be lost, but he was not willing either to compel a response of love and obedience from man. Therefore, his intervention was in a word that expressed his mind and will and could be the means of the most intimate fellowship with himself and yet that left to man the freedom to respond or to rebel. But because God is the Father of all men, the word that called an Abraham or a Moses or an Israel into fellowship with him was recognized as having a blessing in it that belonged to all mankind. It could not stop with Abraham or Moses or Israel. To receive this word and the life in covenant with God that it made possible was to be committed to a mission: to be a people in the service of this word in which the secret of God's purpose for the world would be disclosed. The stories of Abraham in Genesis are a profound expression of this consciousness of destiny and mission in Israel. In Gen., chs. 1 to 11, the descent of mankind into chaos is portrayed. A world is pictured that has fallen a prey to confusion and death because of its determination to be sufficient in itself for life. But God is not willing to leave his world a prey to death. Therefore, his call of Abraham in Gen., ch. 12, is the beginning of a history within history by which he means eventually to overcome the resistance of man and to restore his creation to its true life with him. To be " the called of God " is a costly destiny for Abraham in which he dare not let his own son, who seems to be the only hope of the fulfillment of God's purpose in the future, come between him and God. And Israel in the centuries of its history learned that to be the called of God was not to be the recipient of special favors from God but rather to be constantly bereft of all human securities and forced ever afresh to venture out into the unknown with only God's promise as security and guide. When God's word ceased to be heard, Israel rapidly shaped its life in the pattern of all other nations and settled down to live a " normal " life like other peoples, but always a voice was raised anew to recall Israel to its destiny as the Servant of the Word. Therefore, it can be said that Israel was the people of God not because it chose to be the people of God but only in so far as it responded to a call and choice of God.

Israel in the Old Testament is a foreshadowing of the church, but a foreshadowing in flesh and blood that was also a foretaste of the reality yet to come, and in it the lines of the coming church can be dimly seen. In the fullness of time the Word in which God intervenes to open the way for the return of a revolting world became man in Jesus Christ. No longer was the word just a call to man to return, but the Word in which God called was one with the man who responded to the call. Jesus Christ was both the offer of God's love and the human response in love and obedience to that offer. In his obedience the rebellion of the human self was overcome, and a new Israel living in the strength and joy of a new covenant with God was born. In him the creation was restored to its Creator, and a humanity cut off from life because it was cut apart from God was reconciled to God. No longer was this a mere possibility or hope: it was reality in Jesus Christ. A new man was born and a new humanity was begun. A new day dawned not just for Israel but for the human race and for the world. But Jesus was only the first-born of this new humanity. If God's purpose was to be fulfilled, there had to be a new people of God in fellowship with Jesus Christ, drawing its life entirely from him, its alienation from God overcome by him, sharing with him the wholeness of a life in God but sharing with him also his willingness to let himself be entirely at the service of the redeeming, life-transforming word of God. Faith in Jesus Christ was entrance with him into a new world and a new life, and it belonged to the very nature of that new life that it was intended for all men. It was the restoration not just of Israelites to their true life as Israelites but of man to his true life as man, the life for which he was created, reflecting the nature and so the glory of his Creator. It may have taken some of the disciples some time to recognize the ultimate destination of the gospel and of the life that had been entrusted to them, but the mark of the world's Creator and of his universal purpose was stamped deeply upon every detail of the gospel and upon the life that flowed from it. To receive it was to be put in debt to all mankind, for one had now in his possession a truth and life without which man was not only without a knowledge of the one true God but was unable to be his own true self or to find his own true place within God's world. To believe in Jesus Christ was therefore to be so bound into one with him and with all who had their life from him that the whole of life henceforward could be nothing but a sharing of his ministry. To withhold oneself from him, to wish to have the benefits of his gospel without the responsibilities, would be a denial of faith itself. The church is therefore the inevitable outcome of faith in Jesus Christ, and its ministry, which is its willingness to be the instrumentality through which Christ continues to speak and act and be what he is for all mankind, is an institution not of men but of God. To say No! to *this* church is to say No! to Jesus Christ, and to say No! to Jesus Christ is to say No! to God.

With equal truth it can be said that to believe in the Holy Spirit is to believe in the church and to be the church. God the Holy Spirit is not the private possession of any man. God the Holy Spirit is the God who made all men to have the fullness of their life only in him, so that to receive the Holy Spirit as the cen-

ter and the source of one's life means an unconditional openness
not only toward God but toward all men. He who is our life is
the only hope of life of every man we meet. We have his life in
trust for him, and we must be such in our relations with him
that we may fulfill our trust and his life may pass from us to him.
His sins and all that might repulse us in him must be not a barrier that shuts us out from him but rather a sign to us of the sickness from which he suffers, the absence of God's Spirit from him,
a sickness that we understand because it constantly recurs in us.
But what we offer him is not our broken life and broken light
but the life and light that are present with us in Jesus Christ and
come to us ever afresh in the Holy Spirit. We beseech him in
Christ's stead to be reconciled with God. The Holy Spirit is also
the source of the fellowship we have with other Christians. Our
oneness with them within the church is not based upon the con-
geniality of our personalities or the completeness of the agreement of our principles and practices, but upon the centering of
our existences in the one Spirit. The church is not a human fellowship held together by human ties; at least, if it is no more than
this, it has nothing to distinguish it from any other human society and it is not the church of God. The members of the church
of God are bonded together at a point beyond themselves, and
yet within themselves, by their acknowledgment that the sovereignty over all things in their life belongs not to themselves but
to the Spirit of God. It is significant that in the New Testament
the Holy Spirit is given first not to individuals but to the
church, and that at the receiving of the Holy Spirit by converts,
the hands of representatives of the church are laid upon them.
The communion of the Holy Spirit and the fellowship of the
church are inseparable, and the one is not to be had without the
other. To receive the Holy Spirit is to be bound together into one
and to have one's life in oneness with all who have belonged to
God through all the ages. It is clear, then, that to set the church
aside or to think that one can be a Christian and live the Christian life without the church is a serious error, since there is no
way in which to believe in Father, Son, and Holy Spirit without

already being committed to life in the church of God by that belief.

The objection may be made that though this is true of the church of God, it does not commit us to the church in our community, in which we cannot recognize the church of God. Since the beginning there has never been a church that was not in some respects unfaithful to its nature. The church of the first disciples at Jerusalem remained so fettered with Jewish customs and regulations that most of us would be likely to find it uncongenial. The church at Corinth, rich as it was in gifts of the Spirit, was plagued with problems that were the source of real distress to Paul. The history of the church is not only the history of the triumphs of God's grace and truth but also a history of human blindness, stubbornness, and stupidity. Churches are composed of sinful men, and the strength of sin is such that it is never wholly conquered in this life. God has left the thorn of sin in our flesh to keep us humble that we may not make his work of grace in us the basis for a new form of confidence in ourselves. The church of God therefore exists and has always existed within a sinful and unfaithful church and in spite of that sin and unfaithfulness. In other words, the church of God exists by God's grace and not by its own strength or virtue. And we can never have our life in the church of God except within that sinful and unfaithful church that so offends us. But will it so offend us if once we recognize how much the church is the mirror of ourselves and that, in us as in the church, all that is Christian exists by God's grace in spite of our sin and unfaithfulness?

THE DEFINITION OF THE CHURCH

The creed defines the church as holy, catholic, and the communion of saints. What these terms mean has already been suggested, but it needs to be spelled out more clearly. The term "holy" is used to designate anything or anyone that belongs peculiarly to God and so is separated from the world. The priests of God are holy because they have to do with God. So also are the instruments of their ministry. The ground on the mountainside where God appeared to Moses was made holy by that appearance. God himself is thrice holy in Isaiah's vision. And the Spirit of God who dwells in man is called the Holy Spirit that he may not be confused with any of the higher expressions of the human spirit. The holiness of the church is therefore not a quality that pertains to it of itself but denotes, rather, the presence of God himself in it and its character as the place where God meets with man, speaks to man, gives himself to man, and takes man into a life with himself. The same term " holy " is applied to individual Christians when they are called " saints." This word in its New Testament use is almost unknown to men today, so much so that they would be embarrassed to be called saints as Paul called the members of his churches saints. The Roman usage of the word dominates men's minds, which makes it signify a Christian who has reached perfection and become sinless, a form of limited utopianism that contradicts the New Testament's humble expectation that only in the Last Day when Christ returns will evil lose its power and his people be like him. Paul's saints were also sinners and this was no contradiction, for they were sinners in whose very selves God's Holy Spirit was a living and transforming presence. Their sanctity was not a quality in themselves but a character lent to them by the presence of God.

The church loses its holiness when it becomes merely an association of men, women, and children for moral and religious purposes, when preaching becomes merely hints and helps for the improvement of our characters and our community life, when teaching becomes merely a discussion of life's problems, and there is no longer any expectation of an actual confrontation with God. The life and worship of such a church is flat and superficial, for the dimension of depth is gone; the mystery of the unseen has been dismissed.

The church is catholic, or universal, because the God for whom it speaks is the one God, Creator of heaven and earth, and the Jesus Christ who is its life is the promise of life to every man. The new day that dawned upon the world in him was not a new day just for some one portion of mankind but for all mankind. Therefore, the church that is faithful to its Lord must exist for every man without distinction. It is not catholic merely by geographical ubiquity, by providing that there are churches everywhere. Catholicity must mark its existence in every segment of its life so that wherever there is a church, there will be fellowship with God and man, open to all without regard to race or class or color. Protestant churches have been singularly tempted to betray their catholicity. So many of them have been organized as national churches and have tended to become churches for people only of that one nation, or have allied themselves exclusively with one race or color. These are not slight flaws in the church that can be tolerated as long as the church is sound in other respects. It is the love of God in the midst of his people that is at stake in the church's catholicity, and, as Paul stated in classic form, the church may be rich in all spiritual gifts and graces and yet by lack of love be reduced to nothing in the sight of both God and men. Another sin against catholicity of which the Roman Church and some Protestant churches are guilty is sectarianism, the defining of the church as though the true church were to be found only within the borders of some one institution. There can be but one church of God. The body of Jesus Christ cannot be divided. The Holy Spirit is not given to one body of believers and withheld from all others. And where God is in the midst of his people, who are we to withhold our fellowship from them? We may not approve their doctrine or their practices, and yet we may be open to recognize a unity with them beyond all differences. These problems which relate to the unity and universality of the church already show their faces even at the lower levels of the church school, and the answer that is given them in the character and spirit of the school as well as in its teaching can have a profound influence far beyond the pupils. But let these problems be evaded and no longer can the church command the respect of its keen-eyed young people who recognize so quickly the discrepancy between the church's profession and its practice.

"The communion of saints" suggests the length and breadth and height and depth of the fellowship that is open to us in the church. There is nothing like it in all the earth: an unbroken fellowship that stretches through all time and today reaches out into every corner of the earth. The little group of children in the classroom, or of worshipers in a church, need to have the walls of time and space broken away for them so that they may see themselves as members of a mighty army that spans the ages, participators in the four-thousand-year drama of God's invasion of a rebellious world. They are now the pioneers standing on the dividing line between past and future with the responsibility of being the church of God in this particular age. They are one church with Christians in other lands, with much to learn from them and much to give to them. But, before all else, what must be given and received is mutual recognition and understanding, that the communion of the saints may be a source of strength and encouragement to Christians everywhere, but particularly to those who have their life in embattled situations.

Perhaps it would bring more life and reality into the reading of the Scriptures if Christians regarded the Bible as a doorway into fellowship with people like ourselves who in Old and New Testament times were called into a special closeness with God. Many of them are nameless, as in the psalms, and yet they open their very souls to us that God may be to us what he was to them. Others, such as the prophets, come before us with greater vividness. Paul and Simon Peter and John Mark walk out of the ancient world into our world and become our companions in the faith. To live in communion with them is to live in confrontation and communion with their God. We need also to get the doors of history open, history as the story of those who before our time have wrestled with the great questions of Christian faith and living. We were not ever intended by God to live on the frugal resources of our immediate circle or in the narrow compass of our local Christian fellowship.

Yet this wider communion counts for little if there is not in the immediate and local scene a fellowship that is the communion of saints. It is often from the people whom we have closest to us that we withhold ourselves most completely. The years provide untold offenses to build barriers between people who have long lived together. It is often easier for strangers to be of help to each other than for men who have known each other forty years. Not every congregation of people who know each other's names is a communion of the saints. The building of such fellowship is one of the deepest and most searching works of God, but it makes no progress until a gospel is preached and taught that brings men out of isolation and by laying them open to God breaks down the barriers between them among themselves. When once the barriers are down, there is a sharing of faith and understanding and courage that becomes a constant, though not always a conscious, factor in the members' lives. Each Christian stands no longer alone but with the consciousness of being supported and sustained by the communion of the saints.

There is a danger as we thus define the church that the impression may be conveyed, particularly to children, that the church is a finished structure, complete in every detail, with all its doctrines codified and all its practices determined at some time in the past. Sometimes its history is narrated in such a way as to suggest that all its thrilling battles have been fought and all its great controversies settled, so that nothing remains for a new generation but to carry forward what has been established. No impression could be more unfaithful to the reality. The foundations of the church have been laid in Jesus Christ, together with his prophets and apostles, and "other foundation can no man lay" except he intend to build another church than that of Jesus Christ. Through the centuries some stones have been well and surely laid upon these foundations, but other structures have proved insubstantial and from time to time have had to be cleared away and the work begun anew. The more closely we study the pattern of the church's life disclosed in the gospel, the more we become convinced that in twenty centuries we have taken only the first few steps in the building of the church. How long the total task will take is not for us to know, but we may depend upon it that it will be until the end of time, and each new age will have its urgent task in the building of the whole. We live upon the growing edge of the church, and if our teaching and training of the rising generation is to be relevant, it must prepare them to face the decisions and the tasks that belong to a church that is the instrument of God's redemptive purpose in such an age as ours.

One of the church's greatest dangers is of being content if only it can preserve itself — with sufficient growth to count itself successful. But it exists not for itself but for the world beyond it. God's love is for the world, not just for the church, and he has no love for a church that does not share his love and care and outreach to a world that is lost in its endeavor to find its life within itself. The church deceives itself if it thinks it can have a spiritual security and peace in detachment from the dilemmas of mankind. It merely becomes irrelevant and uninteresting both to God and man. Just as Jesus took into himself the sins and sorrows and anxieties of men, so must his church let itself be burdened and tortured by the distresses of mankind. There is a cheap grace and an illusory peace of mind that Christians sometimes take to themselves by retiring into quiet sanctuaries where the clamor of the world is stilled and where they make themselves feel peaceful by repeating carefully chosen phrases from the Bible. But where Jesus Christ is present in the midst of his people, Christ crucified, there is a willingness to be exposed to the most painful dilemmas of man, that the Physician may be where he wants to be, which is with the sick, and that the Savior may be where alone his saving power is meaningful, which is with sinners. A classroom may be a place of escape from the world, or it may be the burning point where Jesus Christ once more meets and understands and conquers and redeems the world.

16.

. . . *The Forgiveness of Sins*

It has been remarked, with justice, that Jesus in his preaching and teaching does not have much to say about sin. There is no trace, in the instances available to us of his approach to men, of the pattern long familiar to us in evangelistic preaching and teaching: first to convince the man that he is a sinner lost in the darkness of his sin and with fearful punishments threatening him, and then when he has been reduced to an appropriate state of contrition, to offer to him the hope of salvation from his sin through the gospel. The preaching of John the Baptist shows something of this pattern but not the preaching of Jesus. Jesus seems rather to reverse the order and to begin by proclaiming to men God's forgiveness. The palsied man, carried by four friends, did not first hear from Jesus a lecture on his sins and then a word of forgiveness, but before all else there sounded in his ears the gracious words, " Son, thy sins are forgiven thee." Jesus' first act in relation to Zacchaeus was to accept him and offer himself to him in fellowship: " Zacchaeus, come down, for I am going to stay with you today." Jesus " received sinners and ate with them," and it is inconceivable that preparatory to this free association with them he had a talk with them about their sins! The Pharisees who stand opposed to Jesus seem to have had much more to say about men's sins than Jesus did. They had an eagle eye to spot the sins of their fellows and considered it their duty to expose the sins of men wherever they were found. The constant concern of their daily life was to keep free of sin. To maintain the purity of the religious

208

community, they excluded from it any persons who seemed to have grown careless about the keeping of the law. It was, perhaps, in conscious contradiction to the Pharisees and their harsh legalism that Jesus had so little to say to men of their sins and so much to say to them of God's mercy and goodness and the finding of a new life under God's rule.

It would be false to deduce from this that Jesus took sin less seriously than the Pharisees or John the Baptist. The opposite is true. Implicit in all his teaching and in the character of his mission is a consciousness of the colossal tragedy of sin in human life. He sees it in its full dimensions — not as petty breaches of the law that bring unnecessary disorder into the religious community and could be avoided if men would give their minds to it, but as a cruel imprisonment of the human self by the powers of evil, an enslavement that destroys a man in both soul and body and from which he has no power to free himself. The Pharisees saw in the lawbreakers only willful and irresponsible unbelievers with whom nothing could be done. Jesus saw in them sick men who were being destroyed not only by the sickness of their sin but also by the harsh judgments of their brothers whose judgment was taken by them to be the judgment of God. It was a judgment in which there was no hope for the sinner, and, as we see it pictured by Jesus in the attitude of the older brother in the parable of the prodigal, its severity was not relaxed even when the sinner returned to God.

Nothing provoked Jesus more than the presumption of religious people in making themselves the judges of the sins of other men. They were confusing themselves with God and their minds with God's mind, so that they forgot completely that they too were under the judgment of God. It was a blasphemous exaltation of themselves in which they were blinded to the reality of their own sin. Their consciousness of righteousness in themselves was the consequence of measuring themselves alongside those who seemed to be less righteous than themselves instead of letting their lives lie open before God in whose presence no man can be confident of his own righteousness. How could it be otherwise than that Jesus would see all men in their relationship to God under that searching light from which nothing can be hidden, and that he would know the hidden truth of every man's being: that between him and God there were many things that were not right? When he set Simon the Pharisee and the sinner woman alongside each other in a parable, representing them as two debtors, the one with only a small debt and the other with a great debt but neither of them with any resources to discharge the debt, he was disclosing to Simon the deepest truth about his situation which he dared not acknowledge lest it destroy the fragile structure of his self-righteousness. Yet even with Simon, Jesus did not speak directly of his sin but only held up to him a mirror in which it was possible that he might see himself.

This indirectness of Jesus' approach to men's sin is most significant for our understanding of it and for our approach to it in teaching. The truth of every man's existence in his relationship with God is that he is a sinner and that his sin disrupts the order of his life. The magnitude of the sin is secondary, because in essence sin is a resistance of the human self to God that breaks the relationship to God not just at one point but totally, and the self, broken apart from the source of its life in God, is a broken self. But this truth, since it has to do not just with facts about man's conduct but with a relationship to God that is so hidden that he is not conscious of it himself, cannot be communicated to any man as so much information about himself. It is hidden from him as God is hidden, and it has to be revealed to him as God has to be revealed. He cannot know either God or himself except by revelation, by the lifting of the cloud that conceals from him the nature of the relationship that is the source and origin of his life. No one by mere telling can convey to any man a knowledge of God, and so also no one by mere telling can convey to any man a knowledge of himself. In fact, the attempt at direct communication in each case creates a semblance of knowledge that is not a Christian knowing. There is a vast difference between the man who knows of God only because he has been told and the man who knows God and is known by God in personal relation. So also there is a vast difference between the man who knows of sin only because certain elements in his attitude and conduct have been branded sinful and the man who knows himself alienated from God, imprisoned by his own desires, thoughts, and acts within a self that is unendurable to him and shut out from those heights and depths of life in human relationships which should be his in God. It is an offense against the truth to speak glibly of God, but it is also an offense against the truth to speak glibly of sin. The Pharisees were too certain and secure in what they thought they knew of God and sin. The mystery of both God and man was deeper than they comprehended in their doctrines. Their vision failed to reach either into the depths of the abyss of sin in every human life or into the depths to which divine grace is willing to go in order to rescue man from sin. The Christian teacher must follow in the footsteps not of the Pharisees but of Jesus Christ, not prattling seriously yet superficially of sin, but in all relations with his pupils speaking out of an understanding of the dilemmas created by the involvement of the human self in sin and out of a compassion that will go to any length to help anyone to the victory of faith.

THE NATURE OF SIN AND FORGIVENESS

The first difficulty a teacher faces is that his pupils are likely to have a quite unbiblical and unchristian conception of both sin and forgiveness. Sin is a term reserved by them for the more serious offenses that men commit against God's law and against society: acts of violence, irresponsible drunkenness, sexual dissoluteness, flagrant dishonesty. Then there are lesser sins that seem to be less ruinous and less reprehensible, more easily excused as weaknesses or acts of mistaken judgment. Beyond these are the errors and imperfections that are so common that they are regarded as inevitable in human nature: " I'm only human." So firmly fixed is this scale of sins in most communities that for a well-behaved Christian to call himself a sinner seems a form of exaggerated humility, and for a minister to preach a sermon to a congregation of Christians calling them to repentance for their sins seems slightly ridiculous, if not insulting. The prayer of confession is lost upon many people in Christian worship because they are not conscious of any really serious sins to confess and are not inclined to beat upon their breasts and implore God's mercy for themselves as sinners. So also the pupil in the church school class who comes from a family of respectable Christians is likely to be puzzled by what he hears concerning sinners and forgiveness and to feel that this is one aspect of the Christian faith that has little relevance for him. He knows of people in the community who are ruining themselves in sin and who need a gospel that can save the lost, but he is not one of them. And yet these very people who have no consciousness of sin have the reality of sin day after day as the cardinal problem of their existence. They need to throw away their chart of sins against which they measure themselves and answer honestly before God a few simple questions concerning their relationship with him and with each other. God is not interested in how respectable they are. He asks, rather: "Do you love me with all your heart and mind and strength? Do you worship me alone and seek your life from me alone, or do you scatter the worship of your heart in many quarters and reap a disunity of life? Do you love your neighbor as yourself or do you love yourself and your family and give only the crumbs of your love to any neighbor? Do you love truth, my truth, so that you hold it fast, however painful and costly it may be, or is that for you a counsel of perfection?" These are the questions which meet us in the Scriptures and are like knives thrust into our souls.

Sin must be redefined before it can be recognized. Everywhere in Scripture it is primarily the rupture by man of his relationship with God that brings in its train a perversion of his relation with his fellows and with the world. But how can any man know what he has lost unless first he knows something of what life would be in unbroken fellowship with God? Whence comes this dream of an Eden at the beginning and at the end of time in which there is no sin or evil to cast a shadow over the life of man? Is it only the ancient Hebrew writer who remembers that he was made

in the likeness and image of God, or does he speak for man and
set down in words what is written by the hand of God deep in
the existence of every man? The prodigal in the far country could
forget for a time that he was his father's son, but he could not
cease *to be* his father's son. Even in the moments when all relation with his father seemed obliterated, the knowledge of who
he was was buried deep within him. So is it with every man, and
this remembrance of the Father and of the Father's home, which
is our rightful home, however dim it is, remains to haunt and
plague us, a fleeting vision of another self and another world that
might be ours, a consciousness of something lost without which
we never can be whole. No man can know that he has fallen
unless he has known at least something of the strength and peace
and joy of fellowship with God. No man can recognize the aw-
fulness of God's wrath in judgment unless he has tasted the blessedness of a relationship of trust. No man can understand that
sin has imprisoned him in death unless he has breathed in some
measure the air of freedom that belongs to life in God. We are
made for fellowship with God and with each other, and the de-
sign of our existence, while it can be perverted and concealed,
can never be destroyed, and since it is the mark of God upon us,
the stamp of the Creator who refuses to surrender or abandon
his rights in anything he has created, it reminds us where we
have come from and what we have lost.

The story of the fall of man, whether we read it in the third
chapter of Genesis or in the parable of the prodigal or in Paul's
letter to the Romans, is the story of a universal tragedy from
which no man is spared. The desire of Adam and of the prodigal
to be free from the restraints and responsibilities of a life in fellowship, to be masters of themselves, to have no authority beyond
them to which they must bow, is the desire of every man. But
since man with the center of his existence in himself and cut
apart from God is no longer man but only half a man, a broken
man, a wounded man, he can no longer keep order in the world
as God's representative but is himself the most prolific source of
disorder and destruction. The primary expression of man's sin is

therefore not some violent and disgraceful conduct but simply his self-centeredness, which seems at first a just demand for freedom to satisfy his desires and carry out his purposes but soon reveals itself as the drive of the human will to be master not just of its own existence but far beyond. What makes this definition of sin hard to grasp and easy to misunderstand is that there is a legitimate and necessary self-assertion. The child whose will is broken by a discipline that refuses him the right to have any thought or action of his own is likely to be stunted and crippled in his development. The adolescent dare not be branded as specially sinful because he sometimes finds it necessary to rebel in order to pass from a childish state of dependence to a maturity in which he thinks for himself and makes decisions. We do not get free of all sinful self-centeredness by letting ourselves be pushed around by everyone we meet. Christian humility is not spinelessness. Self-assertion is not necessarily sin when our will conflicts with another human will but only when it conflicts with the will of God. Sin is the determination of man to have his own way in spite of God and therefore is the usurping by man of the place of rule that in his life and beyond him belongs to God alone.

The disorder that sin creates is first in man himself. He is in contradiction to himself and so in tension with himself. The self he is and the self that he can never quite forget are at enmity with each other, creating self-disgust and self-hatred. This drives him to all manner of devices to silence and obliterate the buried self that keeps him from content with the self that he has become. But since that buried self is the mark upon him of his Creator, it will not die. It is, however, in his human relationships that man sees reflected most clearly his relationship with God. God meets him not just in the depths of his own being but also in his brother. If he has ceased to know or care about God's mercy, it will be evident in the lack of mercy in his dealings with his brother and, what is more disturbing, in his brother's dealings with him. If he has closed his heart against God, doors are closed tightly also in his most intimate associations with those about him. The conflict of his will with God becomes a painful conflict with every human will that seems to reflect the will of God. Hatred of God and of himself expresses itself in hatred of all who resist his will, and in hatred of the world because at so many points it frustrates his will. The No! of God to sin is not written only in Scripture and is not heard only in the church. If it were, we could escape it easily by leaving the Scriptures closed and absenting ourselves from church. The No! is written into the fabric of life itself, so that there is no escape from it. The structure of human existence and of human relationships, in the largest as well as the smallest units of society, is such that sin engenders a disorder that is a warning sign of death.

Only when we see the reality of sin in these dimensions do we understand why it occupies the place in the creed that it does. Having confessed our faith in God as Father, Son, and Holy Spirit and in the church as the fellowship of faith and the instrument of God's purpose in the world, we would expect next to hear something of the Christian life before the confession is concluded with the triumphant assertion of faith in life eternal. But we hear only of the forgiveness of our sins! The educator may think it would be more constructive if the creed made room for growth in Christian character and progress in the solution of the problems of a Christian society. How can this be a comprehensive description of the Christian life — the forgiveness of sins? Do we never get beyond this? Or is this the transformation at the roots of life itself that alone brings growth in Christian character and makes possible more justice and mercy in men's dealings with each other? Sin is the problem beneath all the other problems of human life, the poison that keeps breaking out in new and unexpected forms of sickness to rob man of his life, and forgiveness is God's answer to the problem in the gospel. Sin is not *a* problem but *the* problem of man, and forgiveness is not just one aspect of God's grace; it *is* God's grace.

Corresponding to the superficial estimate of sin that prevails among many Christians is an equally superficial understanding of forgiveness. It belongs within a legalistic framework in which each action is assigned its own appropriate reward. Evil actions must be punished in order to discourage them in future. For God or man to withhold the punishment would seem to endanger the moral order of society. But in some instances, where there is no danger of encouraging evil, the offender may be forgiven, the solid substance of the forgiveness being that there is no punishment. From this standpoint men are wise to be sparing in their forgiveness, and the less said about the forgiveness of God for sinners the better. When children or adults offend, they must be " taught a lesson " that they may not repeat the offense; they must not be encouraged to think that God is like an indulgent and irresponsible parent who will forgive anything. A legalistic, moralistic Christianity therefore speaks little of forgiveness — like Pharisaism in New Testament times. It inculcates high standards of virtue by word and example but unfortunately makes no provision for moral failure, in short, takes no account of the universality of sin. It hopes to stamp out sin by disapproval and punishment, but it succeeds only in dividing men into two classes: those who have minimized their sin to the point that they feel free to trust in their own righteousness and those who in the knowledge of their sin can only despair. Many alternate between self-trust and despair and are divided souls.

We can understand why Jesus seemed to the Pharisees to be an encourager of immorality. He did not condemn sinners by his words and attitude but accepted them and ate with them. He forgave them before ever he had proof of their repentance. And he acted as though good religious men were in more hopeless straits than those who were living openly in sin. What the Pharisee had no eyes to see was that Jesus' whole life and ministry and gospel was an assault upon sin at a deeper level where alone there was hope that it might be overcome. The forgiveness he proclaimed was no easy escape for men from the consequences of their sin and no encouragement to sin again, because it was *God's* forgiveness, which laid bare the infinite hatefulness of sin. The forgiven man was conscious that his sin had shut him out from God and thereby from his own true life. To receive God's forgiveness was to be accepted into fellowship with God, to be restored to the relation with him that has the promise in it of a life of infinite and eternal richness. It was the man who was forgiven who first knew how far he had fallen in his sin, and in his thankfulness was ready to respond to God with an unconditional love and obedience. But to have God's forgiveness was to have God, the God of infinitely forgiving love, as the sovereign center of one's life, and therefore to deal with other men's sins and offenses as one's own had been so effectively dealt with by God. The mark of the forgiven man was his willingness to forgive his fellow man. Forgiveness, then, precedes repentance, laying open to the sinner what he has lost by his sin and offering its restoration, but he has to accept the offer, and the acceptance, the response to love with love, is in itself a repentance that tears sin up by the roots. Forgiveness is God's one effective way of destroying sin. Punishment restrains it, but only for a time. God's providence has established in the order of our life a pain that sin brings in its train, that man in his blindness may not utterly destroy himself. But his mercy and forgiveness make the sinner hate the sin that robs him of his true humanity.

Perhaps now we understand with what justice it can be said that the gospel is comprehended in this one word "forgiveness." The purpose of Jesus' coming into the world can be described as "to save his people from their sins." And it is this and nothing else that Paul and Luther find at the center of the gospel in their doctrine of justification by faith alone through grace alone. The sinner is redeemed not by anything he does but by God's acceptance of him in Jesus Christ. He can come to God because God has first come to him in love and offered him the gift of life, which he does not and cannot ever deserve. Jesus Christ is God's invasion of our humanity to conquer the sin that holds it prisoner and perverts it into inhumanity, and the weapon of his conquest is his infinitely forgiving love. There is no other weapon strong enough or that can reach deep enough to gain the victory.

The place of love's decisive victory over sin is Calvary, and therefore it is forevermore the place where men most readily and most profoundly find repentance and forgiveness. The cross for

Jesus was his final and decisive giving of himself *to* men which could not be separated from a giving of himself *for* them. His forgiveness was no easy speaking of the words, "Thy sins are forgiven," but was an acceptance of the sinner in love in which he took the sin into himself and bore it for the sinner. He had to give himself in a fellowship with the sinner in which he carried the sinner's burden as his own that the sinner might receive from him his (Christ's) joy and strength and peace in God. Jesus entered into the sinner's life that the sinner might enter into his life. That was his way of conquering sin and reconciling the sinner with God. The cross, then, is the climax in that work of grace that was the secret of his entire life, that strange and marvelous exchange in which he takes our place in condemnation that ours may be the life in God in which there is no condemnation. He speaks no word of condemnation from the cross — for the judges, for Judas, for the shrieking mob, for Peter who denied him, or for our humanity that willed that he should die — but when we see him on the cross and know why he is there, we judge ourselves. His death is God's judgment upon us, stripping us bare of all self-righteousness by which we might have justified ourselves. And we can endure that judgment which is the death of our old sinful self because the cross is Jesus' giving of himself to us in which he takes us into his own life in God and creates in us a boundless hope of what our life may be in God through him.

Sometimes forgiveness is conceived merely as the beginning of the Christian life. The man who was a sinner is forgiven through the grace of God in Christ, and beyond this point of forgiveness or justification or conversion, whichever it may be called, he proceeds to build with confidence the Christian life. God has laid the foundation, and now man, the redeemed man, must build upon it. He *was* a sinner who could put no confidence in himself, but now he has been redeemed from sin and can put considerable confidence in his own judgment and beliefs and works. This can be the basis of a new form of self-righteousness and self-assurance which is all the more obnoxious because it uses with such freedom the language of Christian piety. It has been forgotten that the forgiven man remains a sinner. The universality of sin is not canceled by the forgiveness of the sinner, but, much rather, is established. He is a sinner who has been accepted into fellowship with God in spite of his unworthiness and whose sin is now exposed and overcome in his relationship with God through Christ. But this relationship makes him all the more acutely conscious of those elements in himself, in his church, and in the society that is inseparable from his life, which are in contradiction to the will of God. He is aware how powerful and subtle are the forces that unconsciously restore self to the place of rule, justifying its restoration perhaps by the fact that it is now a Christian and forgiven self, and so negate God's sovereignty. His constant need of worship is that he may be exposed to the word and Spirit of God that uncover to him ever afresh the resistance of his human self to God, that in a constantly renewed repentance God's conquest of his sin may open to him new vistas in the Christian life. He never reaches a plateau where he can begin to have assurance in himself that, through God's cleansing of him from his sin and his fellowship with God, he now is righteous and wise and able to wield God's sword of judgment upon his fellow men. That comfortable plateau is a continuation of the religion of the Pharisees and is the perpetual temptation in varying forms of religious and moral earnestness. There is no safety from it except a daily confrontation with Jesus Christ in which we never cease to marvel and give thanks for the way in which he humbles us with his forgiveness and separates us from our sin by coming in between its shadow and our life.

17.

. . . The Resurrection of the Body
and the Life Everlasting

The Reality of the Unseen

The creed is an affirmation from beginning to end that life has its source, and the center from which alone it makes sense, not in things that are seen but in things that are unseen. The world resists the attempts of the human mind to make sense of it and remains an impenetrable mystery until it is revealed to faith that the world does not exist as a thing of itself but is the creation of a God whose purpose is the secret of the world's existence and whose presence moment by moment is the source of the world's life. A world separated from God, seeking to find its significance and its vitality in itself, is a perverted and distorted world, turned inward upon itself and bent upon its own destruction. The whole of the Old Testament is testimony to the reality of this unseen Source and Center of life. Israel as a people comes into being at the command of a Voice out of the unseen, the voice of a God who calls it into a life of unfaltering fellowship with himself. "Keep covenant with me and live," says this Voice; "break covenant and die!" And the centuries of Israel's history are evidence that these were no empty words invented by priests and prophets. In so far as Israel was faithful to the covenant, it had a meaningful history and could not be shattered even by the most overwhelming catastrophes, but in so far as Israel forgot its covenant with God and sought its life in the more immediate resources and satisfactions of the world, its history lost all distinctive meaning and the nation itself was threatened with absorption into the surrounding world. In short, it was only through the presence and power of the unseen God that Israel was delivered from a stifling imprisonment in the world into a freedom to live a uniquely human life.

Already in Israel there was an awareness that this dependence upon the unseen God for the power to live was not peculiar to Israel, but was the secret of man's life universally. The secret was entrusted to Israel, but only that it might eventually reach all men and become for them the possibility of the fulfillment of their life. Man as man was created for fellowship with God, to reflect the very nature of God in his nature and to order the world as God's representative. But there has been a tragic rupture in man's relation with God that has blinded him and incapacitated him for his true function within the creation. In his blindness he worships elements and powers in his world as though they were his God and the source of his life, and no longer has he his ear attuned to a word that comes to him out of the unseen. To this " man without God," the world is a curse and not a blessing.

The Christian church had its origin in events that we have described as a decisive inbreaking of the unseen world of God upon man's world. Man has always been tempted to think of the visible and tangible world as real and the invisible and intangible as unreal. And even when he is persuaded of the existence of the unseen God and of another world than this one, he tends to set a vast gulf between the seen and the unseen as though they were two completely separate realities with no very intimate relation between them. He lives for a time in the visible, tangible world; then he dies and begins a different life in the invisible world. Also, the unseen God, who has his existence in that unseen world and whose will is known through his revelation, remains a distant God whom man serves at a distance. But in Jesus Christ the gulf between the two worlds is bridged, and the power of the unseen is the primary reality of his existence. The events of his life are explicable only as the working of the power of God's Spirit in him. The Kingdom, which he proclaims as near to every man and ready to become the realm in which man has his life, is visible only to the eyes of faith, and yet it transforms the significance of the day-by-day experiences of Christians in the world. Life in the Kingdom is life in fellowship with God, with an infinite hope of what is yet to be. Life outside the Kingdom is life in darkness and emptiness, with no prospect except death. To set one's heart upon the world and the things of the world is to be enslaved to the world and deprived of one's true life, but to deny oneself and to affirm God and God's Kingdom as one's only source of life is to be set free for God, for one's fellow man, and for a right use of the things of the world.

The seen and the unseen are therefore not two separate worlds that exist apart, but belong together in such intimacy that no man can enter into his true possession of the visible, tangible world until he learns to deal with it as the creation of the invisible and intangible God, and no man can be himself as a truly human being until he finds the source and center of his existence beyond himself in the unseen God. The ultimate origin of all forms of inhumanity, of man's scorn for his fellow man, his conflict with his fellow man, and his subjection of his fellow man, is man's determination to be the master and director of himself, a lust for power that always reaches beyond the man himself because of the involvement of other lives with his. To be master of himself, he has to cast off the restraints and turn a deaf ear to the commands and appeals that come to him out of the unseen. But when he has so asserted what he takes to be himself, he is left with what is only a broken and dying fragment of himself. He loses his grip upon his life in this world when he loses his relationship with the source of his life in the unseen world. Thus, Jesus is so completely himself, so completely man, because in him the visible humanity is so completely ruled by invisible divinity. And he creates a new humanity like his own in other men when his Spirit takes possession of them and masters them so that henceforward they live with their being centered in the unseen.

The resurrection of Jesus has to be understood as the decisive revelation of the primacy and power of the unseen world of God in the midst of this world which is marked by the sign of death. The death of Jesus set a question mark not only against his person but also against his gospel. Death stamps all that it touches as belonging to time and therefore as mortal, transitory, unenduring, not eternal, not divine. God cannot die. But when beyond the cross a living Lord manifested himself in unbroken relationship with his disciples, the question mark was set against death instead of against Jesus and his gospel. It was not a vague, ghostly Jesus whom the disciples knew during the forty days but the same person who had companied with them in the flesh. The wholeness of his being had comprehended his flesh, but the wholeness remained without the flesh. In his resurrection they were given eyes to see the glory of his divine being that during his earthly life had been for them unseen and to some extent uncertain but that was now for them the truth of all truths that had in it the hope of humanity's redemption. They, and the whole early church with them, lived in constant expectation of a new inbreaking of God's world upon this world. What we must see clearly is that a church that had experienced a transformation of human life through the discovery of its true center in the unseen was eager for the whole world to be transformed through a new, complete, and final invasion from beyond. It dare not be forgotten that the church that expected Christ's return at any moment was a church in which to be a Christian was to be unconditionally open to the presence and power of the Spirit who was the Spirit of Jesus Christ. The joy of Christians in what they knew of Christ in the Spirit made them impatient to know him face to face.

It is fitting, then, that the creed should close with the triumphant assertion that the life that the believer has through faith in Jesus Christ is not just an improved moral and spiritual existence. He shares with Jesus Christ his victory over death and his eternal life with God. Eternal life is not a life that begins beyond death so that it stands in radical antithesis to our life in time. Eternal life is life in fellowship with God. To be indwelt by God's Spirit is to have our life in God and in God's eternal Kingdom. The life of Jesus Christ in its oneness with God is life eternal. The inbreaking of God's unseen world upon man is the inbreaking of God's eternity into time. To live with life's center in the unseen in God is to lay up treasures in heaven, where moth and rust do not corrupt and where the thieves of time cannot break through to steal. To receive the gift of life from Jesus Christ is to be received into a life with Jesus Christ, into his life with God, which is eternal life. Faith, as we have already seen, is not faith about Jesus Christ, but faith in him in which we let ourselves be bound into one with him in life and in death, that his life may be ours, and our life, our time, our possessions, our talents, may be his. Any hesitation to let ourselves be bound to him is a denial of our faith. His death becomes our death to self. But if we die with him, we shall also rise with him into a life that confounds the imagination of men. It is therefore in this oneness with Jesus Christ that we believe in the resurrection of the body and the life everlasting.

Misconceptions Confront the Teacher

This final article of the creed provides peculiar difficulties for the teacher, but most of them arise from misconceptions of what is signified by the words of the article. "Resurrection *of the body*" seems to mean the resuscitation, or re-creation, of the disintegrated physical body, and "life everlasting" seems to mean a life that goes on and on beyond the point of death. The first misconception is inevitable in an environment in which "body" signifies the flesh and bones with which we are clothed. But the use of the term in the creed has as its background the very different Biblical significance of "body." The Hebrew had no capacity for abstractions: for him, a man and his body were one and could not be conceived in separation. The Greek might think of God as a vaguely diffused, bodiless, universal mind, but not the Hebrew. To the Hebrew, God was a person with hands and feet, eyes and ears and mouth. And yet, in this there is no denial of the spiritual nature of God. It was simply that a person without a body was inconceivable to him. Therefore, to speak of the arm or eye or ear or mouth of God was to speak of God in the various aspects of his relation with man. And to speak of the heart or hands or eyes or ears or body of man was to speak of the self of man. To lift up his eyes to God is to turn his whole being toward God. To open his ears to God's voice is to respond in faith and obedience to God's call, and to present his body as a living sacrifice to God is to present himself. The resurrection of the body is thus the resurrection of the whole self, distinguishing the resurrection life as personal in contrast to all vague and ghostly conceptions of the afterlife. The resurrection of the believer is like the resurrection of his Lord, because it is a sharing in that same resurrection life.

A further difficulty sometimes arises from the fact that Jesus' physical body is reported to have vanished from the tomb and the wounds in it to have been visible to the disciples. Does that not show that his resurrection body was a physical body, and, if our resurrection is to be like his, must not we too be reclothed in the same body? But the same stories tell of Jesus entering and leaving rooms that were locked and barred, and appearing and disappearing, which reveals the consciousness of the disciples that the resurrection body was different in kind from the earthly, physical body of Jesus. There is no suggestion of a physical presence in the various accounts of Paul's experience of the risen Lord. He saw a blinding light and heard a Voice speaking to him out of the light, which is remarkably similar to Moses' hearing of the voice of God out of the fiery bush. For Paul, the resurrection body is a celestial body in distinction from the terrestrial body and far exceeding it in glory.

" Life everlasting " unfortunately sets the emphasis upon the element of unendingness rather than upon the perspective of an infinitely increasing enrichment in the nature of life. It is not unusual to hear people say that they cannot bear the thought of a life that goes on and on. This is a symptom of a static and complacent view of life. They consider themselves to be Christians who have attained a life of moral and spiritual worth that should qualify them for heaven, but they are not sure they want the prize. For them, the Christian life is not a journey out of the depths into the heights, a sequence of repentances in which they are delivered from their old selves to find a new and more fruitful life in God, a growth in grace in which they are being changed from likeness to likeness as Christ is shaped in them. Rather, it is a careful maintenance of a superior quality of life — or what they take to be a superior quality — a virtue and a piety that they are confident should make them acceptable to God, what Paul calls " man's own righteousness," which is a righteousness of works. What must puzzle them, as it puzzled the Pharisees, is why such a life, if it is acceptable to God, has not more joy and strength and satisfaction in it. The fact must be faced that the legalistic, moralistic, pietistic life in which a man builds merit for himself with God is a life of insufferable dullness. It is not life in God with boundless hope of what it yet may be, a constant invitation to adventure, but rather a course of life by which one attempts to play safe with God, preserving for him in a reasonably unspotted though largely unused condition the life that was entrusted to one's care. Everlasting life is an uninviting prospect for the person who sees in it only an endless continuation of the stagnant existence that is all he has ever known.

Perhaps, however, the commonest misconception both within and outside the church is that anyone who has lived a reasonably decent life should be able to count on a life beyond death. Man's soul is by nature immortal, and there should be a happy immortality for all except the most depraved. Certainly no good-living Christian need have any fear of the outcome, and since it is human goodness that fits a man for immortality, it is not by any means essential that he be a Christian. In the funeral services of some fraternal orders, one hears the faith professed that man by his virtue becomes imperishable. But also in the church school it often happens that the teacher in order to reassure the pupils in the face of death and to incite them to virtue encourages them to think that by virtue and piety they become worthy of the life everlasting. How deeply entrenched this way of thinking is among Christians will be evident to us if we ask ourselves the question: If we have confidence in a life beyond death for ourselves, on what do we base our confidence? At once the mind begins to assemble all the credits in the moral and spiritual inventory that should make us acceptable to God. The confidence is in ourselves, in our merits, in our achievements, and belief in a future life thereby becomes the ultimate consolation of man's belief in himself. In contrast to this, the New Testament gospel destroys all basis for man's confidence in himself and in his own merits and achievements, that he may learn to put his confidence wholly in God and in God's work of grace in him. There is no easygoing belief in the immortality of man in Scripture. Man dies no matter how virtuous he is. But God has revealed himself in Jesus Christ as the God who brings life out of death, and to belong to him wholly and unconditionally is to have a life in him that is beyond the reach of death. The only immortality that man can know is life in God and God's life in him. To be cut off from God is death, not just in eternity but also in time. And to be reconciled with God through Jesus Christ and brought into fellowship with him is a resurrection life that triumphs over death both in time and in eternity. It is clear, then, that the whole Christian faith is at stake in these contrasted confidences concerning immortality. Here it becomes evident whether a man's belief is in God or in himself.

Between Life and Death

A teacher must be prepared also to meet indifference to the subject of life's dimensions beyond time and even the outright denial of the existence of any such dimensions. Death is a singularly convincing fact. The wall between this world and anything that lies beyond is impenetrable, and the attempts of spiritualists to get messages from beyond have made no significant breaches in it. It is not surprising that some thoughtful pupils question the existence of a future life just as they question the existence of God. In some instances they may be reacting against the common conceptions with which they are familiar — heaven as the place of endless enjoyment where you go if you have been good, immortality as the reward of complacent virtue — and may know nothing at

all of the real nature of the Christian hope in its total context in
the Christian faith. Or again, they may be passing through a ra-
tionalist phase in which it seems to them dishonest to accept anything as true that they cannot demonstrate by rational argument.
The temptation, then, is to attempt to furnish them with proofs
that life is not bounded by birth and death, which may lead them
to think that the truth of the Christian doctrine depends upon the
validity of such proofs. It may be helpful to point out to them how
few of the convictions on which their daily lives are based have
been reached by rational argument or can be proved true by
reason. To take just one instance, their choice of friends, and perhaps one day of a lifetime partner in marriage, is not determined
by a process of logical proof but is a decision of a more mysterious
kind that involves the total person. No one can prove to them that
there is a future life or that there is a God, but if they are open to
know God, to know him in a personal relationship in which he
speaks and they respond, to know him as one who comes to them
and fills the emptiness of their life, his life in them will be the
only evidence they need of the reality of a life that is eternal.

Indifference to the subject may be more frequently encountered
than direct denial. Various factors both in the church and in the
development of our society have combined to push the question
of life beyond death into the background. Not many generations
ago it was characteristic of evangelical Christianity to define salvation as salvation from a hell of eternal torment with assurance
of a blessed life in heaven. The question, Are you saved? could be
elaborated as, Where will you spend eternity? And only too often
this fixing of the gaze upon the world beyond involved a blindness to the concrete problems of the individual and of society in
the present time. But with the recognition that both in the Old
Testament and in the New the interest and focus is upon the situations and decisions that confront man in his life in the world
and that salvation is the deliverance of man primarily from present evils, there has been a powerful reaction from the otherworld-
liness of the earlier time. Salvation is interpreted in terms of transformation of personal and social life, and its implications for a life

beyond the grave seem by comparison to be of little importance. In some quarters it would be regarded as most unhealthy and neurotic for anyone to be concerned about what will happen to him after death. This focus upon the present rather than upon the future is also encouraged by the character of our society in which the rapidity of new developments, the fascination of new inventions, and the possibilities of personal advancement all combine with the multiplication of the media of communication to keep our attention fixed upon what is happening today and tomorrow. We cannot look away long enough to ask, " What happens after death? " and perhaps we are so engrossed and entranced by the interests of our world that we are genuinely indifferent to what lies beyond. Death becomes merely a shadow that falls across life from time to time to spoil the fun. Therefore, everything possible must be done to disguise and conceal the shadow. Those who die must be made to appear as though they have not died until they can be placed out of sight. The fact of death must not be allowed to disturb the minds of children — though it is not taken into account that children may be more disturbed by their parents' attempts to conceal the fact of death than by the fact itself.

Death refuses to be concealed. Moreover, the Christian is more concerned about the profounder and more painful reality of the death that is experienced in life than about the death that merely terminates man's earthly life. The outward death is a symbol of the inner and hidden death. And when the symbol is concealed, it is very easy to brush aside the warning that sin has its fruits in death. The death that sin effects is not the dissolution of the body but the dissolution of the relationships with God and man in which man has his life. There is no life in self alone but only death. To be shut out from God and to be no longer capable of relationships of openness and understanding with other people is to have lost not only one's God and one's fellows but also one's self and one's world. How irresponsible it is, then, that young people should be sent out into the world unaware that they face not only the opportunity of life but also the danger of death, and that in the choices they make they will often be choosing between the way of life and the way of death! Death is not just the last enemy who may, by good fortune or good health, be escaped for many years but rather is the ever-present enemy who must be conquered if we are to live today and tomorrow. It is not difficult to recognize the forces of death at work in our world and in ourselves, forces that work through prejudice, suspicion, hatred, misunderstanding, lust, greed, ambition, pride, and in countless other ways to disrupt the relationships in which we live. These are the forces of death that threaten every home, every friendship, every community, every human society large and small. When they have their way with us, it is death that we taste. They shatter not only the order of life in society but also the order of life within the individual.

But if it is important that young people should be prepared for their inevitable encounters with death so that they may not stumble blindly into nothingness, it is yet more important that they should know where to look for life when they find themselves in the midst of death. The time will come when walls of their own making will shut them out from God and man and shut them in upon themselves in despair. It will seem to them as though they were bereft of all that makes life worth living, and they will be sick unto death within themselves. But that can be the hour of understanding when suddenly the words of Jesus, " Those who are well have no need of a physician, but those who are sick," come alive within their minds and speak to them of Jesus' understanding of their situation. They are the prisoners whom he has come to set free, the blind who hope to have their sight restored, the hungry who look to him for food, the dead who wait for him to give them life. And the power that alone can work these wonders is the power of love, the love of God in which we could not believe if it had not been incarnate in this world in the person of Jesus Christ, the love of God, which in the omnipotence of its forgiveness breaks through every wall we build. The wall that shuts us out from God is not able to shut God out from us. In fact, the wall itself that seems to be our death is just the hand of God imprisoning us in a narrow place that we may be made to choose between life and death, between God and self. The life God offers us in love, and that he has brought to our very door in Jesus Christ, is life in fellowship with him, life in response to the love and truth and holiness that meet us in him, and therefore a life that has to be shared beyond ourselves. God breaks open the wall between himself and us, and by his presence with us gives us the power to break open the other walls that shut us in. He restores our life to us by reopening the channels of access from God to man and from man to man. Separation from the love of God is death. Therefore, the coming of Jesus Christ into our human world is love's invasion of the realms of death. Love, as Paul and John knew so well, is not just one among the attributes of God and among the qualities of the Christian life. Love is the fullness of the divine nature, the divine self-giving that is the very life of God. In Jesus Christ this love which is the life of God is revealed to us and comes to us as the only true life of any man. So great is the joy it brings that he who receives it lives ever afterward in perpetual thanksgiving and praise.

Scripture References

The following Scripture references, including verses quoted and passages to which reference is made, are listed by chapter and page number for the convenience of those who wish to examine the way in which particular parts of this book are related to Biblical materials.

1. *Theology and Christian Education*
   p. 14 John 1:14; 14:6. Eph. 4:21
   p. 16 Heb. 11:8-10. Rom. 10:17
   p. 17 II Cor. 5:17, 18
   p. 20 Matt. 16:13 ff.
   p. 22 Matt. 4:4. Luke 4:4. Deut. 8:3
   p. 23 John 15:7, 14, 15
   p. 24 John 1:9-14. Phil. 2:11

2. *I Believe*
   p. 27 Luke 4:18. John 8:32. Gal. 5:1, 13. James 1:25
   p. 30 I Cor. 12:3
   p. 31 John 15:16. Rom. 10:17. Matt. 5:6
   p. 32 Mark 4:26-29
   p. 33 Luke 4:28 ff. Luke 5:30-32. Luke 15:1, 2
   p. 35 Mark 9:24. Job 13:15. Jer. 12:1-6; 20:7 ff.
   p. 36 I Cor. 1:25
   p. 37 Rom. 6:4-11

3. . . . *In God*
> p. 41 James 2:19
> p. 43 Ex. 20:3. Deut. 5:7
> p. 47 Acts 17:16 ff.

4. . . . *The Father Almighty*
> p. 53 Mark 14:36. Luke 23:46
> p. 54 John 14:6. Matt. 11:27. I John 3:1, 2
> p. 55 Jer. 31:9. Mal. 2:10. Hos. 11:1
> p. 56 Isa. 1:2. Rom. 5:14. I Cor. 15:45. I Cor. 11:7. Heb. 1:3.
>   I John 3:2. Mark 14:36. Luke 23:46
> p. 57 Matt. 5:11, 12; 10:16. Luke 15:11 ff.
> p. 58 Luke 12:16 ff. Luke 5:17
> p. 59 Deut. 30:15. John 15:6
> p. 60 Matt. 27:40. I Cor. 1:22. Job 1:9
> p. 62 John 1:14

5. . . . *Maker of Heaven and Earth*
> p. 64 Amos 5:8. Isa. 40:21-23. Ps. 24:1; 50:10
> p. 65 Gen. 1:1
> p. 68 Ps. 19:1
> p. 70 Heb. 11:3. John 1:3. Col. 1:16
> p. 73 I Sam. 2:1-10. Luke 1:46-55
> p. 74 II Kings 6:6. Acts 5:5, 10
> p. 75 Ps. 91. Matt. 4:5-7. I Cor. 3:16, 17; 6:19. II Cor. 6:16
> p. 76 Gen. 1:31. Isa. 45:18. Luke 10:17-19. I Cor. 6:19

6. . . . *And in Jesus Christ, His Son*
> p. 81 Luke 2:52. Heb. 4:15. Matt. 4:4, 6, 10
> p. 82 II Cor. 4:6
> p. 83 Mark 1:15
> p. 84 Mark 1:17. Luke 10:1, 2
> p. 85 John 1:40-42. Luke 24:21
> p. 86 Matt. 26:31-35. Heb. 6:6
> p. 87 Rom. 6:3-11

p. 89 John 10:30. Luke 3:21, 22. Mark 1:6, 7; 8:34, 35; 10:21; 14:22-24

7. . . . *Our Lord*
p. 91 Isa. 9:6, 7; 11:1-5
p. 92 Matt. 4:11, 12. Isa. 48:17-19. Jer. 31:31
p. 93 Rom. 5:10. Heb. 5:8. Mark 14:36. Luke 23:46. Luke 15:1 ff.
p. 94 I Cor. 4:4; 2:16. John 1:4. Gen. 3:5. Luke 15:12
p. 95 Matt. 5:5; 16:24; 4:19
p. 96 Matt. 28:18; 11:27. Phil. 2:10. Rev. 11:15
p. 97 Matt. 7:29; 5:21-27. Luke 10:25; 7:36. Matt. 16:22, 23. Matt. 10:37; 21:12 f.
p. 98 Matt. 21:23 f.
p. 99 John 1:8. Rev. 11:15
p. 101 Matt. 7:21. II Cor. 10:5
p. 102 I Kings, ch. 22

8. . . . *Conceived by the Holy Ghost, Born of the Virgin Mary*
p. 107 Matt. 1:18. Luke 1:35. Matt. 12:46. Mark 6:3. John 19:25. Gal. 1:19. Mark 6:4
p. 108 Mark 3:21. Luke 11:27, 28. Mark 3:31-35
p. 110 John 1:1-14

9. . . . *Suffered Under Pontius Pilate*
p. 117 Mark 1:14
p. 118 Matt. 5:12. Isa., chs. 50; 53. Luke 4:18; 14:28. Mark, ch. 4
p. 119 Luke 4:29. Mark 3:6. Matt. 11:20-24
p. 120 Matt. 10:6; 15:24. Luke 13:34. Luke 10:1. Acts 1:15. Luke 9:55. Matt. 26:72
p. 121 Matt. 26:12
p. 123 Heb. 12:2. Matt. 9:15; 22:2; 11:19
p. 125 John 12:31
p. 126 II Cor. 5:21. John 2:25. Matt. 1:21

p. 127 Phil. 3:10

p. 128 Rom. 5:3. II Cor. 1:5-7

10. . . . *Crucified, Dead, Buried, Descended Into Hell*

p. 130 I Peter 3:19

p. 131 Mark 15:34

p. 134 Acts 20:28

p. 135 I Cor. 1:23

p. 137 Mark 8:31; 9:12. Luke 24:7

p. 138 John 11:50

p. 142 Isa. 6:5; 64:6. Ex. 32:32. Matt. 25:40. Luke 7:37; 19:2

p. 143 Gen. 4:2. Ex. 20:5

11. . . . *The Third Day He Rose Again from the Dead*

p. 146 Gen. 18:1 ff.; 32:24. Mark 15:46; 16:2. Acts 1:3

p. 148 Acts 2:24; 3:15, 16

p. 149 Acts, chs. 9; 22; 26. Gal. 1:11-16. I Cor. 15:8. Acts 9:15

p. 150 Acts 2:17; I Cor. 10:11; 15:26. John 2:22

p. 152 Mark 9:2-8

p. 153 II Cor. 5:16. Phil. 3:10

p. 154 Gen., ch. 3; 28:11 ff. Ex. 3:2 ff.

p. 155 Isa., ch. 6

p. 156 Acts 5:42

12. . . . *He Ascended Into Heaven and Sitteth at the Right Hand of God the Father Almighty*

p. 159 Acts 1:9

p. 160 Ps. 130:1. Isa. 40:10. Acts 2:2. Matt. 3:16

p. 161 Mark 13:29. Luke 21:31. Matt. 28:20. Acts 1:3. I Cor. 15:8

p. 162 Rom. 1:4. John 1:14

p. 163 Eph. 4:22. Col. 3:9. I Cor. 15:28. Acts 10:42. II Tim. 4:1. I Peter 4:5

p. 164 Mark 6:3. Matt. 13:55; 16:14

p. 165 Matt. 16:17. II Cor. 3:17, 18

p. 166 Gal. 2:20. John 20:29

13. . . . *From Thence He Shall Come to Judge the Quick and the Dead*
p. 171 Matt. 10:23; 24:36, 44; 25:13
p. 174 I Cor. 7:25 ff. II Cor. 3:18
p. 176 I Cor. 4:5. Rom. 8:1. Isa. 60:1-5; 61:1-9
p. 177 Isa. 55:11; 51:2; 45:19
p. 178 Heb. 11:10
p. 179 I John 1:1. I Cor. 13:12
p. 180 Matt. 16:18

14. . . . *I Believe in the Holy Spirit*
p. 184 Acts 19:2. John 3:5. I Cor. 14:2. Gal. 5:16
p. 185 I Cor. 12:3
p. 192 Rom. 5:1-5
p. 194 Luke 18:9-14. Matt. 19:17. Luke 7:41, 42

15. . . . *The Holy Catholic Church, the Communion of Saints*
p. 198 Gen. 12:3
p. 199 Gen. 22:1 ff.
p. 200 Rom. 1:14. Matt. 10:40. John 12:44
p. 201 II Cor. 5:20. Acts 8:18. I Tim. 4:14
p. 203 Ex. 3:5. Isa. 6:3. Rom. 1:7. I Cor. 1:2
p. 204 I Cor. 13:1-3; 1:13
p. 206 I Cor. 3:11
p. 207 Matt. 9:12

16. . . . *The Forgiveness of Sins*
p. 208 Mark 2:1-12. Luke 19:5
p. 209 Matt. 7:1-5. Luke 15:29, 30
p. 210 Luke 7:36 ff.
p. 212 Ps. 51:4
p. 213 Gen. 1:26, 27
p. 216 Matt. 9:11
p. 217 Matt. 6:12; 18:21, 22; 18:35

17. . . . *The Resurrection of the Body and the Life Everlasting*

    p. 220 Heb. 11:1

    p. 223 John 11:25; 17:2, 3. I Cor. 15:22

    p. 224 Matt. 6:20. Rom. 6:3-11

    p. 225 Rom. 12:1. John 20:2, 27; 2:26. Acts, chs. 9; 22; 26.
             I Cor. 15:40

    p. 230 Mark 2:17

    p. 231 John 3:16. I John 4:16